Semiha Cemāl:
A Portrait of a Turkish Sufi Philosopher

With the First English Translation of the Prophet of Love

ARZU EYLÜL YALÇINKAYA

Semiha Cemāl: A Portrait of a Turkish Sufi Philosopher

ARZU EYLÜL YALÇINKAYA

ISBN: 979-8-9930815-1-9
This edition published in May 2026.

The Kenan Center Press is the publishing imprint
of The Kenan Center for Turkish Cultural Studies Inc.,
a nonprofit organization dedicated to advancing scholarship
and cultural engagement.

Editor: Adile Sedef Dönmez
Cover Design: Nükte Nur Birol
Page Layout: İbrahim Melik Uyar

THE KENAN CENTER PRESS
210 Highland Avenue, 02494, Needhan MA
+1 617 294-6494

Dr. Arzu Eylül Yalçınkaya is a theologian and historian whose work traverses the intersections of Sufi thought, Ottoman intellectual history, and the ethical architecture of modernity. Trained in Islamic sciences and the history of Sufism, she brings a philological eye and a metaphysical sensitivity to the study of late Ottoman and early Republican texts, with particular attention to figures who straddled spiritual and bureaucratic domains. She is a faculty member at Üsküdar University's Institute for Sufi Studies and the founding director of The Kenan Center for Turkish Cultural Studies in Boston. Alongside her academic appointment in Istanbul, she served as a visiting researcher at Harvard University's Center for Middle Eastern Studies (CMES), where she conducted post-doctoral research on late Ottoman Sufi intellectuals and the bridging roles of Sufi bureaucrats. Yalçınkaya works across disciplines to examine how metaphysical inquiry, aesthetic form, and moral imagination were reconfigured in response to modern secular reforms. A published writer in her fields of expertise, she also contributes to peer-reviewed journals, critical translations, and public lectures, and performs Turkish classical and Sufi devotional music as part of her broader inquiry into embodied knowledge. Her current work explores alternative genealogies of Turkish philosophy through women mystics and thinkers such as Semiha Cemāl, whose writings she positions within a global history of metaphysical literature.

Contents

Preface

At the turn of the millennium, as I mapped the intellectual topography of Turkish women thinkers and Sufi interlocutors, a name began to gather force: Semiha Cemāl (d. 1936). My inquiry had followed the luminous thread of Sāmiha Ayverdi (d. 1993) and through the guidance of Cemalnur Sargut, I learned that Semiha Cemāl had authored a mystical novel in Ottoman Turkish that awaited a translator. The quiet promise in that discovery opened a path. *The Prophet of Love (Aşk Peygamberi)*, Semiha Cemāl's first novel, came into view not as a mere artifact of an earlier script culture but as a compelling question—about language and love, about cultural memory and the fate of spiritual philosophy in a modernizing world. I pursued that question in Istanbul's archives and significant collections until I located the original printing. I held the volume; its Ottoman letters carried both delicacy and intention. My acquaintance with Ottoman Turkish was modest, yet within two weeks I completed a faithful first transcription into the modern Turkish (Latin) script. It was not an academic project. It was, as I later came to see, an encounter.

For years, the translation remained with me, quietly guiding the questions I would later ask as a historian of Sufism and modernity. What does it mean to love with intellect? What does it mean to think with the heart? Semiha Cemāl offered a vision of philosophy grounded in compassion, spiritual rigor, and narrative grace. Her novel reflects a metaphysical idiom that speaks across ruptures—between Ottoman and Republican, between classical and modern, between inherited silence and spoken witness.

This book brings her voice into a broader conversation. It forms part of a larger initiative at the Kenan Center for Turkish Cultural Studies, which I established in Boston to preserve and revitalize Turkish spiritual and intellectual traditions. We publish works that have been overlooked not because they lacked depth, but because they refused the boundaries imposed by genre, gender, or ideology. *The Prophet of Love* belongs to that tradition—of works that remain vital not because they align with dominant narratives, but because they illuminate what those narratives leave behind.

I extend my deepest thanks to my esteemed teacher, Cemalnur Sargut, whose vision and generosity first brought Semiha Cemāl into my world; to my colleagues and friends, whose encouragement sustained this project; and to my parents, who supported this path with quiet love and unwavering prayer. May this book carry Semiha Cemāl's voice to those who are ready to hear it—those who read not only for meaning, but for transformation.

The present volume also inaugurates the Kenan Center for Turkish Cultural Studies, a Boston-based research and cultural initiative, through its Modern Turkish Portrait Series, which is committed to recovering and re-presenting the works of overlooked thinkers, mystics, and writers from the late Ottoman and early Republican periods. Our aim is academic in the fullest, humanistic sense. We invite readers—both scholars and seekers—into a space where Turkish intellectual and spiritual history can be encountered with care, dignity, and interpretive openness.

In that spirit, this book offers itself as a bridge: across languages, across eras, and across hearts. I trust that *The Prophet of Love (Aşk Peygamberi)* will find its way to those searching for more than a narrative. It carries within it the questions and aspirations of a woman who embraced philosophy, cherished silence, and wrote—quietly yet enduringly—toward eternity.

May this book serve her voice well.

July 2025, Cambridge/MA
Arzu Eylül Yalçınkaya

Introduction

Semiha Cemāl Büyükaksoy[1] (1905–1936), early twentieth-century Türkiye's first female philosopher and novelist, emerged as a remarkable voice at a time of radical cultural change. Her writings combined a deep philosophical curiosity with an intimate engagement with Sufi thought, offering readers a unique bridge between inherited traditions and new intellectual horizons. With her powerful pen, she translated foundational works of philosophy into Turkish, enabling the formation of a new intellectual corpus, authored symbolic novels that left a lasting literary mark, and, as a philosophy teacher, shaped a cohort of students. Through these achievements, she established herself as one of the most influential women of her time. Situating her work within the turbulence of her era allows for the rediscovery of her literary and philosophical vision and for reflection on the broader questions of identity, spirituality, and modernity that preoccupied an entire generation.

The early decades of the Turkish Republic (1923–1950) were characterized by an aggressive project of secular modernity that sought to redefine the nation's identity in opposition to its Ottoman-Islamic past.[2] The new republican elites, inspired by European positivism and nationalism, implemented sweeping re-

---

1   After the enactment of the Surname Law in 1934, Semiha Cemāl's family adopted the surname Büyükaksoy.

2   Nazım İrem, "Turkish Conservative Modernism: Birth of a Nationalist Quest for Cultural Renewal", *International Journal of Middle East Studies* 34, no. 1 (2002) 87-112.

forms to break with traditional institutions and belief systems. Among the most consequential was the abolition of the Sufi orders (*tarikat*) and the closure of Sufi lodges (*tekke*) in 1925, which effectively outlawed the public practice of Islamic mysticism.[3] This law symbolically signaled that the mystical orders had no place in the vision of a modern, rational nation-state. In the state-driven narrative of progress, Sufi practices were often recast as relics of superstition or obstacles to enlightenment, and those devoted to spiritual pursuits were marginalized in the official history of Turkish modernity.[4] The early Republican literary sphere echoed this ideological stance: novels and newspapers of the 1920s and 1930s frequently portrayed religious figures and dervish institutions as backward or morally corrupt, reinforcing a binary between the "old" mystical East and the "new" secular West.[5] Such depictions underscored the regime's message that true progress required shedding the Ot-

---

3   Major cultural reforms initiated by the early Republican government included the 1924 Tevhid-i Tedrisat (Law on the Unification of Education), which centralized all educational institutions under the Ministry of National Education; the 1925 abolition of Sufi lodges (tekkes and zaviyes); and the 1928 adoption of the Latin alphabet. These reforms aimed to secularize and modernize Turkish society but often suppressed traditional religious and metaphysical discourses. In the sociopolitical dynamics of the Republic, wherein spiritual and religious expressions were often relegated to the margins: Berna Moran, *Edebiyat Kuramları ve Eleştiri* (İstanbul: İletişim Yayınları, 1991), 97; Erdağ Göknar, *Orhan Pamuk, Secularism and Blasphemy: The Politics of the Turkish Novel* (London: Routledge, 2013), 102-106

4   Binnaz Toprak, "Secularism and Islam: The Building of Modern Turkey," *Macalester International* 15, no. 9. (2005): 28

5   For example, Yakup Kadri Karaosmanoğlu's controversial novel *Nur Baba* (1922) depicted a debauched Sufi lodge, feeding public perceptions of Sufism as decadent and obsolete. Wilson, M. Brett. "The Twilight of Ottoman Sufism: Antiquity, Immorality, and Nation in Yakup Kadri Karaosmanoğlu's Nur Baba." *International Journal of Middle East Studies* 49, no. 2 (2017): 233-253.

toman-Islamic heritage in favor of a Western-oriented, materi-alist outlook.

At the same time, the Republican revolution opened new avenues for women in education and public life under what has been termed "state feminism."[6] Women were envisioned by Kemalist reformers as symbols and carriers of secular modernity, expected to personify the break from the Ottoman past by embracing Western norms of dress, education, and civic involvement. Legal reforms in the 1920s granted urban Turkish women unprecedented opportunities – they gained access to higher education, entered the professions, and after 1934 obtained the right to vote and hold office. However, the celebration of women's emancipation came with ideological strings attached: the ideal Republican woman was generally one who contributed to the nation as a secular, rational, and socially engaged citizen. This ideal often precluded open affiliation with religious mysticism or overtly spiritual pursuits, which were deemed antithetical to the new modern identity.[7]

While a handful of women writers and intellectuals rose to prominence in the early Republic, they typically did so by aligning with the secular nationalist values of the time or by steering clear of "unscientific" subjects.[8] In this context, wom-

6   Hülya Bayrak Akyıldız, "Representation of Women in Early Republic Era Turkish Novels" *Oriental Languages and Civilizations*, eds. Barbara Michalak-Pikulska, Tomasz Majtczak, and Marek Piela (Krakow: Jagiellonian University Press, 2021), 37-46.

7   Hale Yılmaz, *Becoming Turkish: Nationalist Reforms and Cultural Negotiations in Early Republican Turkey, 1923–1945* (Syracuse, NY: Syracuse University Press, 2013), 45–60. Senem Üstün Kaya, "Women Behind the Pens: A Comparative Analysis of Turkish Female Authors From Reform Period to Modernism", *The Online Journal of Science and Technology* 11, no. 4 (2021): 133-141.

8   Hülya Bayrak Akyıldız, "Representation of Women in Early Republic Era Turkish Novels" *Oriental Languages and Civilizations*, eds. Barbara

en who pursued metaphysical or mystical themes in their work found little support and remained on the periphery of the intellectual mainstream. Beneath the surface of this official culture, alternative currents persisted. Not everyone experienced modernity as a stark conflict with faith and tradition. A closer look at the period reveals a more complex landscape of ideas: one in which mysticism and modernism were not mutually exclusive but could quietly coexist and even complement one another.[9]

Recent scholarship has shown that some late Ottoman and early Republican intellectuals did not view Western modernity as wholly alien to their Islamic heritage; rather, they saw it as a "universal civilizing process" continuous with longstanding concepts in Islamic thought.[10] In this vein, certain Sufi thinkers and their followers sought ways to reconcile spiritual practice with the new Republican order. They explored a "third path" that transcended the binary of religious reaction versus secular revolution.[11] These individuals – often operating in subtle or private ways – strived to adapt Sufi ideals to modern life, keeping alive an undercurrent of metaphysical inquiry even as overt religious expression was suppressed. It is within this subtle countercurrent that the subject of this study emerged. These intersecting currents of fundamental secularism and controlled female empowerment form the backdrop for understanding the significance of Semiha Cemāl – a figure

Michalak-Pikulska, Tomasz Majtczak, and Marek Piela (Krakow: Jagiellonian University Press, 2021), 37-46.

9   Kutluğhan Soyubol, "In Search of Perfection: Neo-spiritualism, Islamic Mysticism, and Secularism in Turkey," Modern Intellectual History 18, no. 1 (2021): 70–94.

10   İsmail Kara, Cumhuriyet Türkiyesi'nde Bir Mesele Olarak İslâm, vol. 2 (İstanbul: Dergâh Yayınları, 2016)

11   Homi K. Bhabha, *The Location of Culture* (London: Routledge, 1994), 36–39.

who stands at the crossroads of Sufism, philosophy, and female intellectual history in early Republican Türkiye. Semiha Cemāl's life unfolded amid the tensions between tradition and reform: she came of age just as the Ottoman Empire gave way to the Turkish Republic, and her formative years coincided with the height of the Kemalist cultural revolution. Within a single generation, institutions that had sustained Islamic learning and spirituality for centuries were dismantled, even as Western philosophy and science were newly elevated as benchmarks of progress in universities. Semiha Cemāl's fate and work would be profoundly shaped by this atmosphere.[12] On one hand, she benefited from the Republic's educational reforms that enabled women to study at the highest levels; on the other hand, her deep engagement with Sufi thought and metaphysical questions placed her outside the approved template of the modern Turkish woman. Understanding Semiha Cemāl's legacy thus requires grappling with the paradoxes of her era: she was both empowered and constrained by the sweeping changes around her. The very forces that allowed her to become one of Türkiye's first academically trained female philosophers also ensured that her contributions, steeped in mysticism and spirituality, would be neglected or even consciously forgotten in the march toward a strictly secular modernity.

---

12   The rigid Kemalist perspective and its social consequences were widely debated by early Republican intellectuals, with literature emerging as a key medium for societal reflection. Kemal Karpat argues that early Republican Turkish literature was shaped by the nation's drive for modernization and Westernization, emphasizing that its development cannot be understood without considering the political, social, and cultural forces that influenced its formation. Karpat, Kemal. "Social Themes in Contemporary Turkish Literature Part 1", *Middle East Journal* 14, no. 1, (1960): 29-44; Jale Parla, "The Wounded Tongue: Turkey's Language Reform and the Canonicity of the Novel", *Modern Language Association* 23, no.1, (2008): 31.

REDISCOVERING A FORGOTTEN PIONEER
OF SPIRITUAL PHILOSOPHY

History often remembers the names that sit neatly within its paradigms—the men of reform, the women of the republic, the voices that harmonize with the age. It is less generous toward those who dwell between categories, who write from elsewhere, and who speak in tones not immediately legible to the dominant script. Semiha Cemāl was such a voice: a philosopher and mystic, a woman who lived in the waning light of empire and the austere brightness of a secularizing republic.[13] Her thought refused the binaries of her time—not by negating them, but by quietly weaving them into a singular, contemplative fabric. That she has remained largely absent from the major histories of Turkish literature and intellectual life is not a reflection of her insignificance, but of the questions her legacy continues to ask.

Semiha's intellectual formation unfolded across overlapping worlds: in the *sohbet* (spiritual conversations) halls of the Rifā'ī dervish lodge, under the tutelage of Ken'an Rifā'ī (d. 1950);[14] and in the secular classrooms of Dārülfünūn (now Is-

---

13 There is very limited second literature on the life and legacy of Semiha Cemāl. Primary source to her life is the compiled work by his fellows Samiha Ayverdi, "Kadın Anlayışı ve Semiha Cemāl", *Ken'ân Rifâî ve Yirminci Asrın Işığında Müslümanlık*, eds. Samiha Ayverdi, Nezihe Araz, Safiye Erol and Sofi Huri (İstanbul: Kubbelatı Neşriyat, 2003), 229-248; and introductory parts of her own work, Semiha Cemāl, *Gül Demeti* (İstanbul: İstanbul Bilgi Basım ve Yayım Evi), 6. For A Recent Study, Fulya Bayraktar, "Cumhuriyet Döneminin Öncü Bir Kadın Felsefecisi: Semiha Cemāl Hanim", *Felsefe Dünyası* 52 (2010): 116-125. Also see, Kudret Savaş, *Zaman Sürgünü: Semiha Cemāl Hayatı ve Eserleri* (Çanakkale: Paradigma Akademi, 2022).

14 Ken'ān Rifā'ī (1867–1950) was a leading figure of the Rifā'ī Sufi order during the late Ottoman and early Republican eras. Born in Plovdiv into a prominent bureaucratic family, he was introduced to both state-

tanbul University), where she studied philosophy and served briefly as assistant to the renowned Prof. Mustafa Şekip Tunç (d. 1958).[15] She taught ethics and logic in girls schools while attending Sufi gatherings, translated Greek dialogues while composing novels on divine love, and refused to frame mysticism and modernity as opposing poles. In the quiet margins of her short life, Semiha Cemāl undertook the formidable task of translating Platonic dialogues and possibly Stoic treatises into Ottoman Turkish—work she enriched with her own lucid, context-building prefaces.[16] In her world, Plato could sit beside

craft and Sufism at an early age. His father, Hacı Abdülhalīm Bey, held high-ranking administrative roles, while his mother, Hatice Cenān Hanım—deeply influenced by Shaykh Edhem Efendi and the poetry of Niyāzī-i Mısrī—served as his first spiritual mentor. Educated at the Mekteb-i Sultānī (now Galatasaray High School), Kenʿān Rifāʿī combined classical Sufi learning with modern Ottoman intellectual training. His later career in the Ministry of Education paralleled his deepening engagement with Sufi teaching, producing a distinctive synthesis of spirituality and public service. See, Arzu Eylül Yalçınkaya, "Semiha Cemāl Hanım'ın Dilinden Ken'ân Rifâî'nin Meşreb-i Şerifleri." Presented at the I. Uluslararası Tasavvuf Araştırmaları Lisansüstü Öğrenci Sempozyumu, 2018; Feyza Burak-Adli, "The Portrait of an Alla Franca Shaykh: Sufism, Modernity, and Class in Turkey," *International Journal of Middle East Studies* 56, no. 2 (2024): 207–226.

15   Mustafa Şekip Tunç (1886–1958) was a pioneering Turkish philosopher and psychologist known for his contributions to modern Turkish thought and the institutionalization of psychology and philosophy in Türkiye. He studied philosophy at the Sorbonne in Paris and later became a professor at Istanbul University, where he played a key role in establishing the Philosophy Department. Influenced by Henri Bergson's ideas on intuition and the nature of consciousness, Tunç integrated Western philosophical frameworks with Turkish intellectual traditions. See, Mustafa Şekip Tunç, *Bergson ve Manevi Kudrete Dair Birkaç Konferans* (İstanbul: Muallim Ahmet Halit Kitaphanesi, 1934); Also see, Hayrani Altıntaş, *Mustafa Şekip Tunç* (Ankara: Kültür Bakanlığı Yayınları, 1989).

16   Besides her books and translations, Semiha contributed essays and short pieces to intellectual journals like *Hayat* and *Mihrap*, indicating

Rūmī; truth was neither Western nor Eastern, but a matter of self-purification and disciplined intellect. Her philosophical idiom was hybrid, but never diluted; her voice was contemplative, but never passive.

Semiha Cemāl's name does not appear in most literary histories of the early Republic. Her work is absent from university syllabi, her influence unacknowledged in standard genealogies of Turkish philosophy. Yet her contributions were far from peripheral. In 1927, at the age of twenty-two, she published *Aşk Peygamberi*, a novel that can only be described as metaphysical fiction—infused with Sufi cosmology, Platonic allegory, and ethical inquiry. It was, in essence, a literary act of philosophical resistance. Throughout this volume, we retain the original Turkish title *Aşk Peygamberi*. On its first mention here we note its English sense, *The Prophet of Love*, while also acknowledging that neither "love" nor "prophet" fully conveys the resonance of their Turkish and Islamic philosophical contexts. This approach preserves the layered meanings embedded in the original title while ensuring accessibility for non-Turkish readers. In the index and metadata, both forms appear for clarity and discoverability.

Having noted these linguistic and interpretive considerations, we can return to the historical conditions that shaped the novel's trajectory. The materiality of its publication proved decisive. *Aşk Peygamberi* emerged in 1927, printed in Ottoman Turkish script at the very threshold of the alphabet reform that would reconfigure access to the written word for generations to come. Its script alone consigned it to a rapidly receding ar-

---

her engagement with the literary culture of her time. The renowned sociologist-historian Niyazi Berkes, writing some years later, marveled at Semiha Cemāl's scholarly output – expressing astonishment and admiration that "in such an era, [a young woman] could present us with works so serious and valuable". Berkes, *Unutulan Yıllar*, 2007, 179.

chive, a text instantly marked as belonging to a linguistic order that the new Republic sought to overwrite. Authored by a
young woman whose intellectual audacity unsettled the masculine codes of authorship, the novel carried within it both
the promise of an alternative modernity and the risk of erasure. What followed was less an active repudiation than a quiet
slipping away—into the blind spots of literary memory, into
what we might call the uncurated margins of the canon. Its
absence from university curricula and philosophical genealogies was symptomatic not of insignificance but of a cultural
order unable, or unwilling, to accommodate the metaphysical
voice of a woman writer whose idiom drew simultaneously on
Sufi mysticism and classical philosophy. To recall it now, nearly a century later, is to register more than an act of recovery;
it is to acknowledge the shifting conditions of our own present. The novel's reappearance affirms a widening horizon of
reading, one that recognizes the archive of Turkish literature
as more capacious than its nationalist framings, and one that
welcomes figures once overlooked into the continuum of intellectual history.[17]

That voice was, for decades, nearly lost. Semiha Cemāl
died in 1936 at the age of thirty-one, reportedly after a long
illness. Her published works, printed in limited editions and
in a script soon abandoned, faded into bibliographic silence.
What survived was held in memory—most notably by her
cousin, the writer and Sufi thinker Sāmiha Ayverdi (d. 1993),
who posthumously published *Aşk Budur* (This is Love), an unfinished manuscript Semiha left behind.[18] But even such acts

---

17   Semiha Cemāl, *Aşk Peygamberi*, ed. Nurcan Şen (İstanbul: Çolpan Ki-
      tap, 2023).

18   İlker Aytürk, "Pious and Modern: Women's Islam in the Ayverdi Cir-
      cle," *Journal of Turkish Studies/Türklük Bilgisi Araştırmaları, Festschrift
      in Honor of Özer Ergenç, Part I*, no. 51 (December 2019): 219–236.

of devotion could not secure a place for her in the secular and gendered cartographies of Turkish intellectual history. She lingered, instead, on the margins—invoked as a brilliant young woman who died too soon, but not seriously studied as a thinker in her own right.

The reasons for this erasure are multiple and telling. Semiha did not conform to the prevailing images of womanhood promoted by the early Republic, nor did she perform dissent in ways that the state could easily cast as oppositional.[19] She was not a reformer, but neither was she a traditionalist; she wrote from a space in between, one difficult to narrate in the binaries that organized the intellectual landscape of her time. Her work was spiritual but not nostalgic, modern but not materialist. She left no memoir, no manifesto—only texts that demanded slow, layered reading and an openness to alternative epistemologies.[20] That very complexity may have made her invisible to both secular historians and traditional Sufi biographers.

Why does Semiha Cemāl matter, and what makes her work distinctive? At the heart of her significance lies a bold

---

19 Akyıldız, "Representation of Women in Early Republic Era Turkish Novels", 37-46.

20 Semiha Cemāl Evrenos, "Pervane", *Mihrap* 1, no. 12 (1924): 361-363; "Bahar ve Şifa", *Mihrap* 1, no. 1 (1924): 13-14; "Sabah Ezanını Dinlerken" Mihrap 15, no. 16 (1924): 479-480; "Mihrak-ı Aşkı Sücuda Geldim!", *Mirap* 1, no. 17-18 (1924): 560; "Çölde Bir Secde", *Mihrap* 2, no. 25 (1925): 22; "Çölde Bir Secde", *Mihrap* 2, no. 26 (1925): 79. Semiha Rifâî, "Kurban-ı Aşk", *Mihrap* 2, no. 27 (1925): 117; "Çoban Kızı", *Mihrap* 2, no. 28 (1925): 154-156. Semiha Cemāl, "Züleyha", Güner Dergisi 2 (1927): 6-7; Semiha Cemāl, "Kleopatra", *Hayat Dergisi* 4, no. 96 (1928): 350-351; Semiha Cemāl, "Canana Hitap", *Hilal Dergisi* 1, no. 2 (1958): 14. Some of her translations: Semiha Cemāl (trans.) *Epiktet* (Epictete) by François Thurot (Ankara: Maârif Vekâleti, 1932); Semiha Cemāl, *Kendime: Marcus Aurelius Antonius'un Düşünceleri*, by Gustav Loisel (İstanbul: Devlet Matbaası, 1932).

synthesis of ideas: she bridged the world of Sufi mysticism with the world of Western philosophy, creating a hybrid intellectual framework that was virtually unprecedented among her peers. Semiha Cemāl lived a life in two realms – the dervish lodge and the university seminar – and in her writings, these two streams of influence converged into a unique philosophical perspective. She is perhaps best described as a mystic-philosopher, a thinker who sought ultimate truths by drawing simultaneously from Islamic spiritual traditions and the classics of European thought. In an era when Turkish intellectual life was polarized between ardent secularists and devout traditionalists, Semiha charted an alternative path that refused such binaries. Her work suggests that the pursuit of wisdom (*hikmet*) could transcend the divisions of East and West, modern and traditional, rational and mystical. In this sense, Semiha Cemāl offers us a fascinating case of *intellectual hybridity*: she was a product of her time, yet quietly subversive of its dichotomies.

Crucially, Semiha Cemāl carried out this synthesis as a woman in a predominantly male intellectual arena. Her very presence in these dialogues expanded the possibilities for female intellectual agency in Türkiye. Whereas the republican state tended to celebrate women insofar as they embodied the secular, outward-looking "new woman," Semiha chose a different mode of self-expression – one rooted in interiority, contemplation, and spiritual knowledge. In doing so, she subtly subverted the expectations placed on women of her class and education. She was not content merely to be a model secular educator or a symbol of modernization; instead, she claimed a right to engage with profound existential and ethical questions, traditionally the domain of male scholars and Sufi sheikhs. By translating philosophical texts, she inserted herself into a lineage of knowledge from which women had long been excluded.

By authoring a novel suffused with mystical insight, she assumed the role of a *mürşid* (spiritual guide) in literary form, effectively preaching that love and truth transcend gender-bound roles. Semiha's work thus challenges us to rethink the narratives of both women's emancipation and religious thought in the early 20th century. It suggests that the quest for truth – whether through reason or through love – can defy societal constraints, and that a woman, too, could be a philosopher-mystic illuminating an unseen path.

Only in the past two decades has Semiha Cemāl begun to re-enter scholarly conversations. A pioneering article by Fulya Avcı Bayraktar in 2010 marked one of the first academic attempts to position her as an early female philosopher whose work harmonized Turkish-Islamic ethics with the aspirations of modern thought.[21] Yet even this contribution—important as it was—focused more on classification than on close reading. It was the 2023 reprint of *Aşk Peygamberi*, accompanied by a thoughtful preface from Cafer Şen, that reignited serious interest in the content and significance of Semiha's work.[22] Şen's psychoanalytic reading of the novel opened new interpretive possibilities, and signaled that Semiha's oeuvre might serve as a bridge between philosophy and fiction, between inner life and public ethics, between forgotten voices and the present's hunger for resonance.

This volume continues that unfolding conversation. It does not seek to place Semiha Cemāl neatly into the shelves of established thought, but to consider what those shelves exclude. Her intellectual labor—rooted in love, discipline, intu-

---

21　Fulya Avcı Bayraktar, "Cumhuriyet Döneminin Öncü Bir Kadın Felsefecisi: Semiha Cemāl Hanım." *Felsefe Dünyası*, no. 52 (2010): 116–125.

22　Cafer Şen, "Tasavvufî Bir Romana Psikanalitik Bir Bakış", *Aşk Peygamberi*, Semiha Cemal, haz. Nurcan Şen (İstanbul: Çolpan Kitap, 2023), 5-26.

ition, and inquiry—offers a lens through which to rethink the story of Turkish modernity itself. What if metaphysical longing, rather than being an anachronism, is part of that story? What if the modern subject is not one who leaves the sacred behind, but one who reconfigures it, quietly and courageously? These are the questions Semiha Cemāl leaves us with. And they are, at last, being asked.

SCOPE AND STRUCTURE OF THIS BOOK

This book sets out to restore Semiha Cemāl to her rightful place in Turkish intellectual and literary history and to interpret the deeper significance of her work. In doing so, it illuminates Semiha as a figure of convergence in modern Türkiye: a woman at the meeting point of Sufi mysticism and Western philosophy, of Ottoman cultural roots and Republican reforms. Her story offers a lens onto larger questions—what became of mysticism under a secularizing regime? How did women of her era quietly build bridges between tradition and modernity? By delving into Semiha's life and writings, we uncover an alternative genealogy of Turkish modernity, one running alongside the official secular narrative. Her example reminds us that the spiritual and the rational need not be mutually exclusive, and that a voice silenced in one era may resurface to speak powerfully to another. To explore these themes and reclaim Semiha's legacy, the study unfolds in three parts, combining biography, literary translation, and analysis.

Part I (Chapters 1–4) traces Semiha Cemāl's life and intellectual formation, painting a comprehensive portrait of her journey through a tumultuous era. From the Sufi lodge to the philosophy classroom, we follow her coming of age in late Ottoman Istanbul and her maturation in the early Turkish Republic. This section shows how an aristocratic upbringing steeped in spirituality met a modern education in philosophy, yielding the unprecedented figure of a female Sufi philosopher. We see Semiha as a young woman absorbing the *sohbet* of Kenʿān Rifāʿī's mystic circle even as she excelled at Dārülfünūn in logic and ethics. Part I also highlights Semiha's career as an educator in the 1930s, when she brought philosophical wisdom into her high school classrooms, quietly infusing a positivist curriculum with ethical and spiritual insight. Finally, it examines how such a remarkable thinker fell into obscurity: her works were largely forgotten amid the Republic's push for secular, nationalist literature. By charting the near-erasure of Semiha's contributions—and the few flickers of remembrance that persisted—Part I underscores the patterns of memory and forgetting in intellectual history, setting the stage for why reclaiming Semiha now matters.

Part II (Chapters 5–7) then turns a scholarly lens on *Aşk Peygamberi*, offering in-depth analysis of the novel's themes, style, and place in literature. These chapters unpack the layers of meaning within Semiha's fiction and highlight *Aşk Peygamberi*'s historical and literary significance within the milieu in which it was produced. We begin with a broad philosophical reading of the novel, introducing its plot and characters while examining the bold questions it raises about love, knowledge, and the divine in a rapidly changing world. From there, the analysis dives into the novel's construction: one chapter explores the characters not just as people in a story but as embodiments of ideas (for example, the seeker who represents the restless modern soul, and the "prophet of love" who symbolizes spiritual wisdom). Another chapter dissects the narrative architecture and symbolism of *Aşk Peygamberi*, revealing how Semiha structured the tale as an allegorical journey – filled with imagery of light and darkness, veils and mirrors, gardens and seas – all pointing to deeper metaphysical insights. We then map out the novel's key concepts (such as divine Love, the struggle of the Self, and the ideal of Unity), showing how Semiha translates Sufi doctrines and philosophical notions into literary motifs that a general reader can grasp. Finally, it examines the novel's evocative soundscape and landscape – the use of music, silence, and nature's scenery to mirror the protagonist's inner longing – which adds a poetic, sensory dimension to Semiha's philosophical storytelling. Through this multifaceted analysis, we shed light on Semiha Cemāl's artistry and intellectual depth, situating *Aşk Peygamberi* in context as a bold intellectual novel that ran against the grain of its time. We come to see how Semiha used fiction as a vehicle for ideas, merging emotional narrative with spiritual philosophy in a way virtually unheard of in the literature of early Republican Türkiye.

Part III (Chapters 8-9), In the final part of this book, we offer the first complete English translation of *Aşk Peygamberi*—a novel that reads less like a product of its time than a quiet defiance of it. Written in 1927, during the twilight of Ottoman intellectual inheritance and the dawn of Republican secularism, the work resists easy classification. It is neither a nationalist allegory nor a nostalgic retreat. Rather, it is a metaphysical inquiry disguised as fiction—an intimate meditation on love, selfhood, and spiritual transformation. Translating this text has meant more than carrying words across languages; it has required preserving the philosophical resonance and symbolic depth embedded in Semiha Cemāl's prose. Her Ottoman Turkish—rich in lyrical cadence and layered meanings—carries the echoes of both Qur'anic metaphysics and Greek philosophical ideals. By bringing *Aşk Peygamberi* into English, this volume invites readers into a mode of thinking where spiritual depth and philosophical inquiry advance in concert—each enriching the other. Rather than closing a chapter, the translation opens a renewed conversation with Cemāl's vision, offering love as a way of knowing—an illuminating and disciplined path through which the soul approaches truth with clarity and devotion. This 1920s novel – a rare specimen of metaphysical fiction in early Republican Türkiye – is the centerpiece of Semiha's legacy, yet it has been practically inaccessible to readers until now. By including *Aşk Peygamberi* in its entirety (with annotations to aid modern readers), the book allows us to encounter Semiha's ideas in her own words. The novel itself is a fascinating product of its time and Semiha's dual intellectual world: it follows a protagonist on a spiritual quest guided by a mysterious "prophet of love," unfolding as an allegory about the soul's yearning for truth. Readers will notice how the narrative weaves together Sufi concepts and philosophical dialogues, all couched in the form of a romantic-spiritual tale. Part III thus serves both as a translation and as an invitation into Semiha's imaginative universe, a chance to experience firsthand the blend of mysticism and modern thought that defines her work.

In sum, the book's three-part journey — from Semiha's life, to her own words, to a close reading of her ideas — offers a thorough reexamination of an overlooked pioneer. By combining biography, translation, and critique, we not only rediscover Semiha Cemāl as an individual but also enrich our understanding of Türkiye's modern experience. Her story reminds us that beneath the official history of secular reforms lies a parallel story, one of continuity as well as change, in which spiritual and rational currents intertwined. Ultimately, restoring Semiha to the narrative helps us appreciate a more nuanced portrait of Turkish modernity, one in which the quest for knowledge and the longing for transcendence could coexist, quietly shaping minds and souls even in an age that tried to silence mysticism.

In its entirety, this monograph aims to illuminate the life and work of Semiha Cemāl, framing her not as an isolated curiosity but as a window onto broader themes – including the untold story of spiritual modernism in Türkiye and the contributions of women to intellectual history.

PART I

THE PORTRAIT OF THE FIRST TURKISH
FEMALE SUFI PHILOSOPHER:
SEMİHA CEMĀL (1905-1936)

CHAPTER 1

Thresholds of Transition: Modernity, Sufism, and Women

Semiha Cemāl occupies a singular, though largely overlooked, position within the intellectual and literary history of early Republican Türkiye.[23] Emerging as one of the first Turkish women to engage simultaneously in philosophical and literary production within a predominantly male intellectual milieu, she forged a distinctive synthesis between Sufi metaphysical traditions and classical philosophical thought. Her translations of ancient philosophy—rare undertakings for a woman of her time—stand alongside her original literary compositions as evidence of a profound engagement with universal philosophical inquiries: the nature of love (*aşk*), existence (*vücud*), and the

---

23 There is very limited second literature on the life and legacy of Semiha Cemāl. Primary source to her life is the compiled work by his fellows Samiha Ayverdi, "Kadın Anlayışı ve Semiha Cemāl", *Ken'ân Rifâî ve Yirminci Asrın Işığında Müslümanlık*, eds. Samiha Ayverdi, Nezihe Araz, Safiye Erol and Sofi Huri (İstanbul: Kubbelatı Neşriyat, 2003), 229-248; and introductory parts of her own work, Semiha Cemāl, *Gül Demeti* (İstanbul: İstanbul Bilgi Basım ve Yayım Evi), 6. For A Recent Study, Fulya Bayraktar, "Cumhuriyet Döneminin Öncü Bir Kadın Felsefecisi: Semiha Cemāl Hanim", *Felsefe Dünyası* 52 (2010): 116-125. Also see, Kudret Savaş, *Zaman Sürgünü: Semiha Cemāl Hayatı ve Eserleri* (Çanakkale: Paradigma Akademi, 2022).

self (*nefs*).[24] In this regard, Semiha Cemāl transcended the conventional gender expectations of her period but also positioned herself within a broader, transhistorical conversation on metaphysical themes.

In her sustained engagement with classical Greek philosophy, Semiha Cemāl develops an original philosophical idiom—one that reconfigures Turkish and Sufi traditions through the epistemological and metaphorical frameworks of Platonic and Stoic thought.[25] For Cemāl, writing is a metaphysical negotiation across languages, temporalities, and ontologies. Her work, both her translations and works of fiction, gestures toward an early and ambitious project: cultivating Turkish as a philosophical language capacious enough to articulate universal questions of the soul, love, and ethical conduct. This ambition is most fully realized in her novels, particularly in *Aşk Peygam-*

---

24   Some of her translations: Semiha Cemāl (trans.) *Epiktet* (Epictete) by François Thurot (Ankara: Maârif Vekâleti, 1932); Semiha Cemāl, *Kendime: Marcus Aurelius Antonius'un Düşünceleri*, by Gustav Loisel (İstanbul: Devlet Matbaası, 1932).

25   Platonic and Stoic texts refers to the philosophical writings attributed to two major schools of ancient Greek thought: Platonic texts: These are works by or inspired by Plato (427–347 BCE), a foundational figure in Western philosophy. His writings—often in the form of dialogues—explore themes such as the nature of reality (*forms* or *ideas*), the immortality of the soul, justice, love (*eros*), and the philosopher's role in society. Key texts include *The Republic*, *Phaedrus*, *Symposium*, and *Phaedo*. Stoic texts: These are associated with the Stoic school, founded by Zeno of Citium and developed by thinkers like Epictetus (c. 50 – c. 135 CE), Seneca (c. 4 BCE – 65 CE), and Marcus Aurelius (121 – 180 CE). Stoic philosophy emphasizes rational self-control, virtue as the highest good, and harmony with nature. Its central concerns include ethics, endurance of hardship, and the cultivation of inner freedom. Notable works include Epictetus's *Discourses* and *Handbook*, Seneca's *Letters*, and Marcus Aurelius's *Meditations*. See, Anthony Kenny, *Ancient Philosophy: A New History of Western Philosophy*, Volume 1 (Oxford: Oxford University Press, 2004), 65-115.

beri, where classical ethical paradigms are refracted through a Sufi worldview. Stoic imperatives of self-discipline and Platonic ideals of transcendental love and the soul are interwoven with Sufi concepts such as *ilahi aşk* (divine love), *nefs* (self), and *fenā* (annihilation of the self in God), giving rise to a hybrid discursive space. In this space, metaphysical language—once silenced by the rationalist imperatives of the new Republic—returns not by resistance, but by reimagining its own terms.

Despite the philosophical depth and spiritual resonance of her work, Semiha Cemāl remains marginalized in the history of Turkish literature and intellectual thought—her legacy largely eclipsed by the materialist and nationalist frameworks that shaped the ideological foundations of the early Republican project.[26] This marginalization became especially pronounced in the wake of sweeping cultural reforms: the 1924 Law on the Unification of Education (*Tevhid-i Tedrisat*), which abolished religious schools; the 1925 closure of Sufi lodges, which dismantled institutionalized mysticism; and the 1928 introduction of the Latin alphabet, which rendered much of the Ottoman-language corpus—including Semiha's early works—inaccessible to future generations.[27]

---

26 Feroz Ahmad, *The Making of Modern Turkey* (London: Routledge, 2002), 79.

27 Major cultural reforms initiated by the early Republican government included the 1924 Tevhid-i Tedrisat (Law on the Unification of Education), which centralized all educational institutions under the Ministry of National Education; the 1925 abolition of Sufi lodges (tekkes and zaviyes); and the 1928 adoption of the Latin alphabet. These reforms aimed to secularize and modernize Turkish society but often suppressed traditional religious and metaphysical discourses. In the sociopolitical dynamics of the Republic, wherein spiritual and religious expressions were often relegated to the margins: Berna Moran, *Edebiyat Kuramları ve Eleştiri* (İstanbul: İletişim Yayınları, 1991), 97; Erdağ Göknar, *Orhan Pamuk, Secularism and Blasphemy: The Politics of the Turkish Novel* (London: Routledge, 2013), 102-106.

The early Republican novel, forged in the crucible of revolution and cultural engineering, often functioned as a tool of ideological pedagogy.[28] Literature became a narrative laboratory where the foundational myths of the Republic—secularism, rationalism, civic virtue, and national unity—were rehearsed and reinforced.[29] Heroic protagonists were cast in the mold of ideal citizens, while figures associated with religious tradition, especially Sufism, were relegated to the margins as vestiges of a bygone era. Within this narrative framework, Sufi thought—once a locus of interior transformation—was recoded as a source of social inertia or superstition.[30] Following the 1925 closure of dervish lodges and the accompanying epistemic rup-

---

28   The rigid Kemalist perspective and its social consequences were widely debated by early Republican intellectuals, with literature emerging as a key medium for societal reflection. Kemal Karpat argues that early Republican Turkish literature was shaped by the nation's drive for modernization and Westernization, emphasizing that its development cannot be understood without considering the political, social, and cultural forces that influenced its formation. Karpat, Kemal. "Social Themes in Contemporary Turkish Literature Part 1", *Middle East Journal* 14, no. 1, (1960): 29-44; Jale Parla, "The Wounded Tongue: Turkey's Language Reform and the Canonicity of the Novel", *Modern Language Association* 23, no.1, (2008): 31.

29   Şamil Yeşilyurt, "Cumhuriyetin Erken Döneminde Tarihî Roman (1923-1950)", *Türk Ocakları Derneği Bursa Şubesi'nin Cumhuriyet'in 100. Yılına Armağanı* (2023): 151-171; Yakup Kadri Karaosmanoğlu, *Nur Baba: A Sufi Novel of Late Ottoman Istanbul*, ed. M. Brett Wilson (London: Routledge, 2024).

30   This shift in perception reflects the broader intellectual and political transformations of the late Ottoman and early Republican periods, during which Sufi institutions and discourses came under increasing scrutiny. Reformist thinkers, influenced by modernist, positivist, and nationalist ideologies, began to portray Sufism as an impediment to rational progress, civic virtue, and social modernization. See, Arzu Eylül Yalçınkaya, "From Concept to Novel: Tâhirülmevlevî's (1877-1951) Sufi Engagement and Critique of Teşebbüs-i Şahsî (Individual Initiative) in the Late Ottoman Era", *Kadim* 8 (2024): 23-50.

ture, Sufi discourse was expunged from the authorized spheres of knowledge production.[31] What survived of metaphysical inquiry often did so in veiled form, smuggled into prose fiction or confined to allegory. Even when spiritual themes appeared, they were frequently subordinated to a narrative of moral decline, mirroring the state's portrayal of religious institutions as obsolete and counterproductive.[32]

It is within the charged atmosphere of 1923—a moment dense with the energies of political redefinition and cultural realignment—that Semiha Cemāl's work, and most notably her novel *Aşk Peygamberi* (1927), finds its historical and intellectual resonance. As older forms of spiritual expression gave way to novel configurations of identity and belonging, the novel offers a contemplative response to the shifting epistemological grounds of the new republic. Composed in a moment when the Ottoman Empire's spiritual architecture had been dismantled and its intellectual legacies delegitimized, Cemāl's novel revives Sufi idioms in a register intelligible to the modern reader. Her narrative voice navigates the threshold between secular reason and mystical consciousness, refusing to anchor itself solely inside or outside the sanctioned discursive order.[33] Drawing si-

31 İsmail Kara, *Cumhuriyet Türkiye'sinde Bir Mesele Olarak İslam* (Istanbul: Dergâh Yayınları, 2016), 75-80.

32 For a literary and cultural analysis of how Sufism came to be portrayed as morally decadent and politically obsolete in the early Republican imagination, see, M. Brett Wilson, "The Twilight of Ottoman Sufism: Antiquity, Immorality, and Nation in Yakup Kadri Karaosmanoğlu's Nur Baba", *International Journal of Middle East Studies* 49, no. 2 (2017): 233-253.

33 For a critical examination of how the end of the Ottoman Empire has been represented not as a historical transformation in its own right, but often as a moment absorbed into the founding narrative of the modern Turkish Republic, see, Orçun Can Okan, "Osmanlı'ya Sonlar Yaz((a)ma)mak: İmparatorluk, Devlet ve Ardıllık", Osmanlı Tarihçiliğinde Yani Çalışmalar: Kaynak, Bağlam, Yöntem, eds. Fatma Öncel, Sinem

multaneously from the interiority of Islamic mysticism and the ethical universals of Hellenistic philosophy, Cemāl forges a conceptual hybridity that operates obliquely within the parameters of secular modernity. Her work does not reject the terms of the Republic outright, but insists on the legitimacy of an alternative form of Turkish subjectivity—one grounded in contemplative interior life rather than ideological conformity.

Cemāl's literary intervention is also remarkable for its gendered inflection. In an era when many female authors were celebrated insofar as they mirrored the state's vision of the rational, civically engaged modern woman, Cemāl charts a different path.[34] Her writing does not conform to the pedagogical expectations of Republican didacticism, nor does it reduce womanhood to the performance of public citizenship.[35] Instead, she turns inward—toward metaphysical longing, divine love, and the ontological nature of the self. In doing so, she not only subverts the prevailing disciplinary frames that sought to regulate

Erdoğan İşkorkutan (İstanbul: Vakfı Bank Yayınları, 2023), 245-279. Okan analyzes the narrative and conceptual strategies through which imperial legacies—especially those that do not conform to the secular-nationalist paradigm—are repressed, reframed, or rendered unintelligible. His work offers a useful lens for understanding how Semiha Cemāl's novel reanimates Sufi idioms and metaphysical sensibilities within a literary field increasingly shaped by modernist and republican expectations.

34 Hülya Bayrak Akyıldız, "Representation of Women in Early Republic Era Turkish Novels" *Oriental Languages and Civilizations*, eds. Barbara Michalak-Pikulska, Tomasz Majtczak, and Marek Piela (Krakow: Jagiellonian University Press, 2021), 37-46.

35 For a discussion of how early Republican reforms reshaped female subjectivity around ideals of national duty, self-sacrifice, and moral exemplarity, see, Dikmen Yakalı and Bora Ataman, "Selfless Subjectivities that (Re) Build the Nation: Remaking the 'Modern Turkish Woman' in the Early Republican Period in Türkiye", *Journal of Family History* 48, no. 4 (2023): 432-446.

female expression but also offers a counter-model of female intellectual agency. Her womanhood exemplifies a vision of modernity grounded in spiritual refinement, where inner transformation enriches civic life and redefines progress as a matter of depth rather than display.

Her engagement with Stoic and Platonic thought enriches the foundations of her philosophical vision. Through both translation and fiction, Cemāl offers a transformative reading of classical texts—one that expands their meanings through ethical insight and spiritual depth. She engages the Hellenistic tradition through a Sufi hermeneutic—reshaping its principles in the language of tawḥīd, spiritual love, and inner ethics. Her project is about discovering latent resonances: a philosophical consonance that transcends binaries. In her hands, binaries—secular and religious, modern and traditional, East and West—dissolve into a more fluid intellectual terrain. What emerges instead is a space of convergence—an intellectual topography in which metaphysical inquiry can be reimagined through literary form, precisely because institutional forms had foreclosed it. Viewed in this light, Semiha Cemāl's body of work invites a reappraisal of early Republican intellectual life. She gives voice to a submerged metaphysical undercurrent that persisted beneath the ideological surface of secularism. Her texts—composed in Ottoman Turkish during a period of radical linguistic and epistemic transition—function as palimpsests: bearing traces of a cosmology that was being effaced, yet not entirely erased. To read her today is a way to reclaim an alternate genealogy of Turkish thought—one where philosophy, mysticism, womanhood, and ethical authorship are braided together in defiance of historical amnesia.

1.1. THE HISTORICAL OVERVIEW AND INFLUENCES OF SEMİHA CEMĀL'S FORMATIVE YEARS

Semiha Cemāl's early life was shaped by the cultural and political complexities of a collapsing empire. The late Ottoman period (1789-1918) was marked by a series of military defeats, territorial losses, and internal reform movements aimed at restructuring the imperial order.[36] The political and intellectual elite of the period sought to articulate a vision of national strength through Western-inspired modernization, often emphasizing political centralization, educational reform, and the promotion of a secular Turkish identity.[37] Semiha Cemāl's intellectual formation unfolded within this turbulent context. Educated at *Dārülfünūn*, Semiha Cemāl was part of the first generation of women to enter the formal educational institutions of the new Republic.[38] Her decision to study philosophy, a

---

36   For a detailed overview of the historical and social dynamics of the late Ottoman Empire: Şükrü Hanioğlu, *A Brief History of the Late Ottoman Empire*, (Princeton: Princeton University Press, 2008), 150-203.

37   For the identity politics and discussions of secularism in the first decades of the Turkish Republic, Erik J. Zürcher, *Turkey: A Modern History* (London: I.B. Tauris, 2017), 167-177.

38   Philosophy education at Dārülfünūn, later known as Istanbul University, underwent significant development, particularly after the re-establishment of Dārülfünūn-ı 'Os̱mānī in 1908 under the influence of the Committee of Union and Progress (İttihat ve Terakki). To modernize the institution, new academic chairs were established, students were sent abroad for education, and foreign professors were appointed to address the shortage of qualified instructors. By 1924, courses on Islamic philosophy, moral philosophy (*ahlak*), and logic were introduced in the Faculty of Literature. By 1929, the Philosophy Department was structured into three main chairs: Sociology, Psychology (*Ruhiyat*), and the History of Philosophy, where Islamic philosophy courses were also integrated into the curriculum. See, Tolga Arslan, "Darülfünun'dan İstanbul Üniversitesi'ne Felsefe Öğreniminin Yapılandırılması", *Ankara Üniversitesi Türk İnkılâp Tarihi Enstitüsü Atatürk Yolu Dergisi* 61 (2017): 51-86.

discipline traditionally dominated by men, reflects not only her intellectual ambition but also her willingness to engage with the foundational questions of human existence at a time when Turkish intellectual culture was increasingly shaped by scientific positivism and political materialism.[39]

The 1920s and 1930s witnessed a marked shift in Turkish intellectual life as the Republican elite sought to construct a secular, national identity.[40] The closure of the Sufi lodges in 1925 and the alphabet reform of 1928 were key markers of this rupture, as the state sought to eliminate the symbols of Ottoman-Islamic continuity and replace them with a modern, Western-facing national identity.[41] Literature became a key site of this cultural transformation. The philosophical and spiritual breadth of Cemāl's work distinguishes her from many of her contemporaries. Writers such as Yakup Kadri Karaosmanoğlu (d. 1974) and Halide Edib Adıvar (d. 1964) sought to define the contours of Turkish modernity through narratives that reflect-

---

39   Sait Özervarlı, "Positivism in the Late Ottoman Empire: The "Young Turks" as Mediators and Multipliers", *The Worlds of Positivism*, eds. J., Fillafer, F., Surman, J (Cham: Palgrave Macmillan, 2018), 81-108.

40   See, Nazım İrem, "Turkish Conservative Modernism: Birth of a Nationalist Quest for Cultural Renewal", *International Journal of Middle East Studies* 34, no. 1 (2002: 87-112.

41   The *Regulation on the Closure of Dervish Lodges and Zāwiyas, Attire of the Religious Class, and the Dress Code for Civil Servants*, issued on September 2, 1925, ordered the closure of all dervish lodges, zāwiyas, and tombs. It also revoked the legal status of titles and distinctive attire linked to these institutions, such as those of sheikh, dervish, and disciple. This regulation was reinforced by Law No. 677, *On the Closure of Dervish Lodges, Zâwiyas, and Tombs, and the Prohibition of Certain Titles and Posts*, which was enacted on November 30, 1925.For more information, Cem Apaydın, "Belgeler Işığında Tekke, Zaviye ve Türbelerin Kapatılması Üzerine Bir Değerlendirme", *Yakın Dönem Türkiye Araştırmaları* 16, no. 32 (2017): 149-171; For information on the execution of reforms in early Turkish Republic, Zürcher, *Turkey: A Modern History*, 173-174.

ed the challenges of national identity, secularism, and political progress.[42] Cemāl's work reflects a deeper metaphysical inquiry into the nature of existence and the structure of human consciousness. As a woman engaging with classical philosophical texts and Sufi metaphysics, Cemāl's intellectual position was inherently transgressive—challenging both the patriarchal structures of Ottoman-Islamic tradition and the nationalist-secular frameworks of Republican modernity.

Writing during the early Republican period Semiha Cemāl produced her literary works within a politically fraught and ideologically restrictive environment. The newly established secular regime actively suppressed religious expression in the public sphere. In such a climate, overt engagement with

---

42 Yakup Kadri Karaosmanoğlu (d. 1974) and Halide Edib Adıvar (d. 1964) were prominent figures in early Republican Turkish literature, whose works reflect the complex cultural and political transformations of the late Ottoman and early Republican periods. Karaosmanoğlu's novels, such as Yaban (1932), explored the deep cultural and psychological divide between the urban elite and rural Anatolia, highlighting the tensions between modernization and traditionalism in the formation of Turkish national identity. Similarly, Halide Edib's works, including Sinekli Bakkal (1936), grappled with the interplay of Western influence, Islamic tradition, and gender roles in the context of the newly established secular republic.[2] Both writers contributed to shaping the discourse on Turkish modernity by addressing issues of nationalism, political reform, and social change through their literary narratives. See, Yakup Kadri Karaosmanoğlu, *Yaban* (Istanbul: İletişim Yayınları, 2017); Halide Edib Adıvar, *Sinekli Bakkal* (Istanbul: Can Yayınları, 2019). For detailed analysis on the contribution of these authors, Erdağ Göknar, "Turkish-Islamic Feminism Confronts National Patriarchy: Halide Edib's Divided Self," *Journal of Middle East Women's Studies* 9, no. 2 (2013): 33-34; Kemalism, the word coined to embody the principals and values of the economic, social, political, cultural transformation the new republic envisioned was first used in 28 June 1929 by Yakup Kadri Karaosmanoğlu. Kemalism broadly implied the six arrows: Republicanism, Populism, Nationalism, Secularism, Statism and Reformism. For more information: İrem, "Turkish Conservative Modernism", 87-112.

Sufi doctrine or Islamic metaphysics was discouraged, if not outright censored. Many writers who approached such themes did so within the dominant intellectual frameworks of the new Republic, casting Sufism either as an impediment to national progress or as a sentimental residue of a bygone era.[43] Produced with these dynamics, Semiha Cemāl's work stands out for its quiet defiance and creative subtlety. Rather than confronting these prohibitions head-on, she embedded Sufi and Islamic themes within the framework of fictional narrative, employing a highly symbolic, philosophical language that allowed her to circumvent ideological scrutiny.[44] Her writing harnessed metaphor, allegory, and interior monologue as tools of concealment and revelation. Through the inner worlds and

---

43   Yakup Kadri Karaosmanoğlu's *Nur Baba* (1922), Reşat Nuri Güntekin's *Yeşil Gece* (1928), and *Miskinler Tekkesi* (1946), as well as Refik Halit Karay's *Kadınlar Tekkesi* (1956), share a common critique of Sufi institutions, portraying them as centers of religious exploitation. These works collectively reflect the broader secularist critique of religious institutions during the early Republican period, emphasizing their perceived moral and societal failures. Please see, Yakup Kadri Karaosmanoğlu, *Nur Baba* (İstanbul: İletişim Yayınları, 2023); Reşat Nuri Güntekin, *Yeşil Gece* (İstanbul: İnkılap Kitapevi, 2000); Reşat Nuri Güntekin, *Miskinler Tekkesi* (İstanbul: İnkılap Kitapevi, 2000); Refik Halid Karay, *Kadınlar Tekkesi* (İstanbul: İnkılap Kitapevi, 2010). Also see for a recent edited translation of Karaosmanoğlu's novel, Yakup Kadri Karaosmanoğlu. *Nur Baba: A Sufi Novel of Late Ottoman Istanbul*, ed. M. Brett Wilson (London: Routledge, 2024).

44   For information on the challenges of religious publishing during the early years of the Republic and the single-party period, see İsmail Kara, *Cumhuriyet Türkiyesi'nde Bir Mesele Olarak İslâm* (Istanbul: Dergâh Yayınları, 2017), 415–482; Mustafa Kara, "Cumhuriyet Türkiyesi'nde Tarîkatlar," *Türkiye'de Tarikatlar: Tarih-Kültür*, ed. Semih Ceyhan (Istanbul: İSAM Yayınları, 2015), 103–111. For an overview of the genres of novels and the functions assigned to novels during the Republican period, see Fatih Andı, "Türk Edebiyatında Roman: Cumhuriyet Devri", *TALID Türkiye Araştırmaları Literatürü Dergisi* 8, no. 8 (2006): 165–201.

speech of her literary characters, she conveyed the moral, existential, and cosmological teachings of Sufism—rendering her fiction a discreet yet potent medium of spiritual transmission during a time when public religious discourse had been marginalized. Her command of Ottoman Turkish and her sensitivity to the philosophical nuances of both classical Islamic and Western thought endowed her prose with a distinctive rhetorical texture. Her characters frequently speak in echoes of Qur'anic vocabulary, ethical aphorisms, and metaphysical insights drawn from the Sufi tradition—yet these references remain largely untouched by the predominant ideological binaries of her time.

The neglect of Semiha Cemāl's work in Turkish literary and intellectual history reflects a broader marginalization of spiritual and metaphysical inquiry within the early Republican cultural paradigm. Following the foundation of the Republic, Turkish modernity was increasingly defined through a framework of rupture—an epistemic and civilizational break from the Ottoman-Islamic past.[45] Intellectual legitimacy came to be associated with secular rationalism, scientific positivism,

---

45   Zafer Toprak explores the radical break with the Ottoman past promoted by early Republican cultural politics, particularly through the lens of poet Nâzım Hikmet's (d. 1963) campaign "Putları Kırıyoruz" ("Let's Smash the Idols"). The campaign epitomized the revolutionary zeal of the 1920s, emphasizing a future-oriented nationalism that sought to delegitimize historical continuity. As Toprak highlights, the official discourse of the time explicitly rejected the past as a burden, glorifying instead the youth's duty to sever ties with tradition. One striking slogan from the campaign declared: "Those who reverence their past are those nations who are not interested in their future. [...] The duty of the youth is not to respect the past but to smash it." This iconoclastic rhetoric captured the ethos of a regime determined to redefine national identity through a rupture rather than reform. Zafer Toprak, "Nazım Hikmet'in 'Putları Kırıyoruz' Kampanyası ve Yeni Edebiyat", *Toplumsal Tarih* 261 (2015), 35-36.

and Western notions of historical progress. Within this context, religious and mystical modes of thought were frequently cast as relics of an outdated worldview, incompatible with the forward momentum of the modern nation-state. Semiha Cemāl's corpus complicates and disrupts this dominant narrative. Her writings suggest that philosophical and spiritual inquiry did not vanish in the early Republican period but rather assumed more discreet, symbolically charged forms. Beneath the surface of the new ideological order, her work sustained a metaphysical current that continued to probe questions of selfhood, divine love, ethical responsibility, and ontological unity. In blending Platonic and Stoic philosophical concepts with the deeply experiential and cosmological insights of Sufi metaphysics, Cemāl produced a rare synthesis—one that bridged diverse traditions and subtly contested the reductive secular-materialist foundations of modern Turkish identity. Rather than rejecting modernity, her work reimagines its possibilities. She articulates a form of intellectual and spiritual modernity rooted in continuity that acknowledges the legitimacy of inner experience, intuitive knowledge, and ethical self-cultivation as forms of intellectual labor. In doing so, she reminds us that the formation of the modern Turkish subject was never as ideologically homogenous or spiritually barren as the official discourse.

This subversive metaphysical continuity is nowhere more evident than in Semiha Cemāl's translations and philosophical commentaries on classical Greek thought. Her philosophical vision reflects a bold and sophisticated synthesis of Sufi metaphysics, Platonic idealism, and Stoic ethics—a convergence that offered an implicit rebuttal to the era's narrowing of intellectual horizons. Cemāl's translations of Plato's (427–347 BCE) *Symposium* and *Phaedo* stand as early efforts to reintroduce classical philosophical texts to a Turkish readership increasingly oriented toward scientific and ideological modes of thinking.[46] She approached these works as spiritually resonant texts that could illuminate the inner life of the human being. In her introduction to *Phaedo*, for instance, Cemāl drew direct parallels between the Socratic vision of cosmic harmony and the Sufi doctrine of *tawhīd* (divine unity).[47] She interpreted the Platonic ascent of the soul toward the *eidos*—the realm of eternal forms—as analogous to the Sufi path of spiritual refinement through *fanā'* (self-annihilation) and *baqā'* (subsistence in God).[48] In her view, Socrates' (470 – 399 BCE) calm acceptance of death and his orientation toward the eternal echoed the Sufis' gradual effacement of the ego and union with the Real. Through such interpretive gestures, Semiha Cemāl reframed philosophical inquiry not as a detached, academic pursuit but as an ethical and spiritual discipline—one aimed at aligning the human soul with the metaphysical structure of the cosmos. In doing so, she resisted the growing marginalization of metaphysical thought in Turkish intellectual life, reclaiming a lineage in which philosophy, mysticism, and ethical self-cultivation were inseparable. Her synthesis gestures

---

46 Semiha Cemāl, *Apoloji (Methiye-Sokrates'in Savunması) ve Kriton (Vazife)* (İstanbul: Devlet Matbaası, 1932); Platon, *Aşk ve Ziyafet*, trans. Semiha Cemāl (İstanbul: Devlet Basımevi, 1936).

47 Cemāl, *Apoloji (Methiye-Sokrates'in Savunması) ve Kriton (Vazife)*, 10-12.

48 *Phaedo* is a dialogue written by the ancient Greek philosopher Plato, likely composed around 385–380 BCE. It is one of Plato's most famous works, centering on the final hours of Socrates' life before his execution. The dialogue takes place in the prison where Socrates is held and is narrated by Phaedo of Elis, a student of Socrates. The work explores the nature of the soul, the concept of death, and the immortality of the soul. The dialogue concludes with Socrates' calm acceptance of death, reinforcing his belief in the soul's immortality and the philosophical life as preparation for death. See, Semiha Cemāl, *Apoloji (Methiye-Sokrates'in Savunması) ve Kriton (Vazife)* (İstanbul: Devlet Matbaası, 1932).

toward a vision of knowledge that transcends disciplinary boundaries and reclaims philosophy as a lived practice rooted in both love and *gnosis*.

CHAPTER 2

THE MAKING OF THE FIRST TURKISH FEMALE SUFI PHILOSOPHER

2.1. EARLY LIFE AND FAMILY

Semiha Cemāl was born in the historic Fatih district of Istanbul, a neighborhood long associated with religious learning and cultural vitality.[49] In a household that echoed with both inherited refinement and quiet spiritual resolve, she was raised amid the confluence of Ottoman aristocratic culture and the living rhythm of Sufi learning. Her mother, Nazlı Hanım, descended from the illustrious dynastic house of Evrenos, embodied the sensibility of an educated, contemplative woman whose modern grace harmonized with a deeply rooted spiritual temperament. Her father, Cemāl Bey, was a true çelebi—an Istanbul gentleman distinguished by refinement, generosity, and intellectual poise.

In the final years of the Empire, the family was drawn to the intellectual and spiritual gravitas of Ken'ān Rifā'ī, whose

---

49   Savaş, *Zaman Sürgünü*, 16; Located at the heart of the old city, Fatih has long been central to the Ottoman imperial imagination as both a religious and administrative core, densely layered with mosques, medreses, tekkes, and imperial institutions. On the historical and cultural significance of the Fatih district, see Gözde Çelik, "Tanzimat Döneminde Tarihî Yarımada: Tercihler, Yaklaşımlar, Görünümler," *Türkiye Araştırmaları Literatür Dergisi* 8/16 (2010): 227–258.

tekke and residence in Hırka-i Şerîf (the Holy Mantle of the Prophet Muhammad) had emerged as a luminous gathering place for those seeking ethical clarity and metaphysical depth. As their lives became increasingly intertwined with Ken'ān Rifā'ī's spiritual community, the family's new home near the *tekke* grew attuned to the contemplative rhythm of *sohbet* and the ethos of quiet service. Yet their presence extended beyond the household. In time, they became active participants in the daily life of the tekke complex, offering their energy and care to its educational, devotional, and community-oriented practices. It was within this shared spiritual and moral world—at the threshold between private life and public service—that Semiha Cemāl came of age. Their home soon settled into the daily rhythm of *sohbet* gatherings and quiet acts of service. Nazlı Hanım advanced rapidly on the spiritual path, her keen intelligence matched by a luminous sincerity; Cemāl Bey, with his composed dignity, became one of Rifā'ī's early spiritual successors. Their proximity to the tekke was not symbolic—it was formative. Semiha grew up within reach of both the master's voice and his silence.

It was within this disciplined and affectionate world that Semiha Cemāl began to observe, absorb, and question. Though described in her youth as reserved and inwardly strong-willed, she developed an early sensitivity to the ethical and intellectual atmosphere that surrounded her. Around the age of eighteen, she deepened her commitment to the Sufi path during a series of personal visits to Ken'ān Rifā'ī, often accompanied by her cousin, Sâmiha Ayverdi. The questions they brought—rooted in genuine spiritual seeking—were received by the sheikh with seriousness and warmth. Those close to her recall this moment as a turning point: what had once been respectful proximity turned into reverent participation. Semiha's aristocratic upbringing had encouraged discernment and restraint, yet in Rifāʿī she encountered a depth of wisdom and presence that invited trust. From this meeting, her path of formal *sohbet* began—marking not a break from her past, but the conscious embrace of a lifelong inner journey.

Kenʿān Rifāʿī served as a distinguished Sufi sheikh of the Rifāʿīyye order and held a bureaucratic position within the Ottoman Ministry of Education (*Maʿārif Nezāreti*). His teachings offered a compelling synthesis of classical Sufi wisdom and the evolving intellectual sensibilities of the late Empire and early Republic. Grounded in the inner ethics of Islam, his approach welcomed engagement with contemporary philosophical and literary thought, cultivating a spiritual pedagogy that appealed to a wide spectrum of seekers. His circle brought together writers, educators, artists, and civil servants—individuals drawn to a tradition that spoke not only to personal transformation but to the ethical questions of a society in transition.[50] Semiha Cemāl's mother, Nazlı Hanım, was also an active participant in the spiritual circle surrounding the Rifāʿī lodge.[51] Nazlı Hanım was known for her deep spiritual wisdom, refined sense of love and propriety, and her dervish-like temperament. With a background

---

50   For a detailed information on his legacy and circle, Arzu Eylül Yalçınkaya, *Ken'ân Rifâî: Hayatı, Eserleri ve Tasavvuf Anlayışı* (İstanbul: Nefes Yayınevi, 2021). Also see, Arzu Eylül Yalçınkaya, "Kenʿān Rifāʿī and the Dynamics of Late Ottoman Sufi Poetry: Continuity, Innovation, and Intellectual Engagement", *Journal of the Institute for Sufi Studies* 3, no. 2 (2024): 87-123; Feyza Burak-Adli, "The Portrait of an Alla Franca Shaykh: Sufism, Modernity, and Class in Turkey," *International Journal of Middle East Studies* 56, no. 2 (2024): 207–226. Also one particular study which significantly lays out the influence of Ken'ân Rifâî's in contemporary Turkish Sufi thought particularly how his lineage continued with the work of Cemālnur Sargut, Feyza Burak Adli, "Trajectories of Modern Sufism: An Ethnohistorical Study of the Rifai Order and Social Change in Turkey" (PhD diss., Boston University, 2020).

51   Samiha Ayverdi and Nezihe Araz, "Ken'an Rifâî ve İmanına İştirak Edenlerden Bazıları", 76-77.

rooted in Ottoman privilege, she is said to have turned with clarity and conviction toward a life guided by sincerity, spiritual service. Semiha Cemāl was the youngest child in her family alongside her siblings, Professor Ziya Bey, and Behire Hanım. Semiha Cemāl's brother, Ziya Cemāl (later Büyükaksoy, d. 1953), was one of Ken'ān Rifā'ī's closest disciples and was one of the pioneering figures in modern Turkish dentistry.[52] The fact that her brother, Ziya Bey, pursued an academic career and eventually attained the rank of professor is indicative of the family's strong commitment to intellectual cultivation. From an early age, Semiha Cemāl was thus exposed to both the philosophical and spiritual dimensions of Ottoman intellectual life—a dual inheritance that would shape her literary and philosophical output.

Her early education began at the Çelebi Mektebi, and she continued her secondary studies at Çamlıca Lisesi, a girls' high school that reflected the increasing importance placed on women's education during the early decades of the twentieth century. These institutions provided her with a strong foundation in modern sciences and humanities, complementing the metaphysical and moral education she received at home. Determined to deepen her intellectual pursuits, Semiha Cemāl enrolled in the Department of Philosophy at the Dārülfünūn, the foremost institution of higher learning in Türkiye at the time.[53]

When Semiha Cemāl entered the Dārülfünūn's philosophy department in the early 1920s, she stepped into an institution in transformation. Only a decade earlier, no Muslim woman could study at the empire's sole university – higher education had been

---

52   For detailed information see, Ahmet Efeoğlu, "Modern Türk Diş Hekimliğinin Öncülerinden Prof. Dr. Dt. Ziya Cemāl Büyükaksoy (13 Eylül 1896-6 Ekim 1953)" *Dergi* (2021): 64-68.

53   Founded in the mid-19th century as part of the Ottoman modernization efforts, Dârülfünûn evolved into Istanbul University after the Republican reforms of 1933, representing a key institution in shaping the intellectual elite of early twentieth-century Türkiye.

strictly male. In 1914-15, the Ottoman state had experimented by opening a separate Women's University (Inas Dārülfünūnu), but by 1921, its female students were boycotting their segregated status, demanding integration with the men's classes. Their protests succeeded: during the post-WWI Armistice years, Istanbul's Dārülfünūn began admitting women alongside men – a bold move achieved even before many Western institutions embraced coeducation. Semiha Cemāl was thus among the very first women to receive a full university education in Türkiye, and by contemporary accounts, she distinguished herself as one of the country's first female philosophers. This meant that while she shared lecture halls with male peers, in many ways she was charting unknown territory.

Her presence symbolized a broader cultural shift: the old world of Ottoman tradition yielding to a new Republican vision of modernity – yet Semiha's experience would prove that the transition was not a simple replacement of the old with the new, but rather a complex negotiation between them. Notably, she came from an enlightened family deeply involved in Istanbul's Sufi circles, and her personal mentors believed that women like her could bridge Eastern and Western thought. Indeed, one of the era's celebrated Sufi masters, Ken'ān Rifā'ī, had actively encouraged Semiha's philosophical pursuits – a striking endorsement at a time when many would assume Islamic mysticism and modern philosophy to be at odds. Supported by such forward-thinking guidance, Semiha entered Dārülfünūn not only as a student hungry for knowledge but as a pioneer carrying the aspirations of a generation of educated Ottoman women. Her very enrollment was a quiet revolution, embodying the ideal that the new Turkish woman could be both an intellectual and a guardian of spiritual tradition.

The Dārülfünūn that Semiha encountered was the Ottoman Empire's premier intellectual hub, now being refashioned under the Turkish Republic's reforms. By the mid-1920s, Mustafa Kemal Atatürk's government had overhauled the education system to make it firmly secular and positivist – following the French model by removing religious instruction from curricula and championing science and reason as the basis of knowledge. In Dārülfünūn's Faculty of Literature (which housed the philosophy section), this new vision translated into a curriculum that balanced classical and modern learning. Semiha's coursework spanned the great works of ancient Greek philosophy – studying Plato, Aristotle, and the Socratic tradition in depth – as well as contemporary Western thought, including the latest currents in European philosophy and social sciences. Significantly, the program also introduced psychology (then referred to as *ruhiyat*, the "science of the soul"), reflecting the influence of modern empirical disciplines on the humanities. Semiha excelled in this rigorous program. Under the tutelage of scholars like Prof. Mustafa Şekip Tunç, a Sorbonne-educated philosopher who was a leading light of the department, she and her classmates were exposed to cutting-edge ideas from France, Germany, and beyond.

She graduated in 1926, having received formal training in classical Greek philosophy, modern Western thought, and emerging currents in psychology.[54] What distinguished her was not only her command of this curriculum but her capacity to transpose its frameworks into the metaphysical grammar of Su-

---

54   This official archival document certifies Semiha Hanım's graduation from the Department of Philosophy at the Faculty of Literature, Dārülfünūn (later Istanbul University). It provides crucial evidence of women's participation in higher education and philosophical training during the early Republican period. The document also served as an official credential in her applications for teaching appointments. See Presidency of the Republic of Türkiye, Directorate of State Archives, Ministry of National Education (General), Fonds Code 180-9-0-0, Box 89, File 431, Folder 14.

fism. While the newly founded Turkish Republic was advancing a secular, positivist vision of knowledge, Semiha Cemāl moved between traditions—not as an act of defiance, but of synthesis.[55] Her mind was fluent in contradiction. After graduation, she taught philosophy and psychology at the İzmir Kız Lisesi (Izmir Girls' High School), contributing to the expanding field of female education—a key pillar of the early Republican project. Yet her intellectual gravitation toward Istanbul soon reasserted itself.[56]

2.2. SEMİHA CEMĀL AS EDUCATOR: MERGING PEDAGOGY WITH WISDOM

Semiha Cemāl dedicated herself wholeheartedly to teaching, contributing at a young age to the education of Türkiye's emerging generations… In 1929, she returned to Istanbul to take up a teaching position at the Istanbul Girls' Teacher Training School (*İstanbul Kız Muallim Mektebi*), where she remained until 1935.[57]

---

55 Nazım İrem, "Turkish Conservative Modernism: Birth of a Nationalist Quest for Cultural Renewal", *International Journal of Middle East Studies* 34, no. 1 (2002) 87-112.

56 Following the 1924 Tevhid-i Tedrisat (Unification of Education) Law, the Turkish Republic prioritized expanding girls' education, resulting in a significant increase in female teachers and educational administrators by the 1930s.

57 Kız Muallim Mektebi (Girls' Teacher Training School) was established in 1870 during the reign of Sultan Abdülaziz (r. 1830-1876) as part of the Tanzimat-era educational reforms aimed at modernizing the Ottoman Empire. It was the first official institution dedicated to the professional training of female teachers and played a pivotal role in expanding women's access to education and in shaping the early Republican ideal of the modern, educated woman. See, Mustafa Şanal, "Osmanlı İmparatorluğu'nda Kız Öğretmen Okulu'nun (Dârülmuallimât) Kuruluşu, Okutulan Dersler ve Kapatılışı", *Ankara Üniversitesi Osmanlı Tarihi ve Uygulama Merkezi Dergisi* (OTAM) 26 (2011): 222-244.

Between 1929 and 1935, she taught psychology at the Istanbul Girls' Teacher Training School, a school steeped in its own history of reform. Founded in 1870 under Sultan Abdülaziz, it was the first state institution devoted to the professional preparation of women educators—a bold gesture of the Tanzimat's modernizing spirit. In the Republican era, it evolved into a crucible of female intellectual formation, preparing young women not only for classroom authority but for participation in the secular nation-state's civilizing mission.[58] These schools were among the most prestigious institutions for the education of young women in the early Republican period. Semiha Cemāl's presence there, however, added another layer. She taught not just civic virtue but spiritual inquiry, helping her students imagine a model of womanhood grounded not only in public reason but in private refinement. Her teaching career, though tragically brief, was marked by a deep commitment to cultivating not only intellectual rigor but also moral and spiritual consciousness among her students.

Her teaching coincided with a time when philosophy had only recently been introduced into the national secondary school curriculum.[59] In this context, Semiha Cemāl's presence

---

58   Semiha Cemāl Hanım's early career as a certified assistant teacher (Muallim Muavini) is documented through her examination results, health report, and attestation letter—materials that reflect the bureaucratic protocols for women educators in early Republican Türkiye. For institutional details regarding her appointment and qualification process, see: Presidential State Archives of the Republic of Türkiye, Ministry of National Education (General), Fonds Code 180-9-0-0, Box 121, File 583, Folder 32.

59   Philosophy was formally introduced into the Turkish high school curriculum in the mid-1920s as part of the early Republic's secular educational reforms, marking the first time it was systematically taught at the secondary level. See, Osman Kafadar, "Felsefe Öğretiminin Türk Eğitim Sistemine Girişi ve Tarihi Gelişimi", *Ankara Üniversitesi Eğitim Bilimleri Fakültesi Dergisi* 27, no. 1 (1994): 279-288.

as a female philosophy instructor was groundbreaking. She became known for her disciplined and hardworking nature and was widely respected by her students.[60] Records indicate that she fulfilled her duties with great success at the Istanbul Girls' Teacher Training School and constantly reminded her students that "the soul was ephemeral and the body was transitory".[61] Her classroom was a space of critical engagement and ethical reflection. Students recalled her encouraging them not only to absorb existing knowledge but also to develop their own thinking—an approach rare for the time.

What distinguished her teaching was the integration of philosophical discourse with Sufi-inflected wisdom. She reportedly enriched her lectures with verses from Mevlānā Celāleddīn-i Rūmī (1207–1273) and Yunus Emre (c. 1240–1321), while also quoting from ancient philosophers when discussing moral questions.[62] In doing so, she introduced her students to the intellectual treasures of both Eastern and Western traditions, refusing to draw sharp boundaries between them. For Semiha Cemāl, education was essentially a path toward cultivating a morally perfected human being. Her pedagogy reflected her own integrative personality. She believed that true education involved shaping both the mind and the heart. As a teacher, she aimed to awaken her students' moral awareness and spiritual potential alongside their intellectual capacities.

---

60   Savaş, *Zaman Sürgünü*, 12-13.

61   Savaş, *Zaman Sürgünü*, 12.

62   Mevlânâ Celâleddîn-i Rûmî (1207–1273): Persian-born Sufi poet and founder of the Mevlevi order, buried in Konya. Yunus Emre (ca. 1240–1321): Anatolian Turkish Sufi poet known for his vernacular devotional poetry, associated with early Anatolian mysticism. See, Mustafa Tatcı, "Yunus Emre", *TDV Islâm Ansiklopedisi* (İstanbul: TDV Yayınları, 2013): 43: 600-606; Reşat Öngören, "Mevlânâ Celâleddîn-i Rûmî", *TDV İslâm Ansiklopedisi* (Ankara: TDV Yayınları, 2004), 29:441-448.

Through this multifaceted approach, Semiha Cemāl sought to educate a new generation of students who would not only inherit the values of their national culture but also develop the capacity for universal thought. Her educational philosophy reflected a synthesis of tradition and modernity: while deeply rooted in the spiritual and cultural values of the Ottoman legacy, she remained attentive to the pedagogical methods and intellectual demands of the modern Republic. Unfortunately, her teaching career was cut short in 1935 due to health problems.[63] Even this relatively brief period left a lasting impression on many of her students, some of whom likely went on to become influential figures in their own fields. Semiha Cemāl continued her intellectual pursuits during her teaching years, devoting her free time to writing and translation. Her life bridged both the modern school and spiritual traditions, indicating a synthetic approach that valued both reason and revelation, and she sought to harmonize their strengths in the service of cultivating fully realized human beings.

2.3. THE FORGOTTEN PHILOSOPHER: RECEPTION, OBSCURITY, AND RECLAMATION

Early Republican Türkiye saw women intellectuals primarily in activist and nationalist roles. Leading figures like Halide Edip Adıvar (1884–1964) were celebrated as nationalist writers and educators championing women's emancipation, while Nezihe Muhiddin (1889–1958) became known as a suffragette and feminist organizer.[64] These women mobilized around the new

---

63   Savaş, *Zaman Sürgünü*, 12-13.

64   During the formative years of the Turkish Republic, women intellectuals were largely positioned within the framework of state-led modernization and reform. Figures such as Halide Edip Adıvar and Nezihe Muhiddin were emblematic of this era, using literature, journalism,

Republic's agenda–writing novels and political tracts, founding women's associations, and embodying the ideal of the "enlightened mother" of the nation.[65] In stark contrast, Semiha Cemāl pursued a very different path—one that unfolded not in the public squares of political activism or the institutional arenas of feminist reform, but within the introspective realms of metaphysical inquiry and spiritual authorship, drawing upon Sufi cosmology and classical philosophy at a time when the newly established Republic was actively dismantling the epistemic foundations of the Ottoman-Islamic tradition and promoting a secular, positivist vision of intellectual legitimacy.

Though largely unknown to the broader public, Semiha Cemāl was held in high regard within certain intellectual and Sufi circles. Her writings were published in select literary and philosophical journals during her lifetime, but she never achieved mass readership or popular literary fame. One likely reason was the perceived difficulty and intellectual density of her work, which may have appeared abstruse to the general reading public. Another significant factor was the political climate of the early Republican era, in which Sufi themes were viewed with suspicion and often discouraged by the secularizing state ideology. As a result, Semiha Cemāl remained a figure

and organizational activism to promote women's education, national consciousness, and civic participation. Their prominence reflected the Republic's vision of women as symbols and agents of progress, aligned with secular, nationalist ideals. See, Meral Balcı, and Mervenur Tuzak, "Cumhuriyet'in İlk Yıllarında Nezihe Muhiddin Özelinde Türk Kadınlarının Siyasi Hakları İçin Mücadelesi," *Marmara Üniversitesi Kadın ve Toplumsal Cinsiyet Araştırmaları Dergisi* 1, no. 1 (2017): 43-51; Muzaffer Subaşı and Derya Nazlıpınar, "Halide Edip Adıvar and Her Perception of the 'New Woman'Identity," *Uluslararası İnsan Çalışmaları Dergisi* 1, no. 2 (2018): 374-382.

65   Senem Üstün Kaya, "Women Behind the Pens: A Comparative Analysis of Turkish Female Authors From Reform Period to Modernism", *The Online Journal of Science and Technology* 11, no. 4 (2021): 133-141.

known only within a relatively small, selective community. Over the decades following her death, Semiha Cemāl's name faded from Turkish literary and intellectual consciousness. Although she was a recognized writer in the 1930s, her work remained unpublished in the new Latin alphabet and thus inaccessible to later generations.[66] She was rarely mentioned in literary histories or philosophical anthologies compiled in the 1950s and beyond, effectively relegating her to the shadows of intellectual memory. A survey of contemporary newspapers reveals that her death received little to no coverage, often omitted entirely or noted only in brief, inconspicuous notices. In contrast, the same newspapers regularly featured far less significant stories with far greater prominence. This striking disparity suggests that Semiha Cemāl's identity—as a Sufi-minded female intellectual—did not align with the dominant secular-nationalist image of the ideal Republican subject and may have been deliberately overlooked.

However, evaluating Semiha Cemāl's cultural and historical importance solely in terms of mass visibility risks overlooking her true influence. Her impact, while not widely disseminated, operated through more intimate and enduring channels. For example, her close friend and fellow writer Sāmiha Ayverdi—who would become a prominent public intellectual in the mid-20th century—frequently alluded to Semiha Cemāl's spiritual depth in her memoirs, referring to her as her "spiritual sister" and praising her elevated soul.[67] Though her name may not have appeared often in print, the memory of her character and the traces of her ideas persisted in the lives and works of those

---

66   Her work has been published in Modern Turkish, Semiha Cemāl, *Aşk Peygamberi*, ed. Nurcan Şen (İstanbul: Çolpan Kitap, 2023).

67   Turkish writer and Sufi intellectual, disciple of Ken'ān Rifā'ī, known for her over forty books—spanning historical novels, memoirs, and spiritual essays—and for her deep commitment to the Turkish-Islamic tradition.

she influenced. Some of her students or readers likely went on to shape Turkish cultural life in their own ways, transmitting aspects of her thought through alternative forms.

From the perspective of cultural continuity, Semiha Cemāl can be seen as a representative of a transitional generation—those who inherited the intellectual heritage of the late Ottoman period and carried it into the early Republic. This cohort—which includes influential intellectuals such as Sāmiha Ayverdi, Safiye Erol (d. 1964), Nezihe Araz (d. 2009), İlhan Ayverdi (d. 2009), and Sofi Huri (d. 1983)—represents a distinctive strand of mid-20th-century Turkish thought in which Islamic spirituality and modern intellectual engagement were not seen as mutually exclusive, but as mutually enriching.[68] These women were shaped by the teachings of Ken'ān Rifā'ī and his Sufi circle, which emphasized ethical refinement, inner knowledge (*irfān*), and spiritual responsibility within a changing social order. At the same time, they were highly educated, multilingual, and intellectually cosmopolitan—many having received formal education in Western institutions or possessing a strong command of languages such as French, English, or Arabic.[69]

---

68 Nezihe Araz (d. 2009) was a prominent Turkish journalist, playwright, and author known for her works on the lives of religious figures and her accessible writings on Turkish Sufism. İlhan Ayverdi (d. 2009), a linguist and lexicographer, played a crucial role in the compilation of the Kubbealtı Lugatı and was a key figure in preserving and promoting Turkish-Islamic cultural heritage. Sofi Huri (d. 1983), born in Aleppo, was a literary scholar and translator who contributed significantly to Arabic-Turkish literary studies and was known for her deep engagement with both Islamic and Western intellectual traditions. Safiye Erol (d. 1964) was a notable Turkish novelist and translator of the Republican era, celebrated for her psychologically rich and often autobiographical novels—such as *Kadıköyü'nün Romanı*, *Ülker Fırtınası*, *Ciğerdelen*, and *Dineyri Papazı*. See, Yalçınkaya, *Ken'ân Rifâî*, 167-176.

69 Aytürk investigates how a group of women associated with Samiha Ayverdi (the Ayverdi Circle) navigated and redefined religious prac-

Sāmiha Ayverdi, for instance, authored numerous novels, memoirs, and historical studies that wove together Ottoman memory, Islamic metaphysics, and moral commentary, often in subtle dialogue with contemporary cultural currents.[70] Nezihe Araz (d. 2009), trained in psychology and philosophy, became well known for her writings on Anatolian saints and women mystics, offering accessible and narratively compelling portraits that revitalized public interest in Türkiye's spiritual heritage.[71] İlhan Ayverdi (d. 2009), a philologist and lexicog-

tice within modern Türkiye. Rejecting the common binary between secularist and Islamist feminisms, the author shows how these women crafted a form of "pious modernity"—embracing modern social roles while grounding them in Islamic teachings. By examining their writings, educational activities, and networks, the essay reveals how they simultaneously upheld traditional values and engaged in progressive public life, effectively challenging the perception that religious devotion and modern female agency were incompatible. See, İlker Aytürk, "Pious and Modern: Women's Islam in the Ayverdi Circle", *Journal of Turkish Studies/Türklük Bilgisi Araştırmaları* 51 (2019): 219–236.

70   For recent studies on Samiha Ayverdi see, Elifhan Köse, "Muhafazakar Bir Kadın Portresi Olarak Semiha Ayverdi: Muhafazakarlık Düşüncesinde Kadınlara İlişkin Bir Hat Çizebilmek", *Fe Dergi* 1 (2009): 11-20; İlker Aytürk and Laurent Mignon, "Paradoxes of a Cold War Sufi Woman: Samiha Ayverdi between Islam Nationalism, and Modernity", *New Perspectives on Turkey* 49 (2013): 57-89; Anna Neubauer, "This is the Age of Women: Legitimizing Female Authority in Contemporary Turkish Sufism", *Journal for the Academic Study of Religion* 29 (2016): 150-166; Laurent Mignon, "Du mysticisme au nationalisme religieux: les ambiguïtés de Samiha Ayverdi (1905-1993)", *European Journal of Turkish Studies* 25 (2017): e-journal.

71   These two articles by Ali Pulat and Fatih Bayram examine the major social and gender issues addressed in Nezihe Araz's plays, highlighting her focus on women's roles, struggles, and moral dilemmas in modern Turkish society. See, Ali Pulat and Fatih Bayram, "Nezihe Araz'ın Tiyatrolarındaki Toplumsal Sorunlar", *International Journal of Languages› Education and Teaching* 6, no. 4 (2018): 23-37; Ali Pulat and Fatih Bayram, "Nezihe Araz Tiyatrolarında Kadın Sorunları", *International Journal of Language Academy* 6, no. 26 (2024): 148-161.

rapher, played a central role in preserving Ottoman Turkish and Islamic terminology at a time when state-led reforms had severed linguistic ties with the past.[72] Sofi Huri (d. 1983), an academic and translator, brought a rigorous, often comparative approach to Islamic texts, bridging Turkish religious scholarship with broader currents in global thought.[73] Safiye Erol (d. 1964), was a distinguished Turkish author and intellectual whose novels—such as *Ciğerdelen* and *Ülker Fırtınası*—explore themes of identity, spirituality, and inner transformation, blending psychological depth with a subtle engagement with Sufi metaphysics; educated in Germany and fluent in multiple languages, she also contributed to Turkish literary life as a

72   İlhan Ayverdi's major contribution to the study and preservation of the Turkish language is the Misalli Büyük Türkçe Sözlük, a comprehensive, example-rich dictionary that documents the historical depth and expressive richness of Turkish. Compiled over nearly three decades and published by Kubbealtı Akademisi in 2005, the three-volume work includes tens of thousands of entries, idioms, and contextual quotations drawn from classical and modern Turkish literature. By tracing the etymology of words—whether of Arabic, Persian, or Western origin—and illustrating their usage across centuries, Ayverdi both provided an invaluable linguistic resource and also created a cultural archive that bridges Ottoman Turkish with contemporary usage, offering one of the most authoritative references in modern Turkish lexicography. See, Mustafa Tahralı, "İlhan Ayverdi", *TDV İslâm Ansiklopedisi* (Ankara: TDV Yayınları, 2020), Ek1:149-150; İlhan Ayverdi, *Misalli Büyük Türkçe Sözlük* (Tek Cilt) (İstanbul: Kubbealtı Neşriyat, 2011).

73   Sofi Huri was a multifaceted intellectual who made significant contributions both as a writer on Islamic mysticism and as a prolific translator of philosophical, literary, and religious works into Turkish. Her more than 40 translations, ranging from Rūmī to Western classics, reflect a commitment to cultural mediation and educational outreach across linguistic and spiritual traditions. For her selective works see, Sofi Huri, Hz. Mevlâna ve Yakınları, ed. Ayten Lermioğlu (İstanbul: Redhouse Yayınevi, 1969); Sofi Huri, *İslâm Âleminde İlk Kadın Sufi Olarak Tanınan Râbiat-Ül Adeviye* (İstanbul: Redhouse Yayinevi, 1970).

translator and essayist, shaping the cultural landscape of early Republican Türkiye.[74]

Together, these women formed a unique intellectual milieu: one that was deeply invested in the preservation and reinterpretation of Islamic thought for a modern audience, yet acutely aware of the linguistic, historical, and philosophical shifts of their time. Their work challenged the binary frameworks of East and West, secular and religious, modern and traditional, offering instead a layered and ethically grounded mode of cultural production that remains significant for understanding alternative trajectories of Turkish modernity. In Semiha Cemāl's case, her gender and her synthesis of Sufi and philosophical discourses added further dimensions to her intellectual distinctiveness. Although she may not have influenced large audiences in her time, she now stands—retrospectively—as a pioneering and original thinker whose contributions challenge linear narratives of Turkish modernization. Today, there is a gradual rediscovery of her name in the emerging historiography of women thinkers in Türkiye. As scholars revisit the overlooked intersections of gender, mysticism, and philosophy in early Republican thought, Semiha Cemāl's legacy invites renewed attention as a harbinger of an alternative intellectual path that privileged spiritual interiority over political visibility.

Semiha Cemāl passed away at the young age of thirty-one, marking the premature end of a life filled with intellectual and

---

74   Safiye Erol's novels are marked by a refined psychological insight and a distinctive metaphysical undertone shaped by her engagement with Sufi thought. Her fiction often weaves themes of spiritual longing, national identity, and existential transformation, reflecting both her Western education and deep grounding in Turkish intellectual traditions. Through her literary style and thematic focus, she occupies a singular place in early Republican Turkish literature. See, Safiye Erol, *Ciğerdelen* (İstanbul: Kubbealtı Neşriyat, 2008); Safiye Erol, *Ülker Fırtınası* (İstanbul: Kubbealtı Neşriyat, 2006).

spiritual promise. In the final months of 1935, she was struck by a serious illness that led to an eight-month period of pain and intensive treatment. She died on January 30, 1936, leaving behind a small circle of devoted family, friends, and students who mourned her loss deeply. Her passing was especially devastating to her spiritual sister Sāmiha Ayverdi and to the wider community of Ken'ān Rifā'ī's disciples, for whom she had become a beacon of both learning and sanctity. Her funeral took place in Istanbul, likely attended by her family, friends, and former students. Yet despite her intellectual stature, there is little in the way of written documentation regarding the funeral. As with her life, her death was not widely acknowledged in the public press.[75] A few carried short notices buried in the inner pages, with headlines like "Philosophy Teacher Semiha Cemāl Has Passed Away," but no comprehensive obituary or biographical reflection appeared in the national press. This lack of recognition speaks volumes about the marginal position she occupied in the public sphere, despite the deep esteem in which she was held within certain literary and spiritual circles.

---

75   Savaş, *Zaman Sürgünü*, 12-13.

CHAPTER 3

BRIDGING WORLDS:
THE DUAL INFLUENCES OF PHILOSOPHY
AND SUFISM ON SEMİHA CEMĀL

As both a translator of ancient Greek philosophy and a participant in living Sufi traditions, she stood at the intersection of two intellectual lineages that were increasingly estranged from one another in the early Republican era. What makes Cemāl remarkable is not only that she translated Plato's *Phaedo* and *Symposium* into Turkish at a time when classical metaphysics was being marginalized, but that she did so while writing from within a tradition—Sufism—that had been forcibly expelled from the official domains of knowledge after the 1925 closure of dervish lodges. In a cultural climate where secular rationalism and positivist science had become the new pillars of legitimacy, Cemāl pursued an intellectual path that refused this binary. Rather than choosing between philosophy and mysticism, she wove them together.

Her life and work were shaped by two powerful, yet divergent, pedagogical currents: the metaphysical teachings of Ken'ān Rifā'ī and the philosophical rigor of Şekip Tunç and other university instructors. From Rifā'ī's *sohbet* circles, she inherited a deeply experiential vision of divine unity; from her philosophical training, she gained a language of abstraction and argumentation. These were not parallel influences but interwoven ones. Cemāl did not write apologetics for Sufism, nor did she treat philosophy as a detached academic discipline. Instead, her writings reveal an effort to articulate a unified epistemology—one in which spiritual insight and intellectual reasoning are not merely compatible but mutually illuminating. The chapters that follow explore how Cemāl forged this synthesis, attending closely to the relationships and discursive practices that enabled her to braid ethical self-cultivation, metaphysical inquiry, and philosophical clarity into a singular expression of intellectual agency.

3.1. SOHBET TO KNOWLEDGE: SUFI DISCOURSES AND FEMALE FORMATION IN OTTOMAN LODGE CULTURE

There are moments in a life—and in a nation's life—when the personal and the philosophical converge with almost eerie precision. Semiha Cemāl lived in one such moment. She came of age not only in the literal twilight of the Ottoman Empire but in the conceptual dusk of its metaphysical traditions, just as the Turkish Republic was being born into a new vocabulary of modernity. Her story does not follow the usual path of national allegory. Instead, it winds through a subtler terrain, where the intimacy of spiritual apprenticeship meets the abstraction of philosophical rigor. At its heart lies a singular intellectual friendship—between Semiha Cemāl and her Sufi master, Ken'ān Rifā'ī—a relationship that shaped not only her moral outlook but her metaphysical imagination.

As one of Türkiye's first female philosophers, she distinguished herself through her teaching and her translations of Platonic and Greek philosophical texts into Turkish. Her contributions to Turkish intellectual life were groundbreaking, as she worked to harmonize the philosophical heritage of ancient Greece with the moral and metaphysical foundations of Sufi thought.[76] Yet it was her encounter with Ken'ān Rifā'ī that marked the true turning point in her life, shaping both her intellectual and spiritual development.[77] Before her initiation into the Sufi path, Semiha Cemāl was described as a proud, self-contained, and emotionally guarded young woman, immersed in her own world and largely indifferent to broader social and spiritual concerns.

Even in the quiet corners of family memory, the story of Semiha Cemāl begins with distance—an aristocratic reserve, a luminous mind in search of its mirror. Her cousin, the prolific author and Sufi thinker Sāmiha Ayverdi (d. 1993),[78] would later

76 Bayraktar, "Cumhuriyet Döneminin Öncü Bir Kadin Felsefecisi", 116-125; For discussion on the parallels between Ancient Greek philosophy and Sufism, Kamuran Godelek, "The Neoplatonist Roots of Sufi Philosophy", *The Paideia Archive: Twentieth World Congress of Philosophy* 5 (1998): 57-60; Makoto Sawai, "From Mysticism to Philosophy: Toshihiko Izutsu and Sufism", *Journal of the Institute for Sufi Studies* (2022): 112-121; For a discussion on the Neoplatonic influences on Sufi thought, Annemarie Schimmel, *Mystical Dimensions of Islam* (Chapel Hill: University of North Carolina Press, 2011), 10-11.

77 Cemālnur Sargut, *Ken'ân Rifâî ile Aşka Yolculuk*, ed. Sadık Yalsızuçanlar, (İstanbul: Nefes Yayınları, 2014), 181.

78 Samiha Ayverdi (1905–1993) was a prominent Turkish writer, intellectual, and Sufi figure closely associated with the Rifā'īyye order through her spiritual teacher, Ken'ān Rifā'ī. Her extensive body of work includes novels, essays, and historical studies that reflect her deep engagement with Islamic mysticism, Ottoman history, and Turkish cultural identity. Ayverdi's writings explore the social and spiritual transformations of Turkish society during the late Ottoman and early Republican periods, highlighting the moral and cultural challenges of modernization. Through her literary and spiritual leadership, Ayverdi shaped modern interpretations of Sufism and influenced generations of intellectuals and spiritual seekers in Türkiye. See, Feyza Burak-Adli, "Agent of

trace the arc of her transformation not through milestones or accolades, but through temperament. "Before entering the circle of Ken'ān Rifā'ī's companionship," she wrote, "Semiha Cemāl was a typical child of the aristocracy—beautiful, proud, and indifferent to the larger duties of human life. She was confined to her personal joys and sorrows, unaware of the greater responsibilities that come with existence."[79] The brilliance was there, Ayverdi recalled, but it flickered inward, in danger of consuming itself. "Had her natural gifts not fallen into the hands of a master craftsman," she warned, "she might have lost herself in her own brilliance. She was fortunate that her path crossed with that of a true spiritual guide."[80] The portrait is part caution, part reverence: a record of what it means when an intellect finds its form not through ambition, but through surrender.

Multiple sources attest that Semiha Cemāl was raised in the intimate orbit of Ken'ān Rifā'ī's circle, where the practice of *sohbet*—a form of spiritual discourse rooted in mutual reflection—served as both pedagogical and initiatory space. Her participation was not passive. Known for her boldness and intellectual clarity, she engaged actively in these gatherings, frequently posing complex and nuanced questions. Semiha was an active participant in every sense. Those who knew her recall a presence defined by thoughtful inquiry—a woman whose words, though few, carried the weight of precision and purpose. "Master," she once asked, "why do lovers weep and lament so incessantly? Is it always sorrow that speaks?" The question,

<hr>

Change or Guardian of Tradition?: Sufism, Gender, and Nationalism in Cold War Turkey," *Culture and Religion* 24, no. 2 (2024): 156–181; For a more critical study of Ayverdi's contributions, İlker Aytürk and Laurent Mignon, "Paradoxes of a Cold War Sufi Woman: Samiha Ayverdi Between Islam, Nationalism, and Modernity," *New Perspectives on Turkey* 49 (2013): 57-89.

79   Ayverdi, "Kadın Anlayışı ve Semiha Cemāl", 239.

80   Ayverdi, "Kadın Anlayışı ve Semiha Cemāl", 239.

spare and crystalline, moves directly to the emotional heart of Sufi thought. It reflects a seeking spirit—drawn to the meaning behind longing, attentive to what lies beneath sorrow's surface rather than its appearance.

Ken'ān Rifā'ī, recognizing the depth of her questions and the sincerity of her search, encouraged her development on the spiritual path. Her relationship with her sheikh was characterized by profound reverence and surrender. Those close to her often described her as a rare individual who had "become fully effaced in the presence of her master"—a reference to the Sufi concept of *fanā' fī'l-mürşid*, the annihilation of the self in the spiritual guide as a stage toward union with the divine. Such a state reflects one of the highest degrees in Sufi training, signifying not mere devotion, but the total internalization of the master's ethical and metaphysical teachings. She internalized his teachings, temperament, ethics, and metaphysical vision so fully that her words and actions came to reflect the principles she had deeply studied and absorbed. Their bond was built on trust, yet it moved beyond trust into a shared epistemology—a way of knowing grounded in shared inquiry, mutual respect, and the gradual internalization of an ethical-spiritual framework.

Semiha Cemāl's role in Ken'ān Rifā'ī's circle extended beyond that of a devoted disciple. She played an active part in the preservation of his teachings, contributing to the compilation of his discourses later published under the title *Sohbetler* (Conversations).[81] Alongside a fellow disciple, she undertook the responsibility of recording and organizing these sessions, ensuring that his oral teachings would endure in written form. This task illustrates her dual function: she was both a recipient of spiritual wisdom and a transmitter of it, participating directly in the intergenerational preservation of Sufi knowledge. Through her embodied practice of Ken'ān Rifā'ī's teachings—particular-

---

81   Ken'an Rifâî, *Sohbetler* (İstanbul: Kubbealtı Neşriyâtı, 2000).

ly his understanding of the *insān-ı kāmil* (the perfected human) and the moral imperatives of spiritual life—Semiha Cemāl distinguished herself in both intellectual and spiritual domains.[82] Her Sufi orientation was not an abstract ideal but a lived reality, shaping her demeanor, her writing, and her moral imagination. The deep connection between Semiha Cemāl and her spiritual guide permeated every stage of her life. Her years in the *sohbet* circle left an enduring imprint, forming the metaphysical foundation upon which her later works were built. Those who knew her personally often pointed to the luminous quality of her insight and the serenity of her presence as evidence of the spiritual transmission she had received from Ken'ān Rifā'ī.

Her relationship with Ken'ān Rifā'ī reflected the classical pattern of the master-disciple dynamic, where intellectual and spiritual knowledge is transmitted through direct personal exchange. Ken'ān Rifā'ī's view of Semiha Cemāl as a gifted and sensitive student reflects the depth of their spiritual connection. Upon her passing, Ken'ān Rifā'ī's words—"Of you all, hers was the hardest blow"— capture a moment of profound rupture within his inner world.[83] Far from a simple expression of grief, the statement signifies the singularity of Semiha Cemāl's place

---

82   In Sufi thought, the concept of insān al-kāmil (the Perfect Human) refers to the realized human being who fully reflects the divine attributes and serves as the bridge between God and creation. Rooted in the metaphysical writings of Ibn al-'Arabī, the insān al-kāmil is both the goal and exemplar of spiritual journeying—embodying knowledge (ma'rifa), love (maḥabba), and ethical perfection. This figure is not an abstract ideal but a realized spiritual state in which the individual becomes a mirror of divine unity (tawḥīd) while remaining grounded in human responsibility. In many Sufi traditions, the Prophet Muhammad is regarded as the supreme manifestation of the insān al-kāmil, whose heirs— the saints (awliyā')—continue this perfected model through spiritual guidance. Mehmet S. Aydın, "İnsân-ı Kâmil," *TDV İslam Ansiklopedisi (DİA)*, (İstanbul: TDV Yayınları, 2000), 22: 330–331.

83   Samiha Ayverdi, "Kadın Anlayışı ve Semiha Cemāl", 247.

in his intellectual and spiritual universe. It reflects the emotional weight of her loss and also the depth of their shared vision, cultivated through years of close companionship and philosophical alignment. In retrospect, this remark can be read as an acknowledgment of a loss that was not merely personal but symbolic—a disruption in the continuity of a spiritual lineage and the absence of a voice that had come to embody his ideals with rare clarity and fidelity.

The compiled conversations between Semiha Cemāl and Ken'ān Rifā'ī reveal a deeply pedagogical, metaphysical, and affective relationship structured around dialogic learning, ethical refinement, and shared ontological inquiry. These exchanges, while framed within a master-disciple dynamic, far exceed a didactic hierarchy; they form a co-creative philosophical space where feminine insight and masculine guidance converge in pursuit of divine knowledge (*ma'rifa*) and self-annihilation (*fanā'*).[84] Semiha Cemāl emerges not merely as a receptive interlocutor but as a vital spiritual agent whose questions, commentaries, and observations activate some of the most profound elaborations of Ken'ān Rifā'ī's thought. The relationship is thus best understood as an intellectual companionship (*musāhib*) animated by sincerity (*ihlās*), trust, and spiritual intimacy. In their conversations with Semiha Cemāl as reflected in *Sohbetler*, Ken'ān Rifā'ī's words and hers flow seamlessly, complementing each other with natural harmony.[85] He never dismisses her remarks; instead, he consistently elevates them. While he is known to occasionally challenge or reject the words of others, he always receives Semiha Cemāl's words with respect and affirmation.

Thematically, the conversations reflect a wide range of subjects organized loosely yet coherently around central Sufi con-

---

84   Ken'an Rifâî, *Sohbetler* (İstanbul: Kubbealtı Neşriyâtı, 2000), 246, 296.

85   Rifâî, *Sohbetler*, 224-225.

cerns: the metaphysics of divine attributes (*esmā* and *sıfāt*), the epistemology of love and annihilation, the role of the mürşid, the function of suffering, ethical cultivation (*ādāb*), and the dynamics of *istikāmet* (spiritual rectitude).[86] Classical Islamic figures are interwoven seamlessly with personal anecdotes, mystical poetry, and philosophical reflections. These references are not used merely to illustrate points; they form a living archive through which Ken'ān Rifā'ī instructs and Semiha Cemāl interrogates, thereby reanimating tradition in the context of modern ethical and metaphysical dilemmas. A core preoccupation across the dialogues is the nature of knowledge (*'ilm*) and its ethical implications. Ken'ān Rifā'ī distinguishes sharply between superficial erudition and what he calls "the knowledge of non-being" (*'ilm al-'adem/yokluk*), insisting that spiritual maturity requires not only intellectual capacity but the surrender of that capacity to divine omniscience. In this context, he critiques both the arrogant savant and the blindly pious, upholding instead the ideal of the humble, intuitive seeker. Semiha Cemāl's penetrating inquiries about figures like Socrates and her keen observations on epistemic humility show her adeptness at traversing both philosophical and mystical terrains, indicating a cultivated mind deeply attuned to both classical philosophy and Sufi metaphysics.

Their conversations also foreground the pedagogical method of *sohbet*, as mutual unveiling (*kashf*) of spiritual truths. The dialogic format allows for multi-layered analogies: the fire that leaves no ash (symbolizing pure spiritual combustion),[87] The grafted branch, while it may grow and blossom, symbolizes the limits of transformation—it cannot alter the *kök* (root) or the enduring *tabi'at* (essential nature) of the tree,[88] the child

---

86   Rifâî, *Sohbetler*, 85-86.

87   Rifâî, *Sohbetler*, 93.

88   Rifâî, *Sohbetler*, 94.

longing for the womb,[89] or the night when ships lower their flags (evoking the obliteration of ego).[90] These are not literary embellishments but instruments of *hikma* (wisdom), calibrated to the capacity (*istidād*) of the listener. Semiha often takes the role of interpreter, reflecting, probing, and even contesting—always within the bounds of spiritual etiquette (*ādāb*), but never without intellectual rigor. Particularly noteworthy is how the conversations construct a counter-discourse to superficial religiosity and charismatic theatrics. Ken'ān Rifā'ī, responding to Semiha's astute questions on *karāmāt* (miracles), insists that the true miracle lies not in spectacle but in moral constancy and spiritual depth.[91] This emphasis on inner refinement over external display aligns with the ethos of *malāmatiyya* and provides a critique of both modern rationalism and popular religiosity. Moreover, the emphasis on *fanā'* and the dissolution of duality (*ben-sen*) into unity (*vahdet*) is not merely a theological abstraction but is linked to the very ethics of being.[92] Here, Semiha's reflections on self-effacement, on *nefs* (the egoic self) as the veil, demonstrate her grasp of the ontological stakes of Sufi training.

It was through this sustained and dynamic *sohbet* with Ken'ān Rifā'ī that Semiha Cemāl's intellectual and spiritual identity took shape. Encouraged by her sheikh, she resumed her academic pursuits and began translating philosophical works from Greek and classical Arabic into Turkish, including key texts from the Platonic corpus and works by other major Greek philosophers.[93] Semiha Cemāl's literary works reflected her philosophical and Sufi worldview, blending themes of

---

89   Rifâî, *Sohbetler*, 108.

90   Rifâî, *Sohbetler*, 145-146.

91   Rifâî, *Sohbetler*, 70-73.

92   Rifâî, *Sohbetler*, 145-146.

93   Savaş, *Zaman Sürgünü*, 16.

divine love and human compassion. Her novels and short stories were infused with references to Islamic understanding of unity (*tawhid*), divine love, and Sufi metaphysics.[94] Her fiction explored the tension between human desires and spiritual fulfillment, presenting a vision of human existence grounded in the moral and metaphysical principles of Sufism. The central themes of her work—love for God and compassion for humanity—reflected the spiritual ideals she absorbed through her association with Ken'ān Rifā'ī.

Semiha Cemāl's engagement with Sufi tradition had both a literary and scholarly aspect. Semiha Cemāl's interpretations of Sufi doctrine were informed by her dual identity as a philosopher and a Sufi disciple, allowing her to present complex metaphysical ideas with clarity and depth. Her treatise *Meşreb-i Şerīfleri* (The Noble Dispositions) reflected her intimate understanding of Ken'ān Rifā'ī's spiritual path and philosophical teachings. In this work, Semiha Cemāl emphasized the idea that true human fulfillment lies in both knowledge and moral action. She framed Sufism through a philosophical lens, echoing Aristotle's notion that "knowing is what makes us human." Semiha Cemāl's statement when describing Ken'ān Rifā'ī was, "one of the most beloved things to him is either knowing or teaching what he knows," which reflects a deep connection be-

---

94   She has signed her journal articles as Semiha Cemāl Evrenos and interestingly few of her articles as Semiha Rifâî, cited in Savaş, *Zaman Sürgünü*, 65. Also see. Semiha Cemāl Evrenos, "Pervane", *Mihrap* 1, no. 12 (1924): 361-363; "Bahar ve Şifa", *Mihrap* 1, no. 1 (1924): 13-14; "Sabah Ezanını Dinlerken" *Mihrap* 15, no. 16 (1924): 479-480; "Mihrak-ı Aşkı Sücuda Geldim!", *Mirap* 1, no. 17-18 (1924): 560; "Çölde Bir Secde", *Mihrap* 2, no. 25 (1925): 22; "Çölde Bir Secde", *Mihrap* 2, no. 26 (1925): 79. Semiha Rifâî, "Kurban-ı Aşk", *Mihrap* 2, no. 27 (1925): 117; "Çoban Kızı", *Mihrap* 2, no. 28 (1925): 154-156. Semiha Cemāl, "Züleyha", *Güner Dergisi* 2 (1927): 6-7; Semiha Cemāl, "Kleopatra", *Hayat Dergisi* 4, no. 96 (1928): 350-351; Semiha Cemāl, "Canana Hitap", *Hilal Dergisi* 1, no. 2 (1958): 14.

tween epistemology and spirituality in her thinking. Her writing of his *Meşreb-i Şerīfleri* was as follows:

"One of the things he cherishes most is either to know or to teach what he knows. He often says, "I must benefit, or I must help others benefit." And again, he advises: "Wherever and in whomever you see beauty or goodness, do not hesitate—take it." He also remarks, "The eagerness of those around me to learn is never as strong as my own passion to teach." He cannot tolerate deficiency—even in love. "Desire for others the goodness, the beauty, the joy, the profound love and light that you desire for yourself—only then can you be a true lover," he says. When he utters a beautiful phrase or hears something pleasing, he immediately wishes to share it with all those he loves—or to have it shared. He is true to his word. Even years later, he can recognize something he once said and never forgets where or when he said it. He forgets nothing—except wrongs. He is far more inclined to remember acts of kindness. Keeping his promises is a mark of his dignity. He never forgets even the smallest kindness shown to him, and he has no love for ingratitude or nosiness.

He values punctuality, prefers to act by the clock, and dislikes others going out of their way for him. He constantly reminds those around him not to become a source of burden or distress. He abhors hypocrisy and falsehood. He cannot bear to see others suffer. He loves order and harmony. His power to inspire is immense. Even while discussing an issue, he immediately looks for ways to put it into practice. He quickly grows weary of elaborate daydreams spun around a topic. He never dismisses another's words. If someone says something small, even if others in the room don't hear it or deem it insignificant, he takes an interest—no matter who it is. He asks questions to understand. He dislikes mockery; if he laughs at an incident, it is only because he finds it genuinely pleasing. No one has ever seen him laugh in scorn or derision. He is persistent. If he begins translating a book, for example, he devotes himself to the task and continues with the same enthusiasm until it is complete. The desire he feels at the beginning of a task never fades with time. He dislikes rudeness; he delights in courtesy and subtlety. He forgets the ingratitude shown toward him. He has no taste for resentment; he even feels compassion for those who have betrayed him. He never points out a person's faults to their face; in fact, he avoids them more than the wrongdoer themselves. He takes no pleasure in idle talk. If a pointless or trivial comment is made, he immediately turns his head toward the window. When asked a question and once he has answered, if the same question is posed a second time, his reply then aligns with the other person's heart—no longer reflecting his own thoughts, but rather becoming the property of the one asking. It is contrary to his own desire. He believes that if a word carries truth, it deserves the utmost respect and should not be treated lightly. He always cautions: "Either speak good or remain silent." He cannot endure even a small lapse from those close to him. His sensitivity to faults increases in proportion to the intimacy shared. The closer one is to him, the greater the responsibility."[95]

Semiha Cemāl's portrait of Ken'ān Rifā'ī is both a personal testimony and a literary-spiritual tribute that elevates him as the embodiment of the *insān-ı kāmil*—the perfected human being in Sufi thought. Her description fuses ethical precision with emotional reverence, emphasizing his unwavering commitment to sincerity, his pedagogical devotion, and his metaphysical sensitivity to beauty, love, and order. What emerges

---

95   The original turkish text is available on the following website: https://arsiv.nefesyayinevi.com/semiha-Cemāl-hanimdan-hz-kenanin-mesreb-i-serifleri/ Also see, Arzu Eylül Yalçınkaya, "Semiha Cemāl Hanım'ın Dilinden Ken'ân Rifâî'nin Meşreb-i Şerifleri", *I. Uluslararası Tasavvuf Araştırmaları Lisansüstü Öğrenci Sempozyumu*, 2018.

is a figure whose moral discipline and subtlety of presence do not merely inspire admiration but offer a model of lived philosophy—where teaching becomes a form of service, memory a vessel for gratitude, and silence itself a mode of wisdom. This depiction also subtly mirrors Cemāl's own spiritual aspirations, suggesting that her literary voice is, in part, shaped by the ethical and affective imprint of her mentor. This synthesis of philosophical and Sufi thought reflected a profound exchange of knowledge and spiritual insight between teacher and student. Sāmiha Ayverdi described this exchange in elevated terms: "The connection between them echoed the relationship between Plato and Socrates, between Rumi and Shams, between Imam Ali and the Prophet Muhammad."[96] Ken'ān Rifā'ī himself recognized Semiha Cemāl's exceptional potential, describing her as someone whose intellectual and spiritual gifts reflected both insight and emotional sensitivity.[97]

These intimate intellectual and spiritual relationships—especially those formed between prominent Sufi sheikhs and their learned female disciples—have long drawn both admiration and scrutiny.[98] Far from being unique to the late Ottoman or early Republican moment, such dynamics stretch across the *longue durée* of Ottoman religious life, where the presence of a

---

96 Ayverdi, "Kadın Anlayışı ve Semiha Cemāl", 241.

97 Ayverdi, "Kadın Anlayışı ve Semiha Cemāl", 239.

98 M. Brett Wilson explores how allegations of sexual deviance—particularly orgiastic behavior—have historically been used to discredit Sufi communities, especially in the late Ottoman and early Republican periods. Wilson traces the genealogies of what he calls the "orgy libel", showing how accusations of illicit sexuality were strategically deployed by various actors—reformist bureaucrats, secularist intellectuals, and anti-Sufi polemicists—as tools of moral delegitimization. See, M. Brett Wilson, "Putting out the Candle: Sufism and the Orgy Libel in Late Ottoman and Modern Turkey," *Comparative Studies of South Asia, Africa and the Middle East* 41, no. 1 (2021): 72–84.

spiritually magnetic teacher, often marked by personal refinement and rhetorical grace, could draw close circles of devoted interlocutors, male and female alike. In a society that prized propriety and symbolic order, such relationships—though rooted in longstanding pedagogical and spiritual traditions—sometimes unsettled prevailing sensibilities, subtly exposing tensions around gender, charisma, and authority within a culture undergoing modern transformation.

Ken'ān Rifā'ī, with his cultivated manners, intellectual gravity, and dignified bearing, stood at the center of such a tension. His active encouragement of women's education and inclusion in *sohbet* gatherings was lauded by many as a visionary extension of Ottoman cosmopolitan ethics into a modern frame. Yet, the very novelty of that inclusion—his readiness to teach and engage women in a time of redefined public boundaries—also opened him to whispered judgments. His circle thus became a site where admiration for ethical seriousness coexisted with anxieties about visibility, gendered authority, and shifting communal expectations. That such responses emerged not from the substance of his teaching but from the surface optics of proximity reveals more about the social imaginary of the time than about the nature of the relationships themselves. Rifā'ī, with his erudition, refined manners, and striking presence, exemplified this dynamic as a Sufi master whose influence on educated female disciples both inspired devotion and incited speculation. Though he himself embraced many republican reforms, including women's education and even the ban on Sufi orders, his unorthodox inclusion of women in his circle aroused both admiration and suspicion.[99]

This ambivalence found expression in the literary sphere, where secular modernist writers of the 1920s, such as Yakup

---

99   Feyza Burak-Adli, "The Portrait of an Alla Franca Shaykh: Sufism, Modernity, and Class in Turkey", *International Journal of Middle East Studies* 56, no. 2 (2024): 207-226.

Kadri Karaosmanoğlu (d. 1974), Reşat Nuri Güntekin (d. 1956), and Refik Halid Karay (d. 1965), lampooned Sufi sheikhs as luring naive women into their "lodges" for illicit ends.[100] By casting aspersions of sexual debauchery in the mystical tekke, these writers voiced anxieties not only about Sufism but about the newly visible public role of women. Refik Halid Karay's satirical novel *Kadınlar Tekkesi* (Women's Lodge, 1923) in particular caricatured a seductive sheikh surrounded by society ladies, a scenario widely presumed to target Kenan Rifāī's predominantly female following.[101] Karay denied direct allegory, but the novel's setting closely resembled Rifā'ī's milieu, fueling public suspicions that the sheikh's relationship with his women disciples, notably the brilliant young Semiha Cemāl, was more scandalous than spiritual.

Semiha Cemāl's *Aşk Peygamberi* intensified these misperceptions even as it epitomized a classical Sufi idiom. In this work, Semiha pours forth rapturous, first-person expressions of longing for a *beloved* figure modeled on Kenan Rifâî. To the uninitiated reader, her ardent confessions of "love" and almost erotic yearning for her guide could easily suggest an earthly romance. Historically, some did indeed misconstrue these passages as evidence of a secret liaison or at least improper infatuation

---

100 Wilson, "The Twilight of Sufism", 234.

101 Buğdaycı's article analyzes how Refik Halid Karay's 1956 novel recontextualizes Sufism by framing it as a psychiatric phenomenon. Drawing on Foucault's notions of pathological discourse and power-knowledge dynamics, Buğdaycı shows that the novel employs medicalized language to pathologize Sufi practices—especially among women—as cases of mental aberration, thereby reinforcing a secularist agenda. This shift marks a departure from earlier anti-Sufi rhetoric rooted in moral or religious critique and instead reflects a modern, scientific secularism that constructs Sufism as an object of clinical scrutiny. See, Çiğdem Buğdaycı, "Medicalization of Sufism: the Discourse of Psychiatry, Psychopathology, and Secularity in Karay's Kadınlar Tekkesi," *New Perspectives on Turkey* (2024): 1-20.

between teacher and disciple. However, a deeper, contextually grounded reading reveals that Semiha Cemāl's language belongs to a long mystical love tradition rather than to personal memoir. Her effusive pleas for union and self-annihilation in the beloved's presence mirror the archetypal Sufi motif of *fanā* – the annihilation of the self in love – directed not toward carnal fulfillment but toward the Divine. In Sufi metaphysics, the enlightened guide (*mürşid*) is a mirror to God's attributes; hence loving the guide is ultimately loving God.

Within Sufi circles, however, such relationships were often understood in exalted terms. Contemporary witness Sāmiha Ayverdi likened the bond between Rifā'ī and Cemāl to that of Mevlānā and his disciple Hüsameddin Çelebi (d. ö. 683/1284)– a uniquely intimate *master–disciple* partnership of mutual spiritual nourishment. This analogy, drawn from hagiographic tradition, underscores that what outsiders saw as transgressive intimacy was regarded by insiders as a chaste, transcendental friendship rooted in the Sufi path. Semiha Cemāl's mastery of her teacher's path was not limited to theoretical knowledge; she internalized Ken'ān Rifā'ī's ethical and metaphysical teachings and sought to embody them in her life and work. Her literary and philosophical writings reflect a profound moral sensibility shaped by the principles of Sufism. Ayverdi observed that Semiha Cemāl's moral and spiritual maturity mirrored the ethical perfection she sought in her sheikh.[102]

---

102 Ayverdi, "Kadın Anlayışı ve Semiha Cemāl", 241.

3.2. THE PHILOSOPHER DISCIPLE: REASON, INTUITION, AND THE FORMATION OF SEMİHA CEMĀL UNDER MUSTAFA ŞEKİP TUNÇ AT DĀRÜLFÜNŪN

At a time when Turkish universities were still learning what to make of their first female philosophers, Semiha Cemāl entered the Department of Philosophy at the Dārülfünūn not merely to study but to seek. She brought with her an unusual inheritance: a Sufi vocabulary shaped by spiritual apprenticeship and a rigorous inclination toward metaphysical thought. In classrooms built on the promise of positivist reason, she asked questions anchored in something older, subtler—questions shaped by an inward, ethical longing. Her presence—quiet, sharp, determined—marked her as exceptional not for her novelty as a woman in philosophy, but for the way she thought.

Her formation unfolded under the guidance of some of the early Republic's most prominent thinkers, including the philosopher and psychologist Mustafa Şekip Tunç (d. 1958),[103] the sociologist Yusuf Ziya Yörükan (d. 1954)[104], and the philoso-

---

103   Mustafa Şekip Tunç (1886–1958) was a pioneering Turkish philosopher and psychologist known for his contributions to modern Turkish thought and the institutionalization of psychology and philosophy in Türkiye. He studied philosophy at the Sorbonne in Paris and later became a professor at Istanbul University, where he played a key role in establishing the Philosophy Department. Influenced by Henri Bergson's ideas on intuition and the nature of consciousness, Tunç integrated Western philosophical frameworks with Turkish intellectual traditions. See, Mustafa Şekip Tunç, *Bergson ve Manevi Kudrete Dair Birkaç Konferans* (İstanbul: Muallim Ahmet Halit Kitaphanesi, 1934); Also see, Hayrani Altıntaş, *Mustafa Şekip Tunç* (Ankara: Kültür Bakanlığı Yayınları, 1989).

104   Yusuf Ziya Yörükân (1872–1954) was a distinguished Turkish scholar, historian of religion, and philosopher, known for his contributions to Islamic studies and the sociology of religion. Yörükân joined the Dârülfünûn Faculty of Theology in 1926, where he also served as sec-

pher Mehmet Ali Aynī (d. 1945).[105] Her exceptional aptitude and philosophical acumen quickly attracted the admiration of her professors, who frequently commented on her incisive reasoning, intellectual curiosity, and eloquence. After graduating in 1926, she remained at the university for a brief period as a research assistant to Mustafa Şekip Bey in the Department of Philosophy, participating in its academic and intellectual life. Her professors would later speak of her in glowing terms, recognizing her as one of the most promising minds of her generation and a rare example of a woman whose philosophical depth was matched by her spiritual seriousness.

Among her professors, Tunç had a particularly profound influence on Cemāl's philosophical outlook, especially through their close collaboration when she served as his research and teaching assistant in the psychology (*ruhiyat*) branch.[106] Tunç

retary-general and briefly as acting dean. Following the 1933 university reform, he was appointed to the newly established Institute of Islamic Studies within the Faculty of Literature. See, Hilmi Ziya Ülken, "Yusuf Ziya Yörükân (1887-1952)", *İlâhiyat Fakültesi Dergisi I–II* (1954): 89-95.

105 Mehmet Ali Ayni (1868–1945) was a prominent Turkish philosopher, scholar, and statesman known for his contributions to Islamic thought and philosophy during the late Ottoman and early Republican periods. Born in Manisa, he received a classical Ottoman education, specializing in Islamic jurisprudence (*fiqh*), theology, and philosophy. Ayni held various administrative and teaching positions, including professorships at the Dârülfünûn, where he taught philosophy and Islamic ethics. He was influenced by both Islamic philosophical traditions and Western philosophical currents, particularly those of Henri Bergson. See, Dilek Sarmis, "Conceptualiser le Mysticisme dans une Perspective Académique : La Constitution D'une Histoire Générale du Mysticisme Chez Mehmet Ali Ayni (1868-1945)", *European Journal of Turkish Studies* 25 (2017): 1-26.

106 Savaş, *Zaman Sürgünü*, 20; For the development of academic studies of psychology in Turkish Republic, Şeyma Afacan, "Searching for the Soul in Shades of Grey: Modern Psychology's Spiritual Past in the Late Ottoman Empire", *European Journal of Turkish Studies* 32 (2021): 1-27.

was a leading figure in Turkish philosophical circles during the early Republican period. Educated in France, he was deeply influenced by the works of Henri Bergson (d. 1941) and played a key role in introducing Bergson's vitalist and metaphysical ideas to Turkish intellectual life.[107] Tunç's engagement with Bergsonian philosophy, which emphasized intuition, creative evolution, and the *élan vital* (vital force), challenged the deterministic materialism of the late 19th century by offering a more dynamic and spiritually oriented conception of life.[108] His philosophical framework, which privileged intuition and creative spontaneity over mechanistic determinism, resonated with the ethical and metaphysical dimensions of Ottoman Sufism that Cemāl had absorbed through her relationship with Ken'ān Rifā'ī.

Tunç's position at the Dārülfünūn made him one of the most influential conduits for introducing Bergsonian ideas

107 Henri Bergson (1859–1941) was a French philosopher known for his influential work on time, consciousness, and metaphysics. He challenged the mechanistic and materialist views of reality dominant in 19th-century philosophy, emphasizing the importance of intuition and subjective experience. See, Keith Ansell Pearson and John Mullarkey (eds.), *Henri Bergson Key Writings* (New York: Continuum, 2002).

108 Henri Bergson's philosophy centered on a critique of mechanistic and deterministic understandings of life. He proposed the concept of intuition as a mode of knowing that surpasses rational analysis, allowing direct access to the inner flow of life. His theory of *évolution créatrice* (creative evolution) described life not as a fixed, predictable process but as an open-ended, spontaneous unfolding. Central to this view was the idea of the *élan vital* (vital force), an immaterial and dynamic impulse driving the creative development of all living beings. Bergson's ideas offered a metaphysical alternative to positivist materialism and resonated with thinkers like Mustafa Şekip Tunç, who sought to reconcile modern philosophy with more spiritual and intuitive approaches to knowledge and existence. See, Henri Bergson, *The Creative Mind: An Introduction to Metaphysics* (New York: Dover Publications, 2010), 88.

to Turkish thought, particularly through his exploration of the tension between rational materialism and spiritual idealism.[109] Tunç's emphasis on intuition, moral freedom, and the metaphysical dimensions of existence provided an alternative to the dominant positivist-materialist trends of early Republican Türkiye, which were largely shaped by the influence of Auguste Comte (d. 1857) and Émile Durkheim (d. 1917), especially through the writings of Ziya Gökalp (d. 1924).[110] Tunç encouraged his students to explore the intersections of metaphysical and scientific thought, fostering an intellectual environment where questions of existence, morality, and the nature of reality could be explored through both philosophical and spiritual lenses.

Tunç was closely connected to *Dergâh* journal, which emerged as a significant intellectual platform during the early Republican period, bringing together a circle of prominent thinkers and writers who sought to shape the ideological foun-

---

109 Mustafa Cem Oğuz, "Mustafa Şekip Tunç ve Türkiye'de Bergsonculuk," *Artvin Çoruh Üniversitesi Uluslararası Sosyal Bilimler Dergisi* 1, no. 1 (2015): 90-109.

110 Auguste Comte (1798–1857) and Émile Durkheim (1858–1917) were central figures in the development of positivist and sociological thought, which had a significant impact on early Republican Türkiye through the works of Ziya Gökalp (1876–1924). Comte, known as the founder of positivism, argued that human knowledge progresses through three stages: the theological, the metaphysical, and the scientific (or positive) stage, with the positive stage representing the highest form of knowledge based on empirical observation and scientific reasoning. Durkheim expanded on Comte's positivist framework, establishing sociology as a distinct discipline rooted in the scientific study of social facts — collective norms, values, and institutions that shape individual behavior. See, Türkay Salim Nefes, "Ziya Gökalp's adaptation of Emile Durkheim's Sociology in his Formulation of the Modern Turkish Nation," *International Sociology* 28, no. 3 (2013): 335-350; Alp Eren Topal, "Against influence: Ziya Gökalp in context and tradition," *Journal of Islamic Studies* 28, no. 3 (2017): 283-310.

dations of the new Turkish Republic.[111] Tunç considered *Dergāh* as a vehicle for the dissemination of philosophical and intellectual currents that influenced the trajectory of the Turkish Revolution. Central to Tunç's perspective was the belief that Bergson's philosophy, particularly his concept of *durée* (duration), played a formative role in shaping the revolutionary mindset reflected in *Dergāh*.[112] According to Tunç, the idea of *durée*—which emphasizes the continuous process of becoming and creation—resonated deeply with the transformative spirit of the Turkish Revolution and the intellectual underpinnings of the Republic.[113] He viewed this Bergsonian notion as essential to understanding the dynamic and creative momentum behind the revolutionary project, positioning *Dergāh* as a conduit for introducing and reinforcing this philosophical framework within the emerging Republican intellectual landscape.

The philosophical training she received at Dārülfünūn offered her a comprehensive introduction to both the classical canon of Western philosophy and the emerging currents of modern thought. Although little detailed information survives

111 *Dergâh*, published biweekly from April 10, 1921, to January 5, 1923, with 42 issues, is a key periodical in Türkiye's literary history. It served as an important intellectual and cultural platform during the turbulent final years of the Ottoman Empire, amid the Turkish War of Independence and the Allied occupation of Istanbul. See, Abdullah Uçman, "Dergâh", *TDV İslâm Ansiklopedisi* (İstanbul: TDV Yayınları, 1994), 9:172-174.

112 Nazım İrem, "Undercurrents of European Modernity and the Foundations of Modern Turkish Conservatism: Bergsonism in Retrospect", *Middle Eastern Studies* 40 (2004): 79-112.

113 In Bergson's philosophy, durée (duration) refers to the inner, qualitative experience of time as a continuous flow, distinct from the measurable, segmented time of clocks. It emphasizes the subjective and indivisible nature of time, where past and present interpenetrate in a dynamic process of becoming. See, Suzanne Guerlac, Thinking in Time: An Introduction to Henri Bergson (Cornell: Cornell University Press, 2006), 42-105.

regarding her undergraduate thesis or specific coursework, her later translations provide strong evidence of her intellectual affinities—particularly with Ancient Greek philosophers and the Stoic tradition. Her exposure to Platonic idealism, Aristotelian logic, and the ethical doctrines of Stoicism laid the foundation for the translations and original philosophical works she would produce in later years. Importantly, Semiha Cemāl did not confine her intellectual formation to academic circles. Rather, she viewed her philosophical education as a foundation for broader cultural and ethical engagement. Her writings reflect an effort to transmit complex philosophical ideas to a wider public, often framing them within literary narratives or contemplative reflections rooted in Islamic metaphysics. In this way, she bridged the realms of philosophy, ethics, and public discourse—carving out a unique space for spiritually grounded thought in an era increasingly dominated by rationalist and secularist paradigms.

Some intellects are carved by tradition, others by revolt; Semiha Cemāl's was sculpted by discipline, contemplation, and a rare faculty for synthesis. The education she received under the leading minds of the early Republic would have offered any student a strong foundation. But in her case, it met with something more: an extraordinary capacity not only to absorb ideas, but to reconfigure them—to pass them through the twin prisms of Sufi metaphysics and philosophical inquiry and return them transformed. She was neither merely a product of her instructors nor a passive vessel of their ideas. Her brilliance was her own, sharpened by effort, magnified by guidance, and disciplined by practice.

Tunç provided her with a language and conceptual framework through which she could engage with Platonic and Stoic philosophy, while Rifā'ī's teachings supplied her with the moral and spiritual foundation that allowed her to reinterpret these philosophical traditions through a Sufi lens. This synthesis is particularly apparent in her translations of Plato's *Apology*, *Symposium*, and *Phaedo*, as well as her work on Stoic texts such as Epictetus' *Discourses* and Marcus Aurelius' *Meditations*. In her introduction to *Apology* and *Crito*, she drew striking parallels between Socratic ideals of cosmic harmony and the Sufi concept of *tawḥīd* (divine unity). By employing terms such as "eternal ideal" and "soul," she aligned Greek philosophical notions with Islamic metaphysics, offering a modern philosophical discourse that subtly critiqued the materialist positivism of the early Republic. Far from echoing the voices of her teachers, Semiha Cemāl composed her own register. Their ideas were not her destination but her departure point. From them, she took structure; from herself, vision. The result was not imitation, but articulation—an intellectual stance as original as it was rigorous.

Her incorporation of Stoic and Platonic discourses and symbolism was also a strategic attempt to create a less politically charged literary space, considering the ideological heaviness of the period. Semiha Cemāl was aware that direct engagement with Sufi doctrine in the aftermath of the abolition of the dervish lodges in 1925 was politically and culturally sensitive.[114] By framing her philosophical explorations through the lens of Platonic and Stoic philosophy, she created a subtle yet powerful platform for conveying Sufi metaphysical insights under the guise of classical philosophical discourse.

Semiha Cemāl's legacy challenges us to reconsider the geography of modern Turkish thought—not as a battleground of binaries, but as a terrain where intellectual rigor and spiritual longing can coexist. In an era that sought to sever metaphysics from modernity, she enacted a quiet defiance: she wrote. Her

---

114 See, Martin Van Bruinessen, "Sufism, 'Popular' Islam and the Encounter with Modernity", *Islam and Modernity* (Edinburgh: Edinburgh University Press, 2009), 125-157.

work speaks in many tongues—Platonic, Stoic, Qur'anic—yet her voice remains singular, shaped by an ethic of refinement and a longing for the Real. She did not merely translate philosophy or narrate mysticism; she embodied a form of authorship that braided contemplation and courage, erudition and intimacy. In doing so, she traced a different genealogy of Turkish modernity—one in which the soul, not just the citizen, is called to account. To read her today is not only to remember what was nearly forgotten, but to glimpse what might have been: a modernity capacious enough to include love, virtue, and the metaphysical dignity of thought itself.

CHAPTER 4

THE PHILOSOPHER SUFI AND THE WRITER: SEMİHA CEMĀL'S INTELLECTUAL AND LITERARY LEGACY

In the early decades of the Turkish Republic, philosophy was not merely a field of study—it was a battleground for competing visions of the future. Was it to remain tethered to centuries of metaphysical inquiry drawn from Islamic and Ottoman traditions? Or would it be redefined, retooled, and reimported as a European enterprise of logic, language, and scientific method? For those at the center of the Republic's institutional reforms, the answer was clear: philosophy would be modern, Western, and resolutely secular. Yet beneath this newly polished architecture, older questions still lingered—about virtue, selfhood, and the moral foundations of knowledge. This chapter turns to the institutional fault lines and philosophical realignments of that moment to understand how Semiha Cemāl quietly reclaimed a metaphysical voice within an epistemic regime that no longer recognized its native tongue.[115]

The story of institutional philosophy in Türkiye did not begin with the Republic, nor did its transformation occur overnight. At the turn of the twentieth century, the Ottoman state

---

115 Nesim Şeker, "Vision of Modernity in the Early Turkish Republic: An Overview," *Historia Actual Online* 14 (2007): 49-56.

had already established the Dārülfünūn as a modern university—complete with a philosophy department where scholars grappled with European systems of thought while attempting to articulate metaphysical concepts in Ottoman-Turkish idioms. It was an experiment in intellectual fusion: French idealism met Islamic cosmology; Aristotle and Avicenna shared the syllabus. This fragile continuity extended briefly into the Republican era. But in 1933, the reformist zeal of the new state culminated in the closure of the Dārülfünūn and the creation of Istanbul University. With this reform came rupture. Dozens of Ottoman-trained scholars were dismissed, and the curriculum was placed under the stewardship of Hans Reichenbach, a German exile and leading advocate of logical positivism.

Reichenbach's arrival marked more than just an institutional shift; it signaled an epistemological reorientation. In his inaugural address, he reportedly declared that philosophy in Türkiye would now proceed along rigorous, empirical lines—severed from its speculative and theological past. Islamic philosophy vanished from the syllabus. In its place stood the austere vocabulary of verification, formalism, and analytic clarity. The transformation was not merely curricular but civilizational: a conscious attempt to break with the Ottoman philosophical tradition and rebuild thought on a Western rationalist foundation. And yet, as the following pages will show, this new architecture still bore within it the ghosts of older questions—and the quiet persistence of voices like Semiha Cemāl's, who had learned to speak across its fault lines.

Cemāl's affinities are especially significant when considering the historical conditions of her time. Her thought was not derived solely from classical texts but was deeply informed by personal mystical experience, thus leaving a profound impact on her readers. Indeed, Professor Ziya's words suggest that her writing carried the scent of revelation. Semiha Cemāl's approach to philosophy aimed to dissolve the boundaries between *hikmet-i tabī'i-*

yye (natural philosophy) and *hikmet-i ilāhiyye* (divine wisdom).[116] In her view, philosophers who searched for truth and Sufis who lived that truth were inspired by the same divine source. This perspective enabled a rich intertextual and intercultural dialogue in her works. Plato's theory of Forms was, for her, a philosophical expression of the Sufi search for the Absolute; Epictetus's idea of freedom paralleled the Sufi discipline of the self; Marcus Aurelius's (d. 180) exhortations to humility and composure found echoes in the Sufi virtues of asceticism and contentment.

Her affinity for ancient Greek philosophy, particularly Platonism and Stoicism, is evident in her pioneering translations. She was the first to render several of Plato's major dialogues into Turkish, including *Phaedo* (on the Immortality of the Soul), *Crito* (on Duty), *Apologia* (Socrates' Defense), *Symposium* (on Love), and others.[117] These translations both introduced key philosophical texts to Turkish readers but also played a formative role in the development of a modern philosophical lexicon in Turkish. In addition to Plato, she translated the *Enchiridion* of Epictetus and Marcus Aurelius' *Meditations* from French into Turkish, adding her own prefaces and reflections. In these writings, Semiha Cemāl interpreted classical notions such as Platonic idealism, Stoic freedom, or Aurelius's inner discipline through the lens of an Ottoman-Turkish intellectual and Sufi. Her introductions contextualized these ancient texts for her

---

116 *Hikmet-i Tabī'iyye* refers to natural philosophy—the study of the physical world and its principles—while *ḥikmet-i ilāhiyye* denotes divine or metaphysical wisdom, concerned with ultimate realities such as the soul, God, and existence. In Islamic intellectual traditions, these were often treated as distinct but interrelated realms of knowledge. See, Seyyed Hossein Nasr, *Science and Civilization in Islam* (Cambridge, MA: Harvard University Press, 1968), 59–62.

117 See, Semiha Cemāl, *Apoloji (Methiye-Sokrates'in Savunması) ve Kriton (Vazife)* (İstanbul: Devlet Matbaası, 1932); Platon, *Aşk ve Ziyafet*, trans. Semiha Cemāl (İstanbul: Devlet Basımevi, 1936).

contemporary audience, interpreting them as moral and spiritual guides in an age of cultural transition.

This integrative vision placed her at a distance from both positivist materialism and rigid traditionalism. For Semiha Cemāl, philosophy and Sufism were not opposing paths but twin routes to the same truth, differing only in language. She also succeeded in carrying these philosophical insights into her literary works. Her novels and essays not only reflect the existential questioning of the early Republican Turkish intellectual but also explore timeless Sufi themes. In this sense, her oeuvre constitutes a rare convergence of historical consciousness, literary expression, and metaphysical depth.

Semiha Cemāl's intellectual legacy is preserved in her philosophical translations, non-fiction works, and novels, which reflect a deep engagement with both classical philosophy and Sufi metaphysics. Her literary and scholarly output demonstrates not only her intellectual command over classical Greek and Stoic philosophy but also her ability to integrate these traditions with the ethical and metaphysical underpinnings of Ottoman Sufism. Through her translations, Semiha Cemāl introduced the Turkish intellectual community to the philosophical insights of Plato and Epictetus while framing these ideas within the ethical and spiritual dimensions of Sufi thought. Her novels, meanwhile, served as allegorical explorations of the human soul's journey toward divine truth, shaped by both Platonic ideals and Sufi conceptions of love and moral perfection.

4.1. WRITING THE SOUL:
THE METAPHYSICAL NOVELS OF SEMİHA CEMĀL

This intellectual and spiritual synthesis was perhaps most evident in her novels. Her fiction explores the moral and existential struggles of her characters as they seek to transcend their lower selves and achieve spiritual unity with the divine. In her portrayal of human relationships, love functions not as an end in itself but as a transformative force that propels the soul toward spiritual fulfillment. The ethical ideals of Stoicism—self-control, acceptance of fate, and rational harmony with the cosmos—are reinterpreted through the moral teachings of Sufism, creating a synthesis that reflects both Greek philosophical rationalism and Islamic spiritual idealism.

Aşk Peygamberi, published in 1927 when Semiha Cemāl was only twenty-two years old, stands as a remarkable testament to her early intellectual and spiritual maturity.[118] More than a conventional love story, the novel functions as a fictional manifestation of her metaphysical worldview—an exploration of the soul's journey toward truth through the transformative power of divine love. At the heart of the novel lies the concept of *aşk* (love), not in its worldly, romantic guise, but as a transcendent, ontological force that illuminates the purpose of human existence. Through a richly symbolic narrative, Semiha Cemāl invites her readers into a world where love is not merely felt, but existentially enacted—a state of *becoming* that unveils deeper layers of reality.

Central to the novel is the spiritual relationship between a seasoned mystic guide (*mürşid*) and a young seeker (*mürīd*), a dynamic that has drawn comparisons by literary critics to the metaphysical companionship between Mevlānā Celāleddīn-i Rūmī and Şems-i Tebrīzī (d. 645/1247 [?]).[119] In this modern

---

118   Semiha Cemāl, *Aşk Peygamberi* (İstanbul: Kitabhane-i Sudî, 1927).

119   The relationship between Mevlânâ Celāleddīn-i Rûm and Şems-i Tebrīzī was one of intense spiritual companionship, marked by a transformative bond that reoriented Rûmî's intellectual and mystical life. Şems served as both mirror and catalyst, awakening in Rûmî a deeper experience of divine love (aşk) and prompting the outpouring of his celebrated poetic works. Their meeting is often seen in Sufi tradition as an emblem of the seeker's encounter with the divine through a human intermediary.

reinterpretation, the guide leads the seeker not merely toward knowledge but toward *ma'rifa*—a direct, experiential understanding of divine truth. Their journey together mirrors the stages of the Sufi path, moving from longing to self-effacement (*fanā'*), and ultimately to union (*baqā'*) with the divine. In this sense, *Aşk Peygamberi* can be read as a spiritual Bildungsroman, wherein the characters mature not through the acquisition of worldly wisdom but by undergoing an inner transformation catalyzed by sacred love. Although written in the early years of the Turkish Republic, the novel departs sharply from the dominant literary trends of the period. Rather than reflecting the materialist and nationalist ethos of the time, it draws from the symbolic repertoire of Sufi tradition—dreams, visions, mystical encounters, and the veiled language of the heart. In doing so, Semiha Cemāl offers a counter-literary narrative that reclaims the mystical voice at a moment when official culture increasingly silenced religious and metaphysical expression. Originally published in Ottoman script, the novel remained largely forgotten for nearly a century. It was not until 2023 that *Aşk Peygamberi* was transliterated into Latin script and republished, allowing contemporary readers to rediscover its literary and spiritual significance. In a critical introduction to the new edition, the novel was praised not only for its thematic richness but also for its historical value as a rare example of metaphysical fiction produced in the early Republican period. The work stands as both a philosophical parable and a cultural artifact—offering insight into a parallel modernity grounded not in secular ideology, but in the Sufi vision of inner transformation.

Semiha Cemāl's second novel, *Aşk* (*Love*), published shortly before her death in 1936, continues her literary project of fusing metaphysical thought with symbolic narrative.[120] Set in

---

120 Semiha Cemāl, *Aşk* (İstanbul: Devlet Basımevi, 1936).

ancient Assyria, the novel recounts the allegorical story of Dol-unay, a prophetic figure who preaches divine unity (*tawḥīd*) to a spiritually fragmented society. Far from a historical recon-struction, the novel constructs a symbolic landscape in which Dolunay's teachings, his interactions with other characters, and the narrative arc itself function as a dramatization of the soul's ascent toward the Absolute. The characters—Dolunay, Ayça, and Uluand—serve as archetypes of spiritual transfor-mation. Each reflects a different stage in the soul's journey: Dolunay as the enlightened guide, Ayça as the yearning seeker, and Uluand as the conflicted ego or *nafs*. Through their un-folding relationships, Semiha Cemāl constructs a metaphysical drama that parallels the Sufi path: from bewilderment (*hayra*) and longing (*shawq*) to annihilation (*fanā'*) and subsistence in the divine (*baqā'*). The novel's treatment of love is thus not emotional or romantic in the modern sense, but ontological—a condition of being that aligns the human heart with the divine order of the cosmos.

One of the most distinctive symbolic elements of the nov-el is the *balag*, an Assyrian wind instrument played by Dol-unay during his spiritual assemblies. The instrument func-tions not merely as a historical artifact, but as a conduit of transcendence, recalling the Sufi concept of *samā'*—spiritual audition—as practiced in Mevlevi and other mystical orders. Through Dolunay's music, Semiha Cemāl suggests that divine realities can be accessed not only through rational inquiry but also through the vibrations of sound and rhythm, which awak-en the soul's latent receptivity to the divine. In this way, *Aşk* extends her earlier work in *Aşk Peygamberi* by further inte-grating aesthetics, particularly music, into her philosophical vision of spiritual evolution.

Aşk Budur (This is Love), Semiha Cemāl's final novel, was published posthumously in 1938 by İstanbul Marifet Printing

House, two years after her untimely death.[121] Begun during the final months of her illness, the novel was left unfinished and later completed by her close friend and spiritual confidante, Sāmiha Ayverdi—a gesture that attests to the intimate intellectual and emotional bond between the two women. As with her previous works, Aşk Budur explores the metaphysical dimensions of love, but here the narrative takes on a poignant intensity, shaped by the author's awareness of mortality and the nearness of her own departure from this world. Set once again within a symbolic, pre-Islamic context, the novel tells the story of Yusuf and Meryem, two figures whose journey toward divine truth unfolds through the trials of human love. Yusuf, a monotheist preacher surrounded by a pagan society, becomes the moral and spiritual axis of the narrative. His presence disrupts the established order, challenging the idolatrous conventions of his milieu—not unlike the role of prophetic figures throughout history. Meryem, initially unaware of the spiritual significance of love, is gradually transformed by her bond with Yusuf. Her awakening reflects not only the Sufi notion of *muhabbet* as a catalyst for spiritual ascent, but also Platonic themes of eros as the soul's yearning for the eternal and the ideal. The novel dramatizes the tension between inner truth and external convention, between divine calling and worldly entrapment. Through richly drawn characters and morally fraught encounters, Semiha Cemāl explores the ethical implications of religious reform, presenting Yusuf's message as one that transcends dogma and emphasizes the moral essence of unity, sincerity, and compassion. In Meryem's journey toward awakening, the reader witnesses the soul's gradual movement from heedlessness to remembrance, from fragmentation to wholeness. Stylistically and thematically, *Aşk Budur*

---

121 Completed posthumously by Samiha Ayverdi, Semiha Cemāl, *Aşk Budur* (Istanbul: Marifet Basimevi, 1938).

completes the philosophical and spiritual arc traced across Semiha Cemâl's literary oeuvre. The novel's harmonization of Platonic idealism with Sufi metaphysics—rendered in a prose style both lyrical and contemplative—demonstrates her rare ability to translate dense philosophical insights into emotionally resonant fiction. That the novel was completed by Samiha Ayverdi further reinforces the sense of spiritual continuity and shared vision that defined the intellectual network surrounding Ken'ân Rifâ'î. As a posthumous work, *Aşk Budur* stands not only as a literary text but as a final testament—a quiet affirmation that divine love, expressed through the human heart, remains the soul's highest path to truth.

Her engagement with Platonic and Stoic philosophy became more pronounced in her translations, beginning with Fedon – *Ruhun Bekası* (Phaedo – *The Immortality of the Soul*), published in 1928 by İstanbul Kitaphâne-i Sudi.[122] This was her first published translation following her graduation from the Dârülfünûn Department of Philosophy. The work was based on the French translations of Édouard Sommer and Paul Lemaire, which Semiha Cemâl compared with the original Greek text.[123]

---

122 Plato's Phaedo is one of his most renowned dialogues, centered on Socrates' final conversation with his disciples before his execution. Set in the confines of his prison cell, the dialogue presents Socrates' philosophical arguments for the immortality of the soul, offering a profound reflection on life, death, and the afterlife. Through a dialectical exchange with his companions, Socrates introduces several key arguments—including the cyclical argument, the theory of recollection, and the affinity argument—to demonstrate that the soul exists before birth and survives after death. The dialogue culminates in a mythic vision of the soul's journey after death and affirms the philosopher's duty to seek truth and virtue as preparation for the soul's liberation from the body.

123 The cover of the work includes the note: "This work has been translated into Turkish by comparing the Greek text with the French translations by E. Sommer and Paul Lemaire", Plato, *Fedon: Ruhun Bekası*, trans. Semiha Cemâl (Istanbul: Orhaniye Matbaası, 1928).

In the preface to Phaedo, she offered a detailed analysis of the philosophical significance of the dialogue, situating Plato's exploration of the soul's immortality within the broader context of Greek metaphysical thought. Her introduction addressed key themes such as the nature of the soul, the relationship between body and spirit, and the philosophical foundations of moral and ethical conduct. What distinguishes Semiha Cemāl's translation is the way she frames these Platonic ideas within the language of Sufism. She frequently employs terms drawn from Islamic metaphysics, such as *ruh* (spirit), *nefs* (ego), and *fani* (impermanence), suggesting a deliberate attempt to reconcile Platonic and Sufi cosmologies. Her decision to translate Phaedo reflects her broader intellectual project of reviving classical philosophical ideals within the moral and metaphysical framework of Islamic thought. The translation was reviewed by Mehmed Emin (Erişirgil) (d. 1965)[124] in "Hayat Mecmuası" in 1928.[125] Erişirgil praises the translation for its literary and philosophical quality, highlighting Phaedo's importance among Plato's dialogues due to its captivating style and philosophical depth. He notes that Şaziye Perin Hanım (d. ?) had previously translated Plato's *Symposium* into Turkish, adding another valuable philosophical work to Turkish literature. In Phaedo, Plato recounts Socrates' final moments and

---

124 Mehmet Emin Erişirgil (1891–1965) was a prominent intellectual and
     educator who taught philosophy, particularly ethics and metaphysics, at
     the Istanbul Dārülfünūn during the late Ottoman and early Republican
     periods. He played a key role in disseminating nationalist and secular
     thought, especially the ideas of Ziya Gökalp, while also drawing on
     Islamic intellectual traditions. Levent Bayraktar, "Darülfünun'da Bir
     Felsefe Hocası: Mehmet Emin Erişirgil", *Felsefe Dünyası* no. 50 (2009):
     64–80.

125 Mehmed Emin (Erişirgil), "Yeni Çıkan Kitaplar: Fedon, Ruhun Bekası;
     mütercimi Dârülfünun Felsefe Şubesinden Mezun Semiha Cemāl
     Hanım," *Hayat Mecmuası* 4, no. 81 (1928): 60.

his philosophical defense of the soul's immortality through a structured dialogue. Erişirgil commends Semiha Cemâl for introducing readers to Plato's metaphysical framework and for producing a successful translation in a refined and literary style, which he considers a significant contribution to Turkish philosophical literature.

In 1932, Semiha Cemâl published her translation of *Epictet* (*Epictetus*), based on the French compilation prepared by French philosopher and professor François Thurot (d. 1832).[126] This work, released by the Ministry of Education, reflects her engagement with Stoic ethical philosophy, particularly the Stoic emphasis on self-mastery, moral discipline, and rational acceptance of fate. In her introduction to the translation, Semiha Cemâl emphasizes the Stoic ideal of inner harmony and moral independence, drawing parallels with the Sufi concept of *riyazat* (spiritual discipline). She presents Epictetus' teachings on acceptance and virtue as moral principles that transcend historical and cultural boundaries, aligning Stoic ideals with the Sufi notion of submission to the divine will. The translation's elegant and refined language reflects her literary sensitivity and philosophical acumen, blending the rational clarity of Stoic ethics with the metaphysical depth of Sufi morality.

Semiha Cemâl's philosophical vision reached its most mature form in her translation of *Apoloji ve Kriton* (Apology and Crito) from Plato's corpus, published by the Istanbul State Printing Press in 1932.[127] This translation was based on Maurice Croiset's (d. 1935) French version and included an extensive introduction in which Semiha Cemâl contextualized Socratic thought within the moral and philosophical traditions of an-

---

126 François Thurot, *Epiktet (Epictéte)*, trans. Semiha Cemâl (İstanbul: Milli Eğitim Basımevi, 1932).

127 Eflatun, Semiha Cemâl, *Apoloji (Methiye-Sokrates'in Savunması) ve Kriton (Vazife)* (İstanbul: Devlet Matbaası, 1932).

cient Greece.[128] Her analysis of Socrates' moral stance in the *Apology*—particularly his defense of moral integrity and his willingness to sacrifice his life for the truth—reflects Semiha Cemāl's deep engagement with the ethical dimensions of philosophical inquiry. In this work, she draws a striking parallel between Socratic moral integrity and the Sufi ideal of *ihsan* (spiritual excellence), suggesting that the pursuit of truth and moral integrity in Socratic philosophy mirrors the ethical imperative of submission to divine will in Sufism. The philosophical and ethical framework of the Apology thus becomes a vehicle for expressing Sufi moral and metaphysical ideals within a Western philosophical context.

In addition to her major works, Semiha Cemāl contributed numerous essays and short stories to leading intellectual and literary journals such as "Mihrâb" and "Hayât".[129] Her writings on moral philosophy, religious ethics, and the spiritual foun-

---

128 Semiha Cemāl's translation of *Apology* was based on Maurice Croiset's French version, which was considered one of the most authoritative interpretations of Plato's dialogues in the early 20th century. Platón, *Apologie de Socrate* (Paris: Librairie Hatier, 1958).

129 "Mihrâb" (1923-1925) was a religious and intellectual journal published in early Republican Türkiye, focusing on Islamic thought, moral values, and religious education. It served as a platform for scholars and intellectuals to engage with contemporary issues in Islam and spirituality, often addressing the intersection of religious tradition and modernity. "Hayât" (1926-1929) was a popular intellectual and cultural journal that covered a wide range of topics, including literature, philosophy, science, and social issues. It provided a forum for both conservative and progressive voices, reflecting the cultural and intellectual currents of early 20th-century Türkiye. See, Erdoğan Erbay, "Mihrab", *TDV İslâm Ansiklopedisi* (Ankara: TDV Yayınları, 2020), 30: 29-30; Abdullah Uçman, "Hayat", *TDV İslâm Ansiklopedisi* (İstanbul: TDV Yayınları, 1998), 17:12-14. The essays and stories "Pervâne" and "Sabah Ezânını Dinlerken", "Mihrâkı Aşkı Sücûda Geldim!", published later in *Gül Demeti*, were originally published in "Mihrâb" magazine in 1924. The story "Kleopatra" was published in "Hayat Mecmûası" on September 27, 1928.

dations of human existence reflect the depth and breadth of her intellectual engagement. Her unpublished treatise *Meşreb-i Şerīfleri* (The Noble Dispositions), which compiles her observations on the spiritual teachings of Ken'ān Rifā'ī, stands as a testament to her lifelong commitment to synthesizing philosophical inquiry with spiritual devotion.[130] Semiha Cemāl's literary and philosophical legacy reflects not only her mastery of classical philosophical traditions but also her profound engagement with the ethical and metaphysical ideals of Sufism. Her works continue to resonate as a model of intellectual and spiritual synthesis, bridging the philosophical insights of antiquity with the moral and metaphysical vision of Islamic mysticism.

4.2. TRANSLATING SEMİHA CEMĀL: PRESERVING A PHILOSOPHICAL AND MYSTICAL LEGACY

Semiha Cemāl's *Aşk Peygamberi* stands as a singular work in Turkish literary history—a meditation on the nature of love, existence, and spiritual transformation that transcends the immediate cultural and political preoccupations of early Republican Türkiye. The novel's philosophical and metaphysical orientation positions it not only within the lineage of Sufi mystical writing but also within the broader intellectual tradition of classical philosophy. Her first published work was *Aşk Peygamberi*, written in Ottoman Turkish and published in 1927.[131] This novel reflects her early literary engagement with the theme of love as a transformative force that elevates human existence

---

130 Yalçınkaya, "Semiha Cemāl Hanım'ın Dilinden Ken'ân Rifâî'nin Meşreb-i Şerifleri", 2018.

131 Semiha Cemāl, *Aşk Peygamberi* (İstanbul: Kitabhane-i Sudî, 1927). Later the book has been published in Modern Turkish, Semiha Cemāl, *Aşk Peygamberi*, ed. Nurcan Şen (Ankara: Çolpan Kitap, 2023).

from worldly desire to spiritual fulfillment. The story follows Sühā, a young man initially immersed in the fleeting pleasures of worldly life, who embarks on a spiritual journey under the influence of Yusuf Cemāl, a masterful artist and moral figure widely admired for his ethical conduct and spiritual depth. Sühā's spiritual maturation parallels the Sufi concept of divine love, in which earthly attachment serves as a catalyst for the soul's ascent toward divine truth. The structure of the novel, framed through the diaries of Sühā and Zehrā, reflects a sophisticated narrative technique that blends personal introspection with spiritual revelation. Sühā's initial envy of Yusuf Cemāl gradually gives way to reverence as he recognizes the transformative power of Yusuf's spiritual guidance. The novel's exploration of love as both a moral and metaphysical ideal reflects Semiha Cemāl's attempt to engage with the Platonic conception of eros as a bridge between the sensual and the divine while also drawing upon the Sufi understanding of love as a means of achieving spiritual union with God.

Cemāl's narrative style is marked by lyrical sensitivity and psychological undertones, revealing the emotional and spiritual depths of her characters' journeys. Cemāl's use of elemental symbolism—water, fire, light, and darkness—reflects a broader metaphysical framework in which natural elements function as symbols of spiritual and existential transformation.[132] The recurring motifs of music and nature function as metaphors for the soul's alignment with the rhythms of the cosmos. In Sufi metaphysics, music and nature are often seen

---

132 Northrop Frye (d. 1991), one of the most important and influential literary theorists of the twentieth century, identifies elemental symbolism as a recurring motif in literary archetypes, where fire and light often symbolize spiritual enlightenment and transformation, while water and darkness represent emotional depth and the unconscious. See, Northrop Frye, *Anatomy of Criticism: Four Essays* (Princeton: Princeton University Press, 1957), 141–156.

as reflections of the cosmic order and divine harmony. *Sama'* (divine audition) is regarded as a means of spiritual awakening in Sufism, where the rhythms and melodies of sacred music align the soul with the divine presence.[133] Similarly, natural rhythms—such as the cycles of day and night or the changing seasons—are perceived as manifestations of the divine order, symbolizing the soul's journey toward spiritual alignment and unity with God.

Translating *Aşk Peygamberi* into English is a significant step in reclaiming Semiha Cemâl's legacy as both a literary and intellectual figure. Edward Said emphasizes that the act of retrieving and reinterpreting literary works outside their original cultural context serves to challenge dominant historical narratives and restore the complexity of intellectual legacies.[134] *Aşk Peygamberi* creates a space of "unbelonging" that resists simplistic categorization within the binaries of nationalist literature or nostalgic traditionalism. Rather than reinforcing fixed ideological positions, it occupies a dynamic third space[135]—one that transcends established political and cultural divides and introduces a more fluid and expansive literary voice. Cemâl's work challenges both the secular-nationalist narrative of early Republican Türkiye and the romanticized longing for Ottoman tradition, offering a philosophical and metaphysical framework

---

133   See, Leonard Lewisohn, "The Sacred Music of Islam: Samā' in the Persian Sufi Tradition", *British Journal of Ethnomusicology* 6, no. 1 (1997): 1-33.

134   Edward Said, *Culture and Imperialism* (New York: Vintage Books, 1993), 176–181.

135   Homi Bhabha's concept of the "third space" refers to a hybrid cultural and intellectual space that emerges when fixed binaries—such as East and West, tradition and modernity—are destabilized. In this space, cultural and intellectual elements are reconfigured, creating new modes of expression that transcend dominant ideological frameworks. See, Homi K. Bhabha, *The Location of Culture* (London: Routledge, 1994), 36–39.

that integrates Eastern and Western intellectual traditions. Furthermore, her exploration of love as a metaphysical and ethical force challenges the materialist and political narratives that have shaped Turkish modernity.[136] This translation is not merely an act of literary recovery but a critical intervention in the intellectual history of modern Türkiye. Cemāl's work complicates the dominant narrative of Turkish modernity as a rupture from religious and metaphysical traditions, revealing that spiritual inquiry endured beneath the surface of early Republican discourse. Her engagement with classical philosophy and Sufi mysticism challenges the assumption that modernization requires the abandonment of religious or metaphysical frameworks. Instead, Cemāl presents an alternative modernity that integrates Western philosophical ideals with Islamic metaphysical thought, positioning love not as a transient emotion but as a cosmic principle governing existence.

Cemāl's philosophical synthesis has broader implications for global intellectual history. The dialogue between East and West has often been framed as a clash between Western rationalism and Eastern mysticism. Cemāl's work transcends this binary, showing that Platonic and Stoic ideals of cosmic harmony and ethical self-mastery align closely with Sufi concepts of unity and spiritual discipline. Her work uncovers a shared philosophical foundation between these traditions, positioning Sufi thought not as an esoteric fringe but as part of a universal search for truth and transcendence. Translating *Aşk Peygamberi* also elevates the visibility of female intellectual and spiritual contributions within Turkish and Islamic thought. As one of the first Turkish women to engage with classical philosophical texts and Sufi metaphysics, Cemāl's work challenges the male-dominated

---

136 Jale Parla, "The Wounded Tongue: Turkey's Language Reform and the Canonicity of the Novel", *Modern Language Association* 23, no.1, (2008): 27-40.

canon of Turkish literature and philosophy.[137] Her articulation of love and spiritual awakening through a female voice adds a vital dimension to the history of Turkish modernity. Reclaiming and translating her work restores a forgotten literary and philosophical voice, reaffirming the place of female intellectuals in Turkish and Islamic thought.

Cemāl synthesizes Platonic idealism, Stoic self-mastery, and Sufi metaphysics into a cohesive philosophical framework that transcends simple classification. Her work bridges Eastern spirituality and Western philosophy, positioning love and moral integrity as central metaphysical forces. Platonic contemplation of eternal Forms, Stoic moral self-regulation, and the Sufi ideal of *'ishq* (divine love) converge in her vision of spiritual fulfillment.[138] This translation offers readers an opportunity to engage with a voice that has long been marginalized—a voice that speaks not only to the historical complexities of early Republican Türkiye but also to the enduring philosophical and spiritual questions that continue to shape human existence.

---

137 Despite the prominence of female figures women's literary contributions were often marginalized within the male-dominated canon of early Republican literature. The growing body of feminist literary criticism has since recovered and reassessed these works, highlighting their central role in shaping modern Turkish literary and intellectual history. See, Gürbey Hız, "The Making of the 'New Woman': Narratives in the Popular Illustrated Press from the Ottoman Empire to the New Republic (1890-1920s)", *Early Popular Visual Culture* 17, no. 2 (2019): 156-177. Also see, Fatmagül Berktay, *Kadın Olmak, Yaşamak, Yazmak* (İstanbul: Pencere Yayınları, 2000), 248.

138 Pierre Hadot argues that both Platonic and Stoic traditions position philosophy as an intellectual pursuit but as a way of life, where moral and metaphysical inquiry shape the individual's existential orientation. See, Pierre Hadot, *Philosophy as a Way of Life: Spiritual Exercises from Socrates to Foucault*, trans. Michael Chase (Oxford: Blackwell, 1995), 102–115.

Bringing *Aşk Peygamberi* into English presents a series of complex linguistic and philosophical challenges. Semiha Cemāl's language is richly layered, blending the formal structure of Ottoman Turkish with the modernizing influences of early Republican Turkish—a linguistic register that reflects the political and cultural transition of her time.[139] Ottoman Turkish, with its heavy reliance on Arabic and Persian loanwords, carries the weight of centuries of Islamic and imperial cultural history. By contrast, the language reforms of the early Republic sought to purge these influences, simplifying the lexicon and promoting a more direct, "national" form of expression.[140] Cemāl's writing resists this rupture, preserving the poetic and metaphysical texture of Ottoman Turkish while simultaneously engaging with the philosophical lexicon of Western classical thought. The translator must navigate this semantic and cultural complexity, preserving the metaphysical resonance

---

139 For the book of Turkish women writers translated to English, Arzu Akbatur, "Turkish Women writers in English Translation", *MonTI* 3 (2011): 161-179. Also for the invisibility of the translator and their translation work, Nur Zeynep Kürük Erçetin, "Halide Edip Adıvar: The Forgotten (Self-) Translator Behing the Writer", *Nesir: Edebiyat Araştırmaları Dergisi* 7 (2024): 123-137.

140 The simplification of the Turkish language and the removal of Persian and Arabic loanwords were central issues in the linguistic and cultural reforms of the early Turkish Republic. The language reform sought to strip Turkish of its Ottoman-era linguistic influences, replacing Persian and Arabic loanwords with words derived from Turkic roots and encouraging the adoption of a more "authentic" and "pure" national language. This effort was closely linked to the broader goal of constructing a modern Turkish identity, as language was viewed as a key marker of national unity and independence from the Ottoman-Islamic past. See, Agāh Sırrı Levend, *Türk Dilinde Gelişme ve Sadeleşme Evreleri* (Ankara: Türk Tarih Kurumu Basımevi, 1972), 247; Ayşegül Aydıngün and İsmail Aydıngün, 'The Role of Language in the Formation of Turkish National Identity and Turkishness', *Nationalism and Ethnic Politics* 10 (2004): 415-432.

of Cemāl's language while rendering it accessible to an English-speaking audience.

Moreover, the poetic and musical quality of Cemāl's prose adds another layer that requires careful attention. The rhythmic cadence of Ottoman Turkish, with its intricate patterns of assonance and alliteration, creates a sonic texture that reinforces the novel's underlying philosophical structure. Cemāl's use of elemental imagery—water flowing, fire burning, the kaval's mournful notes—constructs a soundscape that mirrors the emotional and spiritual journeys of her characters.[141] Translating this sensory dimension requires more than linguistic accuracy; it demands an attunement to the musical and symbolic undercurrents of the text. The challenge lies not only in conveying the literal meaning of the words but in preserving the emotional and metaphysical depth encoded in their sound and rhythm.

As you turn to the text itself, it is worth bearing in mind the layers of philosophical and spiritual inquiry that underlie the narrative. Cemāl's writing invites not only emotional engagement but also intellectual reflection—a dialogue between the human heart and the metaphysical structure of existence. In presenting *Aşk Peygamberi* to an English-speaking audience, this translation seeks to preserve the philosophical and poetic integrity of the original text while introducing Semiha Cemāl's singular vision to a broader readership.

---

141 Murray R Schafer, *The Soundscape: Our Sonic Environment and the Tuning of the World* (Vermont: Inner Traditions, 1993).

PART II

REATING *THE PROPHET OF LOVE*:
A PHILOSOPHICAL AND SPIRITUAL
ANALYSIS

CHAPTER 5

METAPHYSICAL FICTION
IN EARLY REPUBLICAN CONTEXT

Aşk Peygamberi can be situated within the tradition of the metaphysical novel – a literary genre that merges storytelling with philosophical and spiritual inquiry. Critics have described the metaphysical novel as one of the novel's highest and most absolute forms, capable of achieving what neither pure literature nor pure philosophy can accomplish in isolation. In such works, narrative art and metaphysical thought converge to explore existential questions and the "human condition" on a profound level. The French philosopher-novelist Jean-Paul Sartre's *La Nausée* (*Nausea/Bulantı*) is often cited as a paradigmatic example, as it conveys a "metaphysical experience" of being and absurdity through fiction. Similarly, the metaphysical novel in the Turkish context uses story — characters, events, symbols—as a vehicle for examining ontological and spiritual dilemmas that lie beyond the scope of ordinary realist prose. In these narratives, literature becomes, in effect, philosophy by other means: a fused discourse where plot, metaphor, and character illuminate questions of morality, existence, and the divine. This fusion endows the novel with moral-philosophical depth while giving philosophy a new, narrative mode of expression. In short, metaphysical fiction transforms the novel into a dual form: part aesthetic creation, part intellectual exploration, inviting readers to discern truths veiled beneath the surface of the story.

In Turkish literary modernity, the rise of the metaphysical novel coincided with a period of intense cultural transition and contestation. The early Republican era (1920s–1940s) was dominated by a secular-nationalist literary paradigm that foregrounded social realism, reformist ideals, and the construction of a homogeneous national identity. Yet, alongside and sometimes beneath this official literary current, there emerged works that quietly reasserted Ottoman-Islamic cultural memory and spiritual discourse within modern novelistic form. Literary historians have noted that certain novels of this era took on a "dissident" quality, subtly challenging the triumphalist nationalist meta-narratives of the 1930s by reintroducing plural, metaphysical perspectivesFor instance, Ahmet Hamdi Tanpınar's (d. 1962) *Huzur* (1949) – set on the eve of World War II – has been read as a meditation on Istanbul's lost Ottoman soul, a text which challenges the nationalist meta-narrative of its time through its nostalgic mysticism and philosophical introspection.[142] In a similar vein, earlier writers with Sufi or philosophical leanings crafted novels that functioned as counter-discourses to militant secularism, keeping alive questions of faith, morality, and transcendence in a rapidly modernizing society. As Göknar characterizes this recuperation of the Islamicate past in modern fiction as a form of "literary neo-Ottomanism", a turn that refocuses attention on the Ottoman-Islamic heritage as a creative wellspring for

---

142　Ahmet Hamdi Tanpınar, *Huzur* (İstanbul: Dergah Yayınları, 2023). For a critical exploration of how Türkiye's modern literary imagination engages with the legacies of empire, emphasizing the philosophical and temporal tensions embedded in national identity narratives see, Johanna Chovanec, "Literature and the Legacy of Empire: Approaching Turkey's Post-Imperial Condition Through Ahmet Hamdi Tanpınar", *Philosophy & Social Criticism* 50, no. 4 (2024): 608-628.

the contemporary novel.[143] Such works do not simply indulge in nostalgia; rather, they use the Ottoman spiritual legacy – Sufi ideals, Islamic philosophy, and classical poetry – as a rich intertextual palette for reimagining Turkish modernity. In doing so, metaphysical novels of the early 20th century open up a narrative space where vernacular mysticism engages critically with Western modernist thought, producing hybrid texts that speak to Türkiye's fractured identity.

Semiha Cemāl's *Aşk Peygamberi* is exemplary of this metaphysical turn in the Turkish novel. Writing as an educated woman immersed in both Sufi practice and Western philosophy, Semiha Cemāl Hanım bridges intellectual worlds in her work. Her dual influence permeates her novel's thematic fabric. Published in the late Ottoman or early Republican milieu (the narrative itself unfolds around the First World War and the Turkish War of Independence), *Aşk Peygamberi* can be read as a product of its time. On the surface, the novel chronicles the personal transformation of its protagonist, Sühâ, through love and mentorship. But at a deeper level, it operates as a spiritual allegory, mapping Sühâ's journey onto the Sufi path of transcendence. In line with the metaphysical novel genre, Semiha Cemāl interweaves multiple philosophical and mystical strands into her narrative. The story's conceptual vocabulary seamlessly ranges from Sufi notions like *nafs* (the ego-self) and *fanâ* (self-annihilation in God), to Platonic ideals of beauty and love, and even to Stoic themes of virtue and fate. *Aşk Peygamberi* thus tran-

---

143 Literary neo-Ottomanism Refers to the revival or reinterpretation of Ottoman cultural, historical, and aesthetic themes in contemporary Turkish literature, often as a means of negotiating modern identity, nostalgia, or post-imperial belonging within the framework of the Republic. See, Erdağ Göknar, "The Novel in Turkish: Narrative Tradition to Nobel Prize," *The Cambridge History of Turkey, Volume 4: Turkey in the Modern World*, ed. Reşat Kasaba (Cambridge: Cambridge University Press, 2008), 472–503.

scends simple genre categories and instead inhabits a liminal genre that Turkish criticism identifies as metaphysical fiction. Through symbolic imagery, lyrical invocations, and philosophically charged dialogue, the novel constructs an ontological drama – one where the characters' inner quests mirror a larger exploration of truth and transcendence.

Our approach to reading *Aşk Peygamberi* is informed by this understanding of the text as a metaphysical novel. In practice, this means analyzing how Semiha Cemāl deploys Sufi motifs (e.g., the motif of *ışık* and *zulmet*, light and darkness) or Platonic references (the ladder of love, the realm of forms) to structure the novel's narrative arc and thematic development. It means paying attention to how form and content interact – how the narrative architecture (chapters, framing scenes, descriptive passages) itself reinforces the book's spiritual message. Such a method follows the critical perspective that the boundary between "literary language" and "philosophical language" in these works is porous, even deliberately blurred. By tracing the novel's use of allegory, symbolism, and intertextual echo, we aim to illuminate *Aşk Peygamberi*'s place in the genealogy of the Turkish metaphysical novel.

Ultimately, this contextual and close-reading approach will show how *Aşk Peygamberi* functions not only as a story of individual salvation, but as a commentary on the broader search for meaning in an era of disillusionment and change. In the chapters that follow, we will explore the novel's narrative structure, conceptual map, and philosophical underpinnings in detail – situating Semiha Cemāl's work as a bridge between the spiritual wisdom of the past and the existential questions of the modern world. Through this exploration, *Aşk Peygamberi* emerges as more than just a novel of its historical moment; it stands as a Turkish literary palimpsest, where layered traditions of mysticism, philosophy, and modern storytelling coalesce into a unique expression of "love" as both human and divine truth.

5.1. A CITY OF SHADOWS, AN ORCHARD OF LIGHT: SÜHĀ'S JOURNEY FROM BEYOĞLU TO THE DIVINE

Semiha Cemāl's *Aşk Peygamberi* is an exploration of the intersection between human and divine love, framed within the metaphysical and ethical structures of Sufi and Platonic philosophy. The narrative arc of Sühā reflects a classic Sufi trajectory of spiritual awakening, where the protagonist's journey from worldly attachment to divine realization is facilitated by the guidance of a spiritually enlightened figure. Sühā's initial state of restlessness and indulgence in worldly desires symbolizes the *nafs* (the lower self), which in Sufi thought represents the soul's attachment to material and egotistic concerns.[144] His encounter with Yusuf Cemāl — a figure embodying spiritual wisdom and transcendence — marks a turning point, initiating Sühā's spiritual awakening. Yusuf Cemāl serves as a *mürşid* (spiritual guide), a crucial element in Sufi pedagogy where the seeker (Sühā) undergoes *tarīqah* (the spiritual path) under the mentorship of an enlightened master.

The narrative structure follows the classical Sufi paradigm of *sulūk* (spiritual journey), where the seeker moves through stages of purification, self-annihilation (*fana'*), and ultimate union with the divine (*baqā'*).[145] Yusuf Cemāl's role in this

---

144   In Sufism, *nafs* (the lower self or ego) symbolizes the soul's attachment to material elements. It represents the base instincts and selfish impulses that distract the seeker from spiritual truth and union with the divine. See, El-Kuşeyrî, *Kuşeyri Risâlesi* (1981), 222

145   This journey follows the classical Sufi framework of sulūk — the spiritual journey through which the seeker progresses by overcoming the lower self (*nafs*). The process begins with purification of the self from material attachments and egotism, leading to *fanā'* (annihilation of the self) — the moment when the seeker's ego dissolves and individual will merges with divine will. Yet, the path does not end with annihilation. The seeker ultimately arrives at *baqā'* (subsistence in God), where he attains spiritual permanence and union with the divine. *Fanā'* marks

transformation reflects the archetypal function of the *shaykh* (spiritual master) in Sufi tradition — not merely as a teacher but as a conduit through which divine truth is revealed. The moral and existential struggles faced by Sühā symbolize the inner conflict between the material and the spiritual, culminating in his transcendence of the ego and alignment with divine will.

The novel's setting stretches from the urban chaos of Istanbul to the tranquil countryside of Antalya's lemon orchards, creating a deliberate contrast between the fragmented modernity of the city and the harmonious natural order of the rural landscape. The contrasting geographies serve as metaphors for the spiritual dichotomy between worldly disillusionment and metaphysical harmony. In Istanbul, particularly in the dark and morally ambiguous streets of Beyoğlu and Karaköy, the atmosphere is marked by corruption and spiritual emptiness—a reflection of the moral instability of late Ottoman modernity.[146] Terms such as "dark," "crooked," "narrow," and "desolate" are

the death of the ego, but *baqā'* signifies the rebirth of the self in alignment with the divine essence. See, Andrew Wilcox, "The Dual Mystical Concepts of Fanā' and Baqā' in Early Sufism," *British Journal of Middle Eastern Studies* 38, no. 1 (2011): 95-118.

146   In the late Ottoman and early Republican period, Istanbul, particularly areas like Taksim, symbolized both the decaying remnants of an imperial past and the emerging, often unsettling, modernity. The urban transformation was accompanied by significant socio-cultural and moral anxieties. Rapid Westernization, economic instability, and the collapse of traditional communal structures produced a sense of alienation and existential fragmentation among the urban population. This period saw the rise of literary depictions of Istanbul's urban spaces as symbols of moral decline and social disorientation. Urbanite characters in late Ottoman and early Republican novels often embody this existential tension. Their moral depravity is depicted through their disoriented and hedonistic lifestyles, emotional instability, and moral ambiguity. See, Erdağ Göknar, "Reading Occupied Istanbul: Turkish Subject-Formation from Historical Trauma to Literary Trope", *Culture, Theory and Critique* 55, no. 3 (2014): 321-341.

strategically repeated in the descriptions of urban spaces, evoking the psychological and moral fragmentation experienced by the characters. Conversely, the pastoral setting of Antalya represents a return to spiritual purity and moral clarity, mirroring the Sufi ideal of retreat from the distractions of the material world toward spiritual introspection and unity with the divine.

The historical framework of the novel subtly reflects the broader political and social shifts of the period. Although the historical context is not explicitly defined, references to military drafts and national celebrations suggest that the narrative unfolds during the First World War (1914-1918) and the subsequent Turkish War of Independence (1918-1923).[147] Sühā's conscription into the military, along with Suleyman's earlier draft notice, indicates that the events occur in the aftermath of the Great War, while the reference to "the ruins of eight years ago" suggests that the novel is set around 1923, shortly before the official establishment of the Turkish Republic. The historical backdrop underscores the novel's exploration of moral and existential dislocation in a period of profound national and cultural transformation.

---

147 The Turkish War of Independence (1919–1923) was a military and political struggle led by Mustafa Kemal Atatürk against the occupying Allied powers following the defeat of the Ottoman Empire in World War I. After the Ottoman government signed the Treaty of Sèvres in 1920, which partitioned much of Anatolia among the Allied powers, Turkish nationalists rejected the treaty and organized armed resistance. The successful defense of Anatolia led to the abolition of the Ottoman Sultanate in 1922 and the signing of the Treaty of Lausanne in 1923, which established the borders of the modern Turkish Republic. The war marked a foundational moment in Turkish national identity, symbolizing the transition from an imperial system to a secular, nationalist state under Atatürk's leadership. See, Edward J. Erickson, *The Turkish War of Independence: A Military History, 1919-1923* (Santa Barbara: Bloomsbury Publication, 2021), 1-54. For more information on the Occupation of Istanbul please see, Daniel-Joseph MacArthur-Seal and Gizem Tongo, "Representing Occupied Istanbul: Documents, Objects and Memory", *YILLIK: Annual of Istanbul Studies* 4 (2022): 91-98.

5.2. EMBODIED LONGING:
THE CHARACTERS OF *THE PROPHET OF LOVE*

At the heart of the novel's philosophical and spiritual inquiry is the character of Yusuf Cemāl, whose name evokes the Arabic word *jamāl* (beauty), symbolizing his embodiment of moral and spiritual perfection.[148] Yusuf Cemāl functions as a spiritual and moral guide, reflecting the Platonic ideal of the philosopher-king and the Sufi archetype of the *insān-ı kamil*.[149] Yusuf Cemāl inspires an almost religious devotion in those around him, becoming the focal point of admiration and longing for both Zehra and Sühā. Primarily Yusuf Cemāl's relationship with Suzān sets an ideal form of uniting in love, which becomes the exemplary connection which everyone in the novel aspires to achieve. The depiction of Yusuf Cemāl in the novel elevates him beyond his renowned skill as a composer, presenting him

---

148 In Sufism, *jamāl* (beauty) refers to the divine attribute of beauty (*al-Jamīl*) and reflects the harmonious, gentle, and aesthetically pleasing manifestations of God's presence in creation. Rooted in the Qur'anic verse "Indeed, God is beautiful and loves beauty" (Ṣaḥīḥ Muslim, 91), jamāl embodies the aspects of God's nature that are associated with mercy (*raḥmah*), grace, and love. See, Süleyman Uludağ, "Cemāl", *TDV İslâm Ansiklopedisi* (İstanbul: TDV Yayınları, 1993), 7:296.

149 The Platonic ideal of the philosopher-king and the Sufi archetype of the *Insān-ı Kāmil* (Perfected Human) reflect parallel visions of moral and intellectual perfection, though they arise from different philosophical and spiritual traditions. In Plato's Republic, the philosopher-king represents the highest form of political and moral authority. The Sufi archetype of the Insān-ı Kāmil embodies the complete manifestation of divine attributes (al-asmā' wa'l-ṣifāt) and serves as a spiritual guide to others on the path to divine union. Just as the philosopher-king governs by virtue of his understanding of the Forms, the Insān-ı Kāmil leads others through his realization of God's unity (tawḥīd) and his capacity to reflect divine perfection in human form. See, Mark Sedgwick, Western Sufism: From the Abbasids to the New Age (Oxford: Oxford University Press, 2017), 35.

as an extraordinary embodiment of moral and spiritual virtue. Described as "a true human (*insān*) being in every sense,"[150] Yusuf Cemāl transcends the confines of his artistry, reflecting the ideal human described by philosophers like Socrates. His virtues—mercy, generosity, loyalty, and almost divine compassion—position him as a paragon of ethical and spiritual excellence. This characterization aligns him with the prophetic figures of history, as the narrator likens his beauty and moral stature to those of an Israelite prophet (*Benī İsrail'in peygamberi*).[151] Yusuf Cemāl's magnetism draws admiration from both men and women, yet this admiration is explicitly portrayed as directed toward his soul rather than any fleeting or base attraction. His essence cannot be reduced to earthly desires; he is not one to be loved with selfish or possessive passion. Instead, he inspires a love rooted in awe and respect for his inner beauty and perfection. His ability to uplift those around him, particularly the poor and destitute whom he clothes, feeds, and shelters, underscores his alignment with the Sufi ideal of a perfected human being.

Within the plot of *Aşk Peygamberi*, Sühā's transformation from a restless, worldly youth to a seeker of divine love through his encounter with Yusuf Cemāl symbolizes the human potential for transcendence. Sühā's journey reflects the narrative's core theme: the struggle to reconcile modern life's fragmentation with the pursuit of metaphysical unity and moral clarity.

---

150 Cemāl, *Aşk Peygamberi*, 67.

151 Platonic love transcends physical attraction and aims to connect individuals to a higher, abstract form of beauty. It is also historically tied to the homoerotic culture of classical Athens, where it was often expressed in the mentorship dynamic between an older mentor and a younger man. Sabrina Ebbersmeyer, "The Philosopher as a Lover: Renaissance Debates on Platonic *Eros*", *Emotion and Cognitive Life in Medieval and Early Modern Philosophy*, eds. Martin Pickavé and Lisa Shapiro, (Oxford: Oxford University Press, 2012), 134-136.

The seekers, on the other hand, both male and female characters who embark on personal quests for meaning, embody the
universal human struggle for transcendence. Their development aligns with the Platonic and Sufi conceptions of self-realization—moving from corporeal desires to spiritual enlightenment. The seekers can sometimes occupy dual spaces as both
strivers of spiritual fulfillment and sucked into the depravities
of urban life.

Certain figures in the novel, like Zeliha and Zehra, who
represent "the innocent/child figures" within the plot, are the
archetypes inspiring others to reconnect with the simplicity and
authenticity of life, emphasizing the novel's theme of returning
to natural harmony. In this opening invocation, the protagonist presents themselves as a being formed through love—one
whose path is guided by it, whose identity is rooted in it, and
whose search unfolds within its light. This notion aligns closely
with the Sufi concept of divine love, where the lover seeks to dissolve the ego and merge with the beloved, understood as a manifestation of the divine. The protagonist's invocation, therefore,
becomes a kind of metaphysical declaration, asserting that the
work they undertake—whether that work is the writing of the
novel itself or their spiritual journey—is inextricably linked to
the divine force of love.

5.3. NARRATIVE ARCHITECTURE
AND SYMBOLIC DEPTH WITHIN THE NOVEL

Semiha Cemāl's *Aşk Peygamberi* opens with an evocative and
layered invocation, *"O Love, I have made you my basmala,"*
framing love as both a metaphysical principle and a creative
force.[152] The opening scene establishes an ideal cosmos where

---

152 Cemāl, *Aşk Peygamberi*, 29.

love becomes the axis of existence, situating it as the key to understanding both the narrative structure and the spiritual journey of the characters. Love here is not presented as a fleeting emotion or romantic attachment but as an ontological force, akin to the Sufi concept of *'ishq*, where the lover seeks annihilation in the divine beloved.[153] The invocation of *bismillahi'l-aşk* parallels the Islamic practice of beginning all actions in the name of God, but here it is directed toward love, transforming it into the foundation upon which the entire metaphysical order of the novel rests. The poetic language, charged with metaphysical and spiritual significance, reflects the mystical register of Sufi discourse, where love is simultaneously the source, the path, and the destination of existence. The imagery of light and darkness, of the setting sun and the approach of night, evokes the tension between separation and union—a central motif in Sufi thought, where the longing for the beloved reflects the soul's yearning for divine unity.

The scene introduces Suzān as a figure embodying the archetype of the Sufi seeker, whose emotional and spiritual states mirror the metaphysical journey of love. The interplay between sensory and metaphysical experiences is heightened by the poetic imagery of burning, yearning, and blindness. Suzān's longing for the beloved, whose presence and absence are marked by the rhythms of day and night, mirrors the Sufi path's cyclical tension between union and separation. The invocation of the sun's setting as a source of anguish reflects the Sufi understanding of existential separation (*firqat*)—the painful distance between the human soul and the divine source. Suzān's vision of the delicate figure leaning into the flames symbolizes the transformative nature of love, where the fire of desire becomes both a trial and a means of spiritual purification. The repetition of blindness and deafness underscores the Sufi notion that true

---

153   For *'ishq* see, Schimmel, *Mystical Dimensions of Islam*, 136-137.

perception lies beyond the sensory realm—that only through the heart's awakening can the soul recognize the true nature of the beloved.

The figure of the horseman, whose beauty is described as almost otherworldly, introduces the central motif of the divine beloved as the object of metaphysical longing. The horseman is not merely a romantic figure; his bearing and presence evoke the Sufi concept of the *insān-ı kamil,* who serves as both a reflection of and a conduit to the divine. Suzān's trembling anticipation and eventual embrace of the horseman symbolize the moment of mystical union, where the boundaries between self and other dissolve. The language used to describe the horseman's beauty—beyond human, untouched by the elements— suggests a metaphysical reality where the beloved transcends the limitations of the created world. The closing lines, where Suzān questions whether the beloved's body could ever fade or disappear, articulate the Sufi dilemma of permanence and impermanence—whether the experience of divine union can persist within the temporal confines of human existence.

Following the opening invocation, the narrative shifts from the metaphysical to the personal, introducing Sühā, a young orphan who embodies the existential and moral struggles of modernity. Sühā's journey from emotional vulnerability and worldly attachment to spiritual transcendence reflects both Platonic and Sufi models of the soul's ascent. At the beginning of the narrative, Sühā is portrayed as emotionally fragile and morally adrift. His status as an orphan symbolizes his existential alienation—a motif that reflects the broader cultural and philosophical disorientation of early Republican Türkiye.[154] His

---

154 The early Republican period was marked by a rupture in collective memory and identity formation, creating a secular, nationalized subject that was cut off from its Ottoman-Islamic epistemic and affective foundations. See, Orhan Pamuk, *Secularism and Blasphemy: The Poli-*

experiences at a boarding school, where he grapples with loneliness and emotional instability, reflect the human condition of separation from the divine source. Sühā's emotional turmoil is compounded by his struggle to find meaning in the transient pleasures of the material world.

His initial fascination with worldly beauty—particularly his admiration for a young woman—mirrors the Platonic stage of love grounded in sensory attraction. However, even at this early stage, Sühā's emotional sensitivity sets him apart from his peers. Unlike his classmates, who engage in hedonistic pursuits without hesitation, Sühā approaches life's pleasures with hesitation and doubt. His aesthetic appreciation of beauty—whether in the form of poetry, music, or nature—suggests an innate receptivity to higher forms of love. This capacity for aesthetic sensitivity becomes the foundation for his spiritual awakening. Sühā's relationship with Celāl, his closest friend, introduces the first stage of his emotional and philosophical transformation. Celāl functions as a Platonic companion and guide, awakening Sühā's awareness of the moral and aesthetic dimensions of human existence. Through Celāl's influence, Sühā develops an appreciation for art and poetry, which serve as conduits for his deeper engagement with the metaphysical order. However, Celāl's role as a guide is ultimately limited. His influence remains within the realm of human friendship and artistic beauty, which Plato identifies as intermediary stages on the path toward true love. Celāl's death symbolizes the end of this transitional phase and marks the beginning of Sühā's search for a higher, more transcendent form of love.

---

tics of the Turkish Novel (London: Routledge, 2013), 95; Jale Parla, "The Wounded Tongue: Turkey's Language Reform and the Canonicity of the Novel", *Modern Language Association* 23, no.1 (2008): 27-40, 31.

CHAPTER 6

CONCEPTUAL MAP
OF THE PROPHET OF LOVE

Aşk Peygamberi unfolds a rich conceptual map drawn from Sufi mysticism and classical philosophy, shaping the novel's symbolic and philosophical universe. At its core, the narrative operates on multiple levels: it is a love story on the surface, a spiritual allegory beneath, and a commentary on the human quest for truth. Semiha Cemāl Hanım, with her Sufi background and philosophical education, embeds in her fiction a conceptual constellation that guides the reader through themes of love, the self, wisdom, divine unity, and the veil. These key concepts recur throughout the novel as a network of meanings that reflect the author's spiritual and intellectual orientation. This section maps out these concepts and their relationships, illustrating how they function across the novel and illuminate its deeper significance. Brief references to characters and moments – notably the journeys of Sühā and the saintly presence of Yusuf Cemāl – will ground this exploration in the story's events, while drawing connections to Sufi thought (and occasional parallels to Western philosophical ideas) to enrich our understanding. The goal is to equip readers with a conceptual framework to navigate the subtle philosophical language of *The Prophet of Love*, and to show how Semiha Cemāl reworks Sufi metaphysics into narrative form.

6.1. LOVE (AŞK) AS COSMIC PRINCIPLE
AND SPIRITUAL LONGING

Love (*aşk*) is the beating heart of the novel's universe – at once a human emotion, a spiritual force, and the very principle that animates existence. *The Prophet of Love* portrays love as a cosmic and sacred energy that guides souls toward truth. In Sufi tradition, love is often described as the force that draws the lover to annihilate themselves in the Beloved (who ultimately is God).[155] Semiha Cemāl inherits this mystical understanding: the novel's language of passion is suffused with the idiom of Sufi love, using the metaphors of earthly desire – flames, wine, intoxication, and union – to signify the soul's yearning for the Divine. This places her in a centuries-old lineage that includes Rabia al-Adawiyya (d. 801/185), Farīd-al-Dīn Attar of Nishapur (d. 1221 /618), Fuzūlī (d. 1556/963), and Mevlānā Celāleddīn-i Rūmī (d. 1273/672)—figures for whom stories of earthly love commonly served as allegories of the soul's journey toward divine union.[156] By situating *Aşk Peygamberi* in this Sufi context, we recognize that what might superficially seem like a tale

---

155 In Sufi metaphysics, love is a transformative force that propels the seeker toward the annihilation (*fanā'*) of the ego or self in the presence of the Divine Beloved, who is ultimately God. This process of self-effacement is understood as the highest form of spiritual realization, in which individual identity dissolves into the unity of existence (*tawḥīd*), allowing the lover to become a mirror to the Divine attributes. William Chittick, *Sufi Path of Love: The Spiritual Teachings of Rumi* (Albany: State University of New York Press, 1983), 179-180.

156 See Margaret Smith, *Rābiʿa the Mystic and Her Fellow-Saints in Islam* (Cambridge: Cambridge University Press, 1928), 123–26; Aṭṭār, *The Conference of the Birds*, trans. Afkham Darbandi and Dick Davis (London: Penguin Books, 1984), 27–34; Fuzūlī, *Leylâ ve Mecnûn*, trans. Walter G. Andrews (Istanbul: Yapı Kredi Yayınları, 1997), 15–17; and Jalāl al-Dīn Rūmī, *The Masnavi*, Book I, trans. Jawid Mojaddedi (Oxford: Oxford University Press, 2004), 78–80.

of worldly love is a faithful echo of classical mystical love discourse. The title itself – *The Prophet of Love* – signals that love is elevated to a prophetic, guiding truth in the novel's world.

In the narrative, the theme of love operates on two interlocking levels: earthly love as a stepping stone and divine love as the ultimate destination. The protagonist Sühā initially experiences infatuation and desire in a worldly sense (particularly his tumultuous love for Zehrā), but these emotions are gradually revealed as a catalyst for something higher. Under the influence of Yusuf Cemāl (a figure who embodies spiritual love), Sühā comes to realize that his personal love was but a fragment of a greater, more transcendent love. This reflects a common Sufi idea that human loves are mirrors or training grounds for learning the all-consuming love of God.[157] In the novel, characters like Sühā, Zehrā, and Suzān each grapple with longing and attachment, only to be gently directed toward the notion that true love is not possession or attachment to a mortal beloved, but an awe-filled devotion to the eternal. Indeed, Semiha Cemāl positions love not as a fleeting emotion but as "a cosmic principle governing existence", a divine energy that underlies all being. Through the events in the story – Sühā's restless passions, Suzān's idealized union with Yusuf, Zehrā's earnest devotion – the reader is shown how love can transform from a source of personal turmoil into a path of spiritual fulfillment.

---

157 Schimmel, *Mystical Dimensions of Islam*, 131–33. Schimmel explains that in Sufi thought, earthly or human love (ʿishq-i majāzī) is often seen as a preparatory stage for divine love (ʿishq-i ḥaqīqī), functioning as both a mirror and a pedagogical metaphor that trains the heart to yearn for and recognize the Divine Beloved.

6.2. THE SELF (NEFS AND RŪH):
TRANSFORMATION OF THE EGO-SELF

Closely tied to the theme of love is the novel's concern with the self, especially the dichotomy between the lower self (nefs) and the spirit (rūḥ). In Sufi thought, the *nefs* (or *nafs*, often translated as ego, lower self, or carnal soul) represents the base impulses and egocentric identity that veil a person from God, whereas the *rūḥ* or soul is the divine spirit or higher self that yearns to reunite with its source.[158] *The Prophet of Love* dramatizes a journey of the self's transformation: the protagonist Sühā's arc is essentially the taming of the *nefs* and the awakening of the *rūh* under the guidance of love and wisdom.

At the start of the novel, Sühā is portrayed as a restless young man indulging in worldly pleasures and driven by selfish desires. This state corresponds to what Sufis call the *nafs al-ammara* (the commanding self that inclines toward evil or excess) – the ego enthralled by material attachments and personal gratification. Sühā's moral and psychological turmoil, set against the backdrop of a decadent Istanbul, symbolizes the *nafs* in its unrefined form. He moves through dissolute urban spaces (gambling halls, brothels, narrow backstreets) which are de-

---

158　In Sufi thought, the nefs (Arabic: nafs) is the aspect of the self associated with ego, desire, and attachment to the material world. It is often seen as the primary obstacle on the path to spiritual realization, because its inclinations toward self-centeredness and worldly pleasure obscure the presence of God. The nefs must be disciplined and purified through spiritual struggle (mujāhada) in order to awaken the rūḥ, the divine spirit or higher self within each person. The rūḥ is considered a breath from God, bestowed at the moment of creation (Qur'an 15:29), and it constantly longs to return to its source. The journey of Sufism is thus a movement from the domination of the nefs toward the illumination of the rūḥ, culminating in intimate knowledge (maʿrifa) of the Divine. See, Chittick, *Sufi Path of Knowledge*, 94–96; Schimmel, *Mystical Dimensions of Islam*, 112–115.

scribed with words like "dark," "crooked," and "desolate," all reflecting his inner fragmentation and the dominance of ego. In these early chapters, Sühā's self is essentially veiled in darkness – he is alienated from his own higher potential, unable to see beyond immediate lusts or fears.

The turning point comes with Sühā's encounter with Yusuf Cemāl, which is depicted as a moment of awakening or remembrance of the soul. Yusuf, as a spiritually enlightened figure, awakens Sühā's dormant soul. Under Yusuf's almost magnetic influence, Sühā experiences profound shame and yearning – emotions that signal the *nafs* starting to dissolve. He begins to question his ego-driven life and feel the stirrings of a deeper self. In Sufi practices, this is akin to entering the path of purification (*tariqah*), where the seeker's ego is disciplined and the heart is polished through association with a master (*mürşid*).[159] The novel explicitly casts Yusuf as a *mürşid* (spiritual guide) and Sühā as the *murid* (disciple) on the path. Their relationship is not just friendship but an initiatory process: Sühā undergoes an inner journey (*sulūk*) of repentance, self-confrontation, and transformation under Yusuf's guidance.

---

159 In Sufi practices, embarking on the spiritual path—ṭarīqah—entails a disciplined journey of self-purification and inner transformation. The ṭarīqah is not merely a set of rituals, but a structured ethical and spiritual process wherein the seeker (murīd) gradually overcomes the dominion of the ego (nafs) and cultivates the virtues necessary for nearness to God. Central to this path is the guidance of a spiritual master (mürşid), whose role is to discern the inner state of the disciple and prescribe appropriate teachings, practices (adhkār, riyāḍah, mujāhada), and moral training. This relationship of companionship and instruction is essential to Sufi pedagogy, as it is through the master's spiritual insight and presence that the disciple's heart is gradually "polished" (a metaphor often used in reference to the hadith that describes the heart as a mirror tarnished by sin). Over time, this polishing reveals the Divine light already latent within the soul. See, Chittick, *The Sufi Path of Knowledge*, 176-179.

As the story progresses, we witness Sühā's *nefs* being systematically broken down – through heartbreak, loss, and introspection – and his soul coming to the fore. One of the novel's powerful subtexts is *"die before you die,"* a well-known Sufi maxim meaning that one must spiritually die to the ego in order to be reborn in spirit.[160] Indeed, Sühā endures a figurative death of his old self: he loses worldly attachments (even being drafted into war, which separates him from his prior life), and he endures deep suffering and remorse. This process corresponds to what Sufis term *fanā'* (annihilation of the self). By the end, the Sühā we see is radically changed – humble, penitent, and illuminated by faith in the Divine. The novel implies that only by confronting and "burning away" the ego can the true self (*the soul*) emerge into the light. In the novel, Sühā's ego was precisely that veil – it kept him absorbed in petty aims "other than the Real." Once love and spiritual discipline strip that veil, Sühā discovers an identity grounded not in ego but in the divine spark within (often referred to as the *"true self"* or *"secret of the heart"* in mystical terms).

Notably, the transformation of the self is not portrayed as easy or serene – it is tumultuous and often painful. The text uses metaphors of illness and convalescence for Sühā's state; at one juncture, he is physically ill and hallucinates (hearing dogs

---

160   The phrase "Die before you die" (*mūtū qabla an tamūtū*) is a well-known hadith frequently cited in Sufi teachings to express the concept of spiritual death preceding physical death. In this context, "dying" refers to the annihilation (*fanā'*) of the ego-self (*nafs*)—a voluntary surrender of selfish desires, attachments, and worldly identifications—so that the seeker may be reborn in spiritual consciousness and divine proximity. It is an invitation to experience a radical transformation in which the self no longer asserts its own will, but becomes a vessel for divine presence. This inner death is seen as a necessary stage on the path to *baqā'* (subsistence in God), wherein the seeker lives not through their own selfhood, but through the light of divine realization. Alexander Knysh, *Islamic Mysticism: A Short History* (Leiden: Brill, 2000), 86.

howl, seeing ghostly visions), reflecting the fevered "detox" of his soul from the poison of the ego. Through Yusuf's compassionate yet firm influence, and through Sühā's own trials, the protagonist moves from the selfish chaos of his *nefs* to the peaceful clarity of a soul aligned with God. In the final stage of his journey, Sühā's inner voice is no longer the insistent "I, I, I" of the ego, but one of surrender. This echoes the famous utterance of the Sufi martyr Hallāj, *"I am He whom I love, and He whom I love is me,"* signifying that the self has completely identified with the Divine.[161] While Sühā does not claim such ecstatic unity explicitly, the ending suggests he has attained a degree of self-transcendence, understanding that what he truly sought all along was not the satisfaction of his *nafs*, but the fulfillment of his soul in the love of God.

6.3. WISDOM (HİKMET AND MA'RİFA): GNOSIS, PHILOSOPHY, AND INSIGHT

Another pillar of the novel's conceptual structure is wisdom, encompassing both rational philosophy (*hikmet*) and mysti-

---

161   This statement reflects the mystical state of fanā' (annihilation of the self) followed by baqā' (subsistence in God), central concepts in Sufi metaphysics. When Ḥusayn ibn Manṣūr al-Ḥallāj declared, "I am He whom I love, and He whom I love is me," he was articulating an experiential truth of union with the Divine—wherein the boundary between the lover and the Beloved dissolves. In this state, the mystic no longer acts from the limited perspective of the ego (nafs), but from the Divine consciousness that has taken full possession of the self. Such expressions were often seen as ecstatic utterances (shaṭḥiyyāt), controversial in theological discourse, but interpreted within Sufism as manifestations of divine love and unity (tawḥīd) realized at the deepest level of the soul. See, Louis Massignon, *The Passion of al-Hallaj: Mystic and Martyr of Islam*, trans. Herbert Mason, vol. 1 (Princeton: Princeton University Press, 1982), 300–305.

cal insight (*ma'rifa*, or gnosis).[162] Semiha Cemāl merges these two forms of knowledge in her narrative. The Prophet of Love presents true wisdom as a deep understanding of reality—an insight cultivated through inner experience and illuminated by divine awareness, beyond the bounds of formal learning or intellectual skill.

Within the story, Yusuf Cemāl embodies the principle of wisdom. He emerges as both a devout mystic and a man of refined intellect and discerning insight. In conversations, Yusuf imparts knowledge to others in a Socratic or platonic dialogue style – not delivering didactic lectures, but guiding his interlocutors to discover truths through questions and parables. The text explicitly likens him to a *Platonic philosopher-king* – someone who unites intellectual virtue with moral virtue – as well as to the Sufi *insān-ı kāmil* (of which more below).[163] This dual reference is telling: the author is aligning the highest ideal of Western philosophy (the sage or philosopher-king who knows the Good) with the highest ideal of Islamic mysticism (the knower of God who has realized divine truth). Indeed, Semiha Cemāl's synthesis suggests that philosophical wisdom and mystical gnosis ultimately converge. For her, Plato's quest for

---

162 In Sufi epistemology, *hikmet* refers to divinely rooted wisdom that aligns both the intellect and ethical behavior with cosmic order, while *ma'rifa* designates direct, experiential knowledge of God obtained through inner unveiling rather than rational deduction. See, Mustafa Kara, "Hikmet", *TDV İslâm Ansiklopedisi* (İstanbul: TDV Yayınları, 1998), 17:518-519; Süleyman Uludağ, "Marifet", *TDV İslâm Ansiklopedisi* (İstanbul: TDV Yayınları, 2003), 28:54-56.

163 The *philosopher-king*, as described in Plato's *Republic*, is an ideal ruler who governs justly by virtue of philosophical wisdom and moral integrity, having attained knowledge of the eternal Forms—especially the Form of the Good. He embodies the fusion of intellectual contemplation and ethical leadership, making him uniquely qualified to rule. See, Bernard Boulet, "The Philosopher-King", *A Companion to Plutarch*, ed. Mark Beck (Oxford: Blackwell Publication, 2014), 449-462.

eternal Forms or the Stoic pursuit of virtue is not at odds with Sufism's quest for divine reality; both seek the eternal unity of the divine as the ground of truth.

Semiha Cemāl's portrayal of wisdom also carries a subtle critique of purely secular or material understandings of life. By setting up Yusuf's spiritual philosophy against the backdrop of a society in moral disarray, the novel suggests that what truly heals and guides humanity is this higher wisdom connected to the divine.[164] Characters who lack this – for instance, those mired in materialism or cynical modern attitudes – appear shallow or lost. The implicit message is that without spiritual wisdom, one cannot make sense of suffering or love or fate. Yusuf's sage-like presence offers an alternative: he brings clarity, comfort, and purpose to those around him by orienting them to a transcendent perspective.

6.4. DIVINE UNITY (TEVHİD):
ONENESS AS THE ULTIMATE REALITY

All the paths of love, self-purification, and wisdom in *The Prophet of Love* ultimately lead to the realization of divine unity (*tevhid*) – the idea that all existence is one because it originates from and is sustained by the One (God). Tevhid (also spelled *tawḥīd*) in Islamic theology means affirming the oneness of God, but in Sufi philosophy it extends to an experiential

---

164 In early Republican Türkiye, the epistemological authority of rationalism and scientific positivism was institutionalized as part of a broader effort to construct a modern, secular nation-state. The new regime privileged formal education, scientific method, and historical materialism as the sole legitimate modes of knowledge. This rationalization of knowledge marginalized alternative epistemologies, especially the experiential, intuitive, and metaphysical dimensions of Islamic thought. See, Nazım, "Turkish Conservative Modernism", 87-112.

realization that there is no true reality but the Divine Reality.[165] The novel threads this concept throughout its narrative, gradually uncovering the oneness behind apparent separations and differences.

One way the novel conveys *tevhid* is through symbolic contrasts of light and darkness. Repeatedly, we find imagery associating light with truth, unity, and God's presence, while darkness is linked to ignorance, fragmentation, or God's absence. In Sufi literature, God is often described as Light (*nūr*), and realizing God's unity is akin to emerging into light. *The Prophet of Love* echoes this symbolism: Yusuf Cemāl is frequently associated with light – his face, character, and even music have an aura that illuminates others – whereas the corrupt city life or the characters' ego-driven states are depicted in dim or dark tones. The text explicitly notes that *nūr* (light) signifies guidance and divine illumination, while *zulmet* (darkness) represents *"the veils of ignorance, materiality, and separation from the divine."*. Crucially, the narrative suggests that spiritual awakening requires "piercing the veils" of darkness to reach the light of unity. This is illustrated when Sühā finally confronts the "darkness" within himself – his ego and false attachments – and as a result, he perceives the "light" of truth that Yusuf had been pointing him toward. Only by facing the inner darkness (his fears, guilt, and selfishness) can Sühā's heart be flooded with divine light. This journey from darkness to light is nothing other than moving from a sense of separation to a sense of unity.

The concept of *tevhid* also manifests in how the novel portrays nature and cosmos. When the setting shifts from Istanbul to the serene countryside of Antalya (with its lemon orchards and starlit skies), the narrative tone becomes harmonious and reflective. The countryside symbolizes a return to primordial

---

165   See, Süleyman Uludağ, "Tevhid", *TDV İslâm Ansiklopedisi* (İstanbul: TDV yayınları, 2012), 41:22-24.

harmony – an environment where one can sense the underlying oneness of creation. Under the vast night sky or in the tranquility of an orchard, characters like Sühā experience moments of awe and unity: the multiplicity of worldly concerns falls away, and they intuit that all creatures, all elements of nature, and themselves are part of an integrated whole. This mirrors the Sufi idea that the universe is a manifestation of God (*tajalli*), and every part of it is interwoven by the single reality of God's Being.[166] Semiha Cemāl's metaphysical background allows her to infuse the narrative with these contemplative passages that evoke the unity of existence. For instance, late in the novel, Sühā observes the night sky and feels a profound peace – as if he has found his place in the cosmic order. Such moments reinforce *tevhid* by showing that beyond the "noise" of individual dramas, there is a unifying silence or presence holding everything together.

For Semiha Cemāl and her contemporaries influenced by Sufism, *tevhid* was also a response to the existential dislocation of their time. The early 20th century brought wars, the collapse of the Ottoman order, and rapid secularization in the new Turkish Republic. Amid such upheavals, *The Prophet of Love* posits unity as the antidote to chaos. The fragmentation (of values, identities, communities) is implicitly likened to the Quranic idea of *"zulmet upon zulmet"* (layers of darkness), whereas the

---

166　In Sufi metaphysics, *tajalli* (divine manifestation) refers to the continuous self-disclosure of God through creation. The universe is not seen as separate from God but as a locus of His attributes (*şifāt*), revealing aspects of divine reality. This ontological view—especially developed in the thought of Ibn ʿArabī—asserts that all existence is unified through *wujūd* (Being), and the multiplicity of creation is but a veil over the singularity of divine presence. See, Seyyed Hossein Nasr, "God is Absolute Reality and All Creation His Tajalli (Theophany)", *The Wiley Blackwell Companion to Religion and Ecology*, ed. John Hart (Oxford: Wiley Blackwell, 2017), 3-11.

vision of God's oneness restores a sense of purpose and coherence. By having her characters attain inner unity, Semiha Cemāl hints at the possibility of a more unified society grounded in spiritual truth. Thus, *tevhid* operates not only as personal enlightenment in the novel but as a quiet social philosophy: it affirms that despite apparent divisions – religious, cultural, or personal – there is a deeper oneness that can guide humanity forward if realized.

6.5. THE VEIL (HİCAB): ILLUSION AND UNVEILING OF TRUTH

To discuss love, the self, wisdom, and unity is to also acknowledge what obstructs them – in Sufi terms, the veil (*hicab*).[167] Throughout *The Prophet of Love*, the imagery of veils, curtains, and blindness is used to denote anything that conceals the truth from the characters' sight. The concept of *perde* in Sufi literature signifies the myriad veils between the human perception and ultimate Reality: these can be ignorance, ego, worldly distractions, or even the limits of ordinary senses. Semiha Cemāl employs this motif both literally and metaphorically to show the process of spiritual unveiling that her characters undergo.

Early in the story, Sühā is essentially wandering in a world of veils. The debauched nightlife of Istanbul's Beyoğlu district, with its artificial lights and fleeting pleasures, serves as a veil – it seduces the senses and occupies the mind, preventing Sühā from seeing the emptiness of his pursuits. Likewise, his obses-

---

167 In Sufi terminology, the *ḥijāb* (veil) refers to the metaphysical or psychological barriers that obscure the seeker's perception of divine truth. These veils—such as ego, pride, heedlessness, or attachment to the world—prevent the soul from realizing unity (*tawḥīd*) and experiencing divine love and wisdom directly. See, Süleyman Uludağ, "Hicab", *TDV İslâm Ansiklopedisi* (İstanbul: TDV Yayınları, 1998), 17:430-431.

sion with Zehrā at first is a veil of passion that blinds him to the higher love calling him. Even his own reasoning, when divorced from spiritual insight, is a veil; Sühā often rationalizes his actions or clings to pride, which only deepens his delusion. The novel pointedly illustrates this when Sühā, at his lowest, cannot "see" a way out of his misery – a symbolic blindness caused by the thick veil of his ego and grief.

Conversely, as Sühā starts to awaken, the language of unveiling appears. There are moments described as if a curtain is lifted from Sühā's vision – he perceives, however briefly, the folly of his ways and the presence of the divine. One dramatic scene has Sühā visiting a shrine or a spiritually significant place, where he experiences a vision (or an intense dream) laden with symbolic imagery: he sees a desert oasis with water and a mirage-like figure *"veiled in soft white mist"*. He hears voices calling out, and the whole experience is one of uncanny revelation. This can be interpreted as an inner unveiling – a mystical glimpse granted to him. Though couched in poetic language, it marks Sühā's first real intuition that reality is more than meets the eye. The "soft white mist" suggests that the divine truth is near yet still partially veiled; Sühā is on the cusp of clarity but not fully there. Only later, under Yusuf's mentorship and after further trials, does the final veil drop.

The veil concept in the novel emphasizes the distinction between appearance and reality. Characters learn that what they initially see or strive for (surface love, personal glory, others' faults) often obscures the true nature of things. By "tearing down the veil" – a process accomplished through suffering, love, and grace – they come to discern the divine truth that was present all along. Semiha Cemāl thereby enacts a literary *kashf* (unveiling): her narrative gradually lifts layer after layer of illusion, both for her characters and for the attentive reader, until the underlying radiance of *tevhid* shines through. It is a journey from illusion to illumination – once the veil of separation is removed, the seeker finds that the Beloved was "nearer than one's jugular vein" the whole time.

6.6. THE GUIDE AND THE PERFECT HUMAN: MÜRŞİD, PROPHETHOOD, AND THE İNSĀN-I KĀMİL

While the five concepts above form the core of the novel's symbolism, an additional concept emerges organically at their intersection: the idea of the spiritual guide and the perfect human. This is embodied in the character of Yusuf Cemāl, who can be seen as *The Prophet of Love* referenced in the title. Though not a prophet in the orthodox religious sense, Yusuf is portrayed with quasi-prophetic qualities – a human exemplar of divine attributes, guiding others to truth. In Sufi terminology, he represents the *mürşid* (enlightened guide) and the *insān-ı kāmil*.[168]

From the moment Yusuf Cemāl enters the story, he is surrounded by an aura of sanctity and admiration. Other characters regard him with reverence: they sense something "more-than-human" about his presence. His name itself is symbolic – *Yusuf* alludes to the prophet Joseph, famed for his beauty, and *Cemāl* means "beauty" in Arabic. Thus, Yusuf Cemāl literally signifies "Joseph Beauty" or the beauty of Joseph, immediately evoking the Quranic tale of Joseph, whose face was so

---

168 In Sufi thought, the *mürşid* is the spiritual guide who leads the disciple on the path of inner purification and divine realization. When the *mürşid* embodies the highest degree of spiritual attainment, he becomes the *insān-ı kāmil*—the Perfect Human—who reflects all divine attributes and serves as a mirror of God's presence. These two concepts are thus intertwined: the *mürşid* functions as a guide precisely because he has actualized the ontological and ethical fullness of *insān-ı kāmil*, becoming both a model and a conduit for the seeker's own transformation. See, Mehmet S. Aydın, "İnsân-ı Kâmil", *TDV İslâm Ansiklopedisi* (İstanbul: TDV Yayınları, 2000), 22:330-331.

luminously beautiful that it left onlookers astonished. In Islamic mysticism, Joseph's beauty is often interpreted as a reflection of God's beauty (*cemāl*), and those who were captivated by Joseph are likened to souls drawn to the Divine Light.[169] In the novel, Yusuf's physical beauty (his handsome face, graceful demeanor) is a manifestation of his inner perfection. The narrator emphasizes that people are drawn to Yusuf not out of base attraction but out of awe for his *soul*. Women and men alike "love" him, but it is made clear that this love is reverential and pure, aimed at his virtues and compassion. He inspires in them what a prophet or saint would: the desire to be better, to love more deeply, to transcend self-interest.

Yusuf's qualities align with what Sufi lore describes as the *insān-ı kāmil*, the Complete or Perfect Human. This concept, elaborated by figures like Ibn 'Arabī, refers to an individual who has actualized all the potentials of the soul and mirrors the Divine Names and Attributes in their character. Such a being is often called *a friend of God* (velī) or even metaphorically a prophet-like figure for their community (though not bringing new scripture, they renew the timeless truths). In Yusuf's case, the text explicitly calls him *"a true human being in every sense"* and lists his virtues: mercy, generosity, loyalty, and a near-divine compassion. He is selfless to an extraordinary degree – clothing and feeding the poor, caring for the sick, and

---

169   In Islamic mysticism, Prophet Joseph (*Yūsuf*) is viewed as a manifestation of divine beauty (*camāl*), with his physical attractiveness symbolizing the radiant qualities of God. The women who were captivated by Joseph—most famously in the episode with Zulaikha—are interpreted by Sufi commentators as representing souls overwhelmed by the irresistible pull of divine light, illustrating how creation mirrors and draws the seeker toward the beauty of the Creator. See, Ahmad Karimi, Akbar Shahiditabar, and Farhad Morsali Pavarsi, "Narratological Re-reading of Prophet Yusuf and Zulaikha Story," *Interdisciplinary Studies of Quran & Hadith* 1, no. 1 (2023): 90-108.

expecting nothing in return. These actions reflect the Sufi ideal of service (*khidma*) as a mark of the perfected soul.[170] They also resonate with Christ-like or prophet-like imagery (feeding the hungry, healing the sick), suggesting that Yusuf is a Christian or Muslim figure within the narrative.

Yusuf's function as a *mürşid* is crucial to the conceptual map of the novel. In Sufism, the mürşid or shaykh is the guide who has traversed the path and attained *ma'rifa*, and thus can lead others. The relationship between Sühā and Yusuf mirrors this: Yusuf gives *sohbet* (spiritual conversation) to Sühā, imparts practices (like instructing him in prayer or recitation perhaps, though not shown explicitly, we infer he rehabilitates Sühā spiritually), and watches over Sühā's progress with patience. Sühā responds with devotion and obedience, much like a disciple. The novel thereby highlights that no journey to Truth is accomplished alone – the seeker benefits from the light of a guiding friend. Semiha Cemāl, as a disciple of Ken'ān Rifā'ī, surely injects her personal understanding of discipleship here: Yusuf's portrayal may even be inspired by her own teacher's qualities. It's notable that in reality, Semiha Cemāl dedicated *Aşk Peygamberi* to Ken'ān Rifā'ī, and one can see reflections of a Sufi master's wisdom in Yusuf's character. Thus, *The Prophet of Love* can be read on one level as an homage to the author's spiritual guide, cast in fictional form.

One could ask why call the guide figure a "prophet" of love. In Islamic theology, Prophethood ended with Muhammad; yet

---

170 In Sufism, khidma (service) is a spiritual discipline that signifies the soul's maturity and refinement. Far from being a utilitarian act, it is a sacred gesture through which the realized person (insān-ı kāmil) expresses humility, gratitude, and nearness to the Divine by serving creation with reverence, seeing every act of care as directed ultimately toward God. See, Dilaver Selvi, "Tasavvufta Marifetin Meyvesi Rahmet Ahlâkı ve Hizmet", *Kafkas Üniversitesi İlahiyat Fakültesi Dergisi* 4, No. Ek.1 (2017): 85-155.

in Sufi parlance, there is the idea of the "Muhammadan Reality" continuing, meaning the spiritual function of guiding people to God's love continues in the saints.[171] The phrase *"Aşk Peygamberi"* suggests that Yusuf fulfills a prophetic role by delivering the message of divine love to the people around him. He doesn't claim prophecy, but his life itself is the message. Through his being, others come to know God's love. In a moving scene near the end, as Yusuf lies on his deathbed (implied; the novel hints he falls gravely ill or possibly passes away, which often happens to saint characters as a final test for the devotees), those he has guided gather and realize that *Yusuf was the bridge that led them to God.* The sorrow of losing Yusuf is transformed into a profound gratitude – they each carry forward the light he kindled in them. This is analogous to the role of a prophet: to bring people from darkness into light, from ignorance to knowledge of God. Yusuf accomplished exactly that, albeit without miracles or revealed scripture – his tools were compassion, wisdom, and exemplary conduct.

In sum, the concept of the guide/*insān-ı kāmil* in the novel ties together all other concepts: Love finds its highest expression in the person of the guide (Yusuf radiates divine love); the Self's journey is enabled by the guide's influence (he helps strip Sühā's ego veil); Wisdom is channelled through the guide

---

171 The *ḥaqīqat al-Muḥammadiyya* (Reality of Muhammad) is a foundational metaphysical concept in Sufi cosmology, referring to the primordial light or essence from which all creation originates. According to this doctrine, the Prophet Muḥammad is not only the final messenger in historical time but also the first creation in ontological order—the *nūr Muḥammadī* (Muhammadan Light). This light is understood as the divine prototype of all being, encompassing the totality of existence and knowledge. Ibn ʿArabī and other metaphysically inclined Sufis describe it as the locus of divine self-disclosure, through which the Names and Attributes of God are manifest in the cosmos. See, Mehmet Demirci, "Hakikat-i Muhammediye", *TDV İslâm Ansiklopedisi* (İstanbul: TDV Yayınları, 1997), 15:179-180.

(Yusuf transmits philosophy and gnosis); and Divine Unity is witnessed in the guide (Yusuf's being is at one with God's will, demonstrating *tevhid* in human form). Through the five primary concepts, The Prophet of Love offers a rich conceptual map that is deeply rooted in Sufi metaphysics, artfully woven into story form. Semiha Cemāl Hanım reinterprets Sufi ideas in the context of early 20th-century Turkish society, demonstrating their timeless relevance.

For the English-speaking reader, understanding these interlocking concepts will illuminate many otherwise subtle or poetic passages of the novel. What might seem like an overly sentimental line, for instance, could be recognized as a nod to the Sufi idiom of divine love. A character's inner conflict may reveal a stage in the soul's refinement, reflecting its movement toward spiritual clarity and moral depth. The presence of a mentor like Yusuf can be appreciated in light of Sufi hagiography rather than dismissed as an idealization. In other words, this conceptual map enables a deeper hermeneutic engagement with *Aşk Peygamberi*. It shows how Semiha Cemāl, drawing from the well of Islamic mysticism, created a literary work that is simultaneously a spiritual allegory. Her novel invites readers to ponder the nature of love, the ego, wisdom, and the Divine in their own lives. Just as Sühā's story points beyond itself to universal truths, so too does the novel point beyond its plot to a philosophy of living: one where the heart is both student and teacher, love is both path and destination, and the human being is both the veil and the mirror of the Divine.

CHAPTER 7

THE PHILOSOPHICAL AND MYSTICAL UNDERPINNINGS OF *THE PROPHET OF LOVE*

Aşk Peygamberi serves as a confluence of various philosophical and spiritual traditions, most notably Platonism, Stoicism, and Sufism. The novel explores Platonic themes of love and beauty through the protagonist Sühā's ascent from physical to spiritual love—a journey that mirrors Plato's *Ladder of Love* in *The Symposium*. The relationship between Sühā and Yusuf Cemāl, who acts as both mentor and spiritual guide, reflects the Platonic ideal of love, where a superior figure leads the soul toward a deeper understanding of eternal truths. Stoic elements surface in the novel's emphasis on moral endurance and detachment from worldly pleasures, particularly in how the characters confront fate and the limitations of human life. Yusuf Cemāl embodies this Stoic ethos, demonstrating a philosophical resignation and acceptance of life's trials as part of a larger cosmic order.

At the core of the novel, however, is a distinctly Sufi framework, which seamlessly integrates with the Platonic and Stoic influences. The novel is imbued with Sufi metaphors and practices, such as *fanā* (self-annihilation in divine love) and *baqā* (subsistence in divine presence), which guide Sühā's spiritual transformation.[172] Yusuf Cemāl represents the archetypal Sufi master, drawing Sühā away from his initial infatuation with Zehrā toward a higher, divine love. The novel reflects the classic Sufi progression from *Leyla* (the earthly beloved) to *Mevla* (the divine Beloved), illustrating how the transient ultimately gives way to the eternal. Through this synthesis of Platonic, Stoic, and Sufi traditions, *Aşk Peygamberi* presents a complex philosophical exploration of love as a means of self-transcendence and spiritual realization.

7.1. PLATONIC & STOIC UNDERPINNINGS

Sühā's emotional and spiritual development mirrors the Platonic ascent from physical to spiritual love outlined in *The Symposium*. In Plato's framework, love is portrayed as a ladder, where the soul progresses from the appreciation of physical beauty to the love of the soul, and ultimately to the contemplation of eternal, divine forms. Sühā's initial admiration for a beautiful woman reflects the first stage of love as articulated in Platonic philosophy—a stage rooted in sensory attraction. His captivation with physical beauty marks the beginning of a spiritual and philosophical trajectory that aligns with the "ladder of love" described by Diotima in The Symposium.[173] In this model, love begins with the desire for a single beautiful body, then gradually expands toward an appreciation of all beautiful bodies, the beauty of souls, the beauty found in laws and institutions, and ultimately, the contemplation of Beauty itself—eternal, ab-

---

172 Schimmel defines fanā and baqā as essential stages in the Sufi path of love and spiritual transformation. See, Schimmel, *Mystical Dimensions of Islam*, 140-146.

173 Plato, *Symposium*, trans. Alexander Nehamas and Paul Woodruff (Indianapolis: Hackett Publishing Company, 1989), 210a–212b.

stract, and unchanging.[174] This early phase of bodily attraction, or *eros somatikos*, is not dismissed in Platonic thought but is understood as a necessary entry point into deeper forms of love and knowledge.[175] The problem arises only when one remains fixated on the material form and fails to ascend toward metaphysical understanding. In this sense, the novel does more than depict romantic desire—it invokes a classical philosophical structure in which love becomes a path from the visible to the invisible, from the transient allure of the body to the enduring illumination of truth. This progression resonates closely with the Sufi understanding of love, where the seeker begins with earthly attachments (*Leyla*) but is ultimately drawn toward the love of the eternal (*Mevla*).[176]

Initially, Sühā is caught in the throes of material, earthly affection, particularly in his infatuation with Zehrā. His love for Zehrā represents the lower rungs of Plato's ladder of love—a stage characterized by physical attraction and emotional dependence.[177] However, under the guidance of Yusuf Cemāl, his understanding of love begins to transcend physical desire, shifting toward a deeper spiritual awareness. Yusuf Cemāl's role in this transformation mirrors that of Socrates in *The Symposium*, where the figure of the teacher catalyzes the seeker's ascent from superficial attachment to a higher metaphysical truth.[178] Through Yusuf Cemāl, Sühā comes to recognize that true love is not confined to the transient beauty of the physical world but

---

174   Diotima's speech in the *Symposium* introduces this philosophical ascent, often referred to as the "ladder of love," culminating in the vision of the Form of Beauty.

175   Gregory Vlastos, "The Individual as an Object of Love in Plato," *Platonic Studies* (Princeton: Princeton University Press, 1981), 29–70.

176   Schimmel, *Mystical Dimensions of Islam*, 431-432.

177   Vlastos, "The Individual as an Object of Love in Plato", 29-70.

178   Plato, *Symposium*, 204a–210a; Diotima's speech.

reflects a deeper, cosmic reality. As Sühā's journey unfolds, his relationship with Zehrā loses its hold over him, not because of emotional withdrawal but because his understanding of love evolves. What begins as a longing for human connection is ultimately transformed into a recognition of divine presence. The transition from Zehrā to Yusuf Cemāl parallels the Platonic movement from *eros* (physical love) to *agape* (spiritual love), culminating in the recognition that the essence of love lies not in the beloved itself but in the divine source of love.

In the Platonic framework, the philosopher leads the student toward a higher understanding of truth and beauty, guiding the soul from the realm of sensory perception to the contemplation of eternal forms.[179] Similarly, in the Sufi tradition, the *mürşid* (spiritual guide) directs the *murid* (seeker) toward spiritual enlightenment by helping the seeker transcend the limitations of the material world.[180] Yusuf Cemāl's wisdom and spiritual insight gradually awaken Sühā to the realization that his love for Zehrā was only a stepping stone toward a higher, more profound form of love. Initially bound by the desires and limitations of earthly attachment, Sühā's emotional and spiritual maturation unfolds under Yusuf Cemāl's guidance, mirroring the Platonic ascent from physical to metaphysical love. Yusuf Cemāl's role as the Prophet of Love underscores his symbolic function as a conduit of transcendent wisdom—a figure who bridges Platonic and Sufi ideals by revealing that true love is not rooted in the ephemeral, but in the eternal unity of the divine.

The novel's philosophical architecture is also informed by Stoic ethics, particularly in the characters' confrontation with

---

179 Plato, *Phaedrus*, trans. Alexander Nehamas and Paul Woodruff (Indianapolis: Hackett Publishing Company, 1995), 249e–250e.

180 Milad Milani, "Mysticism in the Islamicate World: The Question of Neoplatonic Influence in Sufi Thought", *Later Platonists and their Heirs among Christians, Jews, and Muslims* (Leiden: Brill, 2022), 413-544.

fate and human limitation. Yusuf Cemāl embodies the Stoic sage, embracing principle of *apatheia*—a state of inner tranquility and emotional detachment achieved through acceptance of life's inevitable trials.[181] His calm resignation in the face of suffering and his measured guidance of Sühā reflect the Stoic ideal of moral fortitude in the face of adversity. Throughout the narrative, Sühā's growth involves learning to adopt this Stoic mindset. His early emotional turmoil and attachment to Zehrā reflect a form of existential vulnerability—an untempered response to the contingencies of life. Under Yusuf Cemāl's mentorship, however, Sühā gradually develops a more tempered approach to love and suffering. This shift reflects the Stoic doctrine that true freedom arises not from the fulfillment of desire but from the cultivation of inner resilience and alignment with cosmic order (*logos*).[182]

Yusuf Cemāl's teachings align with the Stoic belief that virtue consists in living in accordance with nature and accepting the world as it is. According to Stoic philosophers, nature operates according to a divine, rational structure, and true wisdom lies in recognizing our place within this order. Rather than resisting or lamenting what lies beyond our control, the Stoic sage cultivates apatheia—inner tranquility—by embracing fate and focusing only on what is within one's power: judgment, intention, and moral choice.[183] Similarly, Yusuf Cemāl's insistence on

181 Edgar M Krentz, "ΠΑΘΗ and ΑΠΑΘΕΙΑ in early Roman Empire Stoics", *Passions and Moral Progress in Greco-Roman Thought* (London: Routledge, 2007), 122-135.

182 Susanne Bobzien, *Determinism and Freedom is Stoic Philosophy* (Oxford: Clarendon Press, 2004), 330-344; René Brouwer, *The Stoics Sage: The Early Stoics on Wisdom*, Sagehood and Socrates (Cambridge: University of Cambridge Press, 2014), 92-134.

183 Marimuthu Prahasan and Mahir I.L.M, "Human Flourishing by Living in Harmony with Nature and Moral Integrity: Insights from Epictetus the Stoic", *American Journal of Arts and Human Science* 4, no. 1 (2025): 89-96.

detachment from worldly possessions and fleeting emotional states is not a rejection of human experience but an invitation to engage with it from a place of spiritual clarity. The Stoic notion that suffering is not to be feared but understood as part of a larger cosmic harmony is echoed in Yusuf Cemāl's counsel to Sühā, who learns that love entails not possession but surrender—a central tenet in both Stoicism and Sufism.

7.2. SUFI UNDERPINNINGS IN *THE PROPHET OF LOVE*

While Platonic and Stoic elements shape the novel's philosophical framework, its spiritual core remains unmistakably Sufi.[184] The relationship between Sühā and Yusuf Cemāl reflects the archetypal Sufi dynamic of the *salik* (seeker) guided by the *mürşid* (spiritual guide). In Sufi thought, the mürşid plays a central role in the seeker's journey toward divine realization. More than a teacher, the mürşid serves as a conduit of divine grace (*baraka*), offering spiritual direction, ethical discipline, and inner purification. This relationship is essential for the seeker to progress from ego-centered existence (*nafs*) to union with the divine through *fanā* (annihilation) and *baqā* (subsistence in God).[185] Yusuf Cemāl's role is not simply that of a teacher but of a mystical companion who directs Sühā toward self-annihilation and union with the divine. Sühā's initial love for Zehrā characterized by emotional intensity and attachment to the physical world. His eventual release from this attachment marks the transition to *ishq* (divine love), where the lover sees beyond the

---

184 For a detailed introduction to the basic understandings of Sufism, see, William Chittick, *Sufism: A Beginner's Guide* (Oxford: Oneworld Book, 2000).

185 For detailed discussions of *fanā and baqā* see, Abu'l-Qasim al-Qushayri, *Al Risala al-Qushayriyya Fi'ilm al-Tasawwuf*, trans. Alexander D. Knysh (Reading: Garnet Publishing, 2007), 89-90.

physical form of the beloved and recognizes the presence of the divine within. Yusuf Cemāl, embodying the wisdom of the Sufi path, teaches Sühā that true love transcends the material and points toward the eternal.

The journey from *Leylā* to *Mevlā* (Leylā'dan Mevlā'ya)—from human love to divine love—is central to Sühā's spiritual maturation. The Sufi tradition frames love as both a trial and a gift, a force that purifies the self through both suffering and revelation. Sühā's eventual detachment from Zehrā is not a rejection of human love but its sublimation; he learns that the love he sought in Zehrā was only a shadow of the divine love that Yusuf Cemāl reveals. The symbolism of *fanā* and *baqā* is woven throughout the novel's final passages. Sühā's renunciation of earthly desire represents *fanā*—the dissolution of the ego in the presence of the divine. His subsequent experience of inner peace and unity reflects *baqā*—the state of abiding in God's presence. In this way, *Aşk Peygamberi* illustrates the Sufi teaching that true love involves both sacrifice and fulfillment—the emptying of the self to make room for divine presence.

7.3. NATURE AS ALLEGORY: THE SYMBOLIC LANDSCAPE OF *THE PROPHET OF LOVE*

Nature functions as a dynamic and multifaceted symbol in *Aşk Peygamberi*, reflecting the spiritual and emotional currents of the characters' inner lives while simultaneously evoking the ontological structure of existence. Through elemental imagery—water, fire, light, and darkness—Semiha Cemāl constructs a metaphysical framework that draws from Sufi metaphysics, Platonic idealism, and Stoic cosmology. The interplay between these symbols reflects the novel's philosophical ambition: to explore the nature of love, existence, and spiritual awakening through the elemental forces that shape both the external world and the soul's interior landscape.

Water, a recurring symbol in Sufi thought, represents spiritual purification, continuity, and divine grace.[186] In the novel, the "Kör Irmak" (*Blind River*) serves as a striking metaphor for spiritual stagnation and the need for divine intervention to restore the flow of grace. The dried-up river reflects the inner desolation of the characters, particularly Sühā's emotional and spiritual emptiness before his awakening. Just as water in Sufi discourse symbolizes the flow of divine love and knowledge, the stagnant river mirrors the soul's separation from this vital source. The imagery of water resurfaces as Sühā's spiritual journey unfolds; his growing awareness of love as a transformative force is marked by the reappearance of flowing water. The sparkling clarity of the stream he encounters upon arriving in Antalya signals the beginning of his inner renewal: "*Pırıl pırıl ne güzel bir su!... Bir müddet daha dinlediler küçük ince sadâsına doyulamıyordu*" (*The water sparkled brightly... they listened to its soft, delicate sound and could never get enough*). The movement of water reflects the progressive opening of the soul to divine grace, aligning with both the Platonic notion of love as a dynamic ascent toward eternal truth and the Sufi understanding of love as a flow that dissolves the ego and unites the soul with the divine.

Fire, in contrast, embodies the consuming and creative dimensions of love. Cemāl draws upon both Stoic and Sufi traditions to present fire as a symbol of transformation, destruction, and renewal. In Stoic cosmology, fire (*pur technikon*) represents the rational and active principle (*logos*) that animates and orders

---

186   In Sufi metaphysics, water is one of the most powerful and multilayered symbols, representing divine mercy, spiritual knowledge, purification, and the flow of love. See, Schimmel, *Mystical Dimensions of Islam*, 5; Esmaeil Radpour, "Symbolism of Water in Daoism: A Sufi Point of View", *Sophia Perennis* 15, no. 34 (2019): 5-17.

the cosmos.[187] The Stoics conceived of the universe as cyclically consumed by fire, only to be regenerated anew—an endless process of annihilation and creation that reflects the ordered structure of existence.[188] Cemāl's invocation of fire reflects this cyclical framework, but she simultaneously situates it within a Sufi metaphysical context, where fire represents the annihilation of the self (*fanā*) and the subsequent subsistence (*baqā*) in divine presence. The *ateş kaya* (*Fire Rock*) in the novel serves as the central symbol of this transformative dualism. When Sühā leads Zehrā to the Fire Rock, he recounts the story of two young lovers who threw themselves into the flames rather than live apart. The Fire Rock thus becomes a site of sacrifice and spiritual renewal—a place where worldly love is consumed to reveal the deeper essence of divine love.

Simultaneously, the novel introduces the dual themes of light and darkness as elemental forces that mirror the journey toward self-realization and spiritual ascension. In Sufi thought, *nur* (light) symbolizes divine presence, guidance, and illumination, while *zulmet* (darkness) represents the veils of ignorance, materiality, and separation from the divine.[189]

---

187 Pur Technikon (πῦρ τεχνικόν) in ancient Stoic philosophy refers to the "craftsmanlike fire" — the intelligent, creative, and organizing fire that serves as the fundamental active principle (archē) in the universe. See, Brouwer, *The Stoics Sage*, 46-47.

188 The Stoics' concept of cosmic cycles, known as *ekpyrosis* (ἐκπύρωσις), posits that the universe periodically perishes in a conflagration driven by the *pur technikon* and is subsequently regenerated in an identical form. This endless sequence of destruction and re-creation embodies the rational, purposeful structure of the cosmos, governed by logos (divine reason), and emphasizes the Stoic belief in a universe that is both living and intelligently ordered. See, David E. Hahm, "The Stoic Theory of Change", *The Southern Journal of Philosophy* 23 (1985): 39-56.

189 Toshihiko Izutsu, *Sufism and Taoism: A Comparative Study of Key Philosophical Concepts* (Berkeley: University of California Press, 1983), 149–153.

Similarly, in Stoic cosmology, light is equated with the rational fire (*logos*) that illuminates and governs the universe, while darkness signifies chaos and the absence of order.[190] Platonic philosophy further emphasizes this dichotomy: light symbolizes the intelligible realm of eternal truths, while darkness represents the shadowy, transient world of physical forms. Cemāl's deliberate use of this symbolic contrast serves as a bridge between these traditions, positioning light and darkness as metaphysical poles that define the soul's ascent from ignorance to knowledge. The narrative's shifting imagery of light and shadow reflects the characters' moral and spiritual struggles. When Sühā stands before the shimmering water, bathed in soft light, he experiences a moment of clarity and peace—a moment of illumination. In contrast, his periods of doubt and emotional turbulence are frequently marked by darkness and shadow. This interplay reflects the Sufi understanding that spiritual awakening requires the piercing of veils that obscure divine truth. Only by confronting the darkness of the self—its attachments and illusions—can the seeker perceive the light of divine unity.

Cemāl deepens this metaphysical tension through the figure of Suzan, the novel's first named character, whose very name signifies "burning" or "one who burns." Suzan's name, derived from Persian, echoes the classical Divan poetry motif of *āteş-i Sūzan* (burning fire), underscoring her association with the consuming and transformative power of love. In one of the novel's most evocative scenes, Suzan sits upon a stone amidst the scorching sands of the desert at sunset, her hands seared by the flames of her passion as she pours her emotions onto paper. The juxtaposition of the arid desert and the cool transparency of the oasis reflects the dual nature of love as both consuming fire and sustaining water. Suzan's identity, consumed and re-

---

190   Hahm, "The Stoic Theory of Change", 47-48.

constituted by love, reflects the cyclical process of annihilation and renewal at the heart of Sufi and Stoic cosmologies.

Suzan's burning desire reaches its culmination when she encounters the figure of a radiant horseman emerging on the horizon—an image that evokes the Qur'anic depiction of Yusuf's beauty in Surah Yusuf (12:31): "This is none but a noble angel." Overcome with reverence, Suzan rises and seizes the reins of his horse, mirroring Züleyha's act of devotion in classical Yusuf and Züleyha narratives. Suzan's exclamation—"*These hands, this body, they do not resemble the created... you are not a creature!*"—reflects the Stoic notion of immanent divinity, where the cosmos itself is a manifestation of God's rational order. For Stoic thinkers like Epictetus, God and the cosmos are one; every entity within the universe participates in the divine essence. Suzan's recognition of her beloved as transcending material existence reflects the Stoic conviction that the divine permeates all of creation.

Cemāl's synthesis of Platonic, Stoic, and Sufi symbols reveals a unified philosophical vision in which love functions as the metaphysical bridge between the human and the divine. Water and fire, light and darkness, presence and absence—all reflect the dynamic forces that shape the spiritual journey. Fire's consuming intensity is tempered by the fluid grace of water; light's guiding clarity emerges only through the contrast with darkness. This dialectical interplay mirrors the seeker's path from material attachment to spiritual freedom—a path that leads, ultimately, to the dissolution of the self and the union with eternal love. Suzan's transformation encapsulates this ontological cycle: consumed by love's fire, purified by love's waters, illuminated by divine light, she transcends the human and dissolves into the eternal.

Through this elemental framework, *Aşk Peygamberi* constructs a profound meditation on the nature of love as both a destructive and creative force. Cemāl presents love not merely as an emotional state but as a cosmic principle—a force that consumes and restores, dissolves and creates, guiding the soul toward the eternal source of being. The novel's philosophical depth lies in this harmonious fusion of classical and mystical traditions—a vision of love that encompasses both the annihilating fire of passion and the sustaining flow of divine grace.

7.4. THE SOUNDSCAPE OF *THE PROPHET OF LOVE*

Music in *Aşk Peygamberi* functions as both a narrative and metaphysical device, intricately woven into the fabric of the novel's emotional and spiritual landscape. Throughout the text, musical references are not merely ornamental but serve as symbolic conduits through which characters confront emotional tensions, experience spiritual transformation, and access metaphysical truths. Semiha Cemāl constructs a carefully orchestrated soundscape where classical Ottoman and Western musical forms, traditional instruments like the kaval and tambur, and the recurring presence of ambient sound—like the flowing of water—create an auditory architecture that parallels the philosophical and mystical undercurrents of the novel. This complex soundscape mirrors the spiritual rhythms of the characters' inner journeys, where music becomes a bridge between the human and the divine, embodying the tension between earthly desire and transcendental love.

The novel is punctuated by scenes of music-making and listening, where the characters engage with music not merely as an aesthetic pleasure but as a medium for spiritual and emotional expression. Western classical music and Ottoman classical forms—particularly the melancholic strains of the Hicaz mode and the romantic elegance of Chopin's waltzes—appear throughout the novel, serving as emotional leitmotifs that underscore the inner states of the characters. In one instance, the sound of Chopin's waltz emerges from the piano in the background, as the characters drift through a charged emotional moment: "At school, Chopin's waltz is played on the piano; even though the characters remain silent, they linger around the instruments". The act of listening becomes a form of silent emotional communion, where music articulates the inner turbulence that the characters themselves cannot express through language. The recurring presence of Chopin's waltz, a piece associated with longing and the transient beauty of human connection, underscores the tension between attachment and detachment, echoing the novel's philosophical exploration of love as both a fleeting human experience and an eternal metaphysical force.

In this interplay between Western and Ottoman musical traditions, Cemāl constructs a subtle philosophical dialogue. Western classical forms, represented by the piano and Chopin's waltz, reflect the Romantic preoccupation with individual emotion and existential longing. By contrast, Ottoman classical music—embodied by the tambur and the melancholic Hicaz mode—invokes the communal and spiritual dimensions of longing within the Sufi tradition. The tambur's deep resonance reflects the cosmic order within Sufi metaphysics, where the harmony of sound mirrors the underlying unity of existence (*wahdat al-wujūd*). The Hicaz mode, with its plaintive and meditative quality, evokes the emotional intensity of the lover's separation from the beloved—a musical expression of the Sufi concept of firāq (separation) and the yearning for reunion with the divine. This dual musical framework reflects the philosophical synthesis at the heart of the novel, where the individual and the universal, the emotional and the spiritual, are held in delicate balance.

The presence of the kaval as Sühā's preferred instrument deepens this metaphysical symbolism. In Sufi tradition, the ney (reed flute) is a central symbol of spiritual longing and the soul's separation from God. The reed, having been cut from the reed bed, sings its mournful song as a lament for its lost origin—a metaphor for the human soul's yearning for reunion with the divine. The kaval in *Aşk Peygamberi* functions in a similar symbolic capacity, representing the internal restlessness of the seeker and the pull toward spiritual fulfillment. Sühā's connection to the kaval is charged with emotional and mystical significance: "I was playing the kaval by the lake shore". The natural setting—the reflective surface of the lake, the softness of the breeze—creates a soundscape where music becomes a form of prayer, blending the physical and spiritual realms.

Yet the kaval is not always responsive to Sühā's touch. At times, it resists his attempts to draw music from it: *"My kaval lay on the grass with its head bowed, exhausted and weary. I don't know why it complains so. I try to play it, but it refuses to sing"*. The kaval's silence reflects Sühā's spiritual struggle, suggesting that the ability to produce music—like the ability to experience divine love—depends on the alignment of the soul with the divine order. In this way, the kaval functions not only as an instrument but as an extension of Sühā's spiritual state, echoing the Sufi belief that the human heart must be tuned to the divine rhythm before it can express the music of love.

Yusuf Cemāl's role as both spiritual guide and musician further underscores the novel's metaphysical alignment between music and spiritual transformation. His compositions are described not merely as music but as manifestations of wisdom and divine harmony: *"Zeliha found some of Yusuf Cemāl's compositions and played them for us on the violin. They were truly masterpieces."* The term şaheser (masterpiece) elevates Yusuf Cemāl's music beyond artistic accomplishment, suggesting that his compositions reflect a deeper metaphysical truth. Just as the Stoics viewed the cosmic order as a divine harmony, and the Sufis understood the music of the ney as an echo of the soul's longing for God, Yusuf Cemāl's music becomes a medium through which the characters encounter the structure of the universe itself.

Simultaneously, the novel constructs a persistent soundscape in which the natural and musical elements merge into a unified auditory experience. The constant presence of water—its rhythmic flowing, its delicate murmur—forms the background of this soundscape, creating a sense of continuity and grace that reflects the Sufi notion of divine mercy (*rahma*) as a flowing current that sustains existence. The novel's sonic texture is reinforced through the repetition of certain phonetic patterns in the characters' names and dialogue. The recurring sounds of soft consonants and liquid vowels create an acoustic foundation that mirrors the constant presence of flowing water. Even in moments of silence, the suggestion of sound remains, aligning with the Sufi belief that divine presence persists beneath the surface of ordinary perception.

Music in *Aşk Peygamberi* thus becomes a symbol of the characters' spiritual development and their movement toward metaphysical unity. Sühā's initial attachment to the sensory pleasures of music reflects the lower rungs of Plato's Ladder of Love, where the soul's desire is bound to material beauty. Through Yusuf Cemāl's guidance, Sühā's relationship with music evolves from sensory enjoyment to spiritual contemplation. His kaval-playing, once an expression of personal longing, becomes a form of prayer—an act of alignment with the divine order. Yusuf Cemāl's music, echoing the Stoic conception of cosmic harmony, reflects the transcendent structure of existence, where individual experience is integrated into a universal symphony. The fusion of Western classical forms with Ottoman modes and Sufi instruments reflects the philosophical synthesis at the core of the novel, where human and divine love are revealed as two dimensions of the same eternal truth.

Ultimately, Cemāl presents music not merely as an emotional or aesthetic force but as a metaphysical principle that bridges the human and the divine. The novel's sonic landscape—constructed from the interplay of flowing water, musical performance, and the silent resonance of sound—becomes a reflection of the cosmic order, where love functions as the underlying rhythm that sustains existence. Just as the Stoics viewed the universe as a harmonious whole governed by the logos, and the Sufis understood existence as a manifestation of divine love, music in *Aşk Peygamberi* emerges as a microcosm of this universal order—a fleeting echo of eternity, vibrating through the characters' hearts and guiding them toward transcendence.

سمیحه جمال

عشق پیغمبری

- ملی رومان -

صاحب وناشری
کتابخانهٔ سودی
استانبول - باب عالی جادهسی

PART III

SEMİHA CEMĀL'S NOVEL:
THE PROPHET OF LOVE

-1-

A SCENE OF LOVE

"O Love, I have made you my *basmala*! My beloved, you are the principle of *Bismillāhi'l Aşk*—the key and essence of the whole universe. The sun is setting now; night is coming again—that dark night which always begins with the burning of my heart for you and always ends with the games of love that unfold between us. Night will separate me from you; I will lose sight of you in the darkness. No matter how radiant the image of you burns within my heart, I still need to see you. This is something that, for the sake of my beloved, must exist here—they have said. And yet my eyes remain blind to it for all eternity, unable to see; my ears remain deaf to its sound.

Do not set, O sun—do not set. Though your setting is more delicate than your rising, this evening I cannot bear the thought of you disappearing from sight. I do not want to see this day—marked by the lingering scent of my beloved upon me and the renewed fire of love it has kindled in my heart— fade away upon the horizon of my life. O my fiery, beautiful beloved—so passionate in your love, so ablaze with fire! Without you, I would remain lost in endless nights, no matter how brightly the sun might rise over the blissful gardens of paradise. Even if they were to bring me the suns of every world that orbits this star, I would still be left in darkness without you. Where are these flocks of birds flying toward the horizon at dusk? Once, I too opened my wings and flew toward unknown and mysterious horizons among such a flock. It was you who crossed my path.

I saw before me a delicate vision, leaning into the sun—a coy sun. Her hands, like yours, stretched toward the flames. Her face was untouched by the elements of this world. Even now, I cannot believe the dream I saw. From time to time, I rub my eyes. I reach out with my hands to feel the image before me. With my lips and my skin, I try to grasp the degree of her presence. Sometimes, in the moon I watch at night, I see this shy and delicate vision—the one I did not know I had loved before. And in that moment, the moon turns dark; the stars dim. The world slips away from my sight, and I weep. Even if this world were a rose, its fragrance would still be yours."

A half-clothed woman sat upon a stone at sunset, writing these words onto a piece of paper. In the distance, beyond a tent stretching out toward the scorched horizon, there was nothing to be seen beneath the fading glow of the sunset. After sitting in silence for a while, listening to the stillness around her, she resumed:

"Once, you asked me about love. I had denied it then," I had answered. And yet, even then, that exquisite vision had already drawn her bow from within the sun, and when the arrow struck, I turned my head toward her. O fire, until my hands were burned, I could not understand what you were. O you— dancing, veiled in crystalline waters amidst the oasis of love in this desert! I have returned to you once again, with a heart scorched and sorrowful. Suzān, Suzān! you say. In this scorched land, this place laid to waste and turned to ash—what land are you seeking? Tell me, what land could be worth transforming this fire, which turns all to roses at the slightest touch? What land are you searching for?"

She rose to her feet. On the sand, footprints were visible. She bent down and kissed them, one by one:

"Come... come, my love. In this body you have nourished with your beauty, there is a garden that you have graced with your constant presence, elevating it in value. It smells of roses and amber, just like the palms of your hands. Come there with me."

Because love... Ah, you do not know what it is—you swear you know, but you do not. If you knew what love was, you would not pass by my door each evening, indifferent, wounding me anew with the songs of your fire. If you knew what love was, you would have dropped the dagger from your hand long ago!"

She listened again. Lying down, she pressed her ear to the sand. The sound of approaching footsteps. Who could possibly pass through here at this hour? It could only be him. Trembling with excitement, she remained on her knees... And then, a horseman appeared—exceedingly beautiful, with a face that seemed almost beyond human. His bearing, delicate and other-worldly, stirred within the soul that singular sensation known only to lovers. The young woman grasped the horse's reins, pulled him down, and embraced him.

"Look, Suzān—look, I've come back!"

A beautiful voice spread across the burnt air of the desert. Arm in arm, they walked toward the tent.

"It feels as though I have not seen you for five hundred years... and yet, it has only been a few hours. I have seen you, I am holding you—and still this longing within my heart remains unspent. Tell me, what should I do? Is there anything beyond this? Here I am, wrapped around you—why, then, does this fire of longing continue to rise rather than fade?"

After watching him for a moment, she covered her eyes with her hands:

"My human nature cannot bear so much beauty. Tell me—your true name is 'Love,' isn't it? You belong to none of the elements—neither air, nor water, nor earth, nor fire. Tell me—these hands, this body—they do not seem created. I see none of the frailty or weakness of creation within you. God forbid—surely you are not a mere creature. My love—can this body of yours truly fade away? This divine form to which I devote my very being—could it vanish from my sight, even for a moment? Until now, I did not know how to speak the language of love. My heart did not know the rhythm of its beat. Frozen and numb, it lay dormant—until you revived it with your touch. And look—these arms wrapped around you… you will not be able to loosen them, will you?"

- 2 -

SÜHÄ'S[191] JOURNAL

MAY 2 (…) HIGH SCHOOL[192]

But oh, how beautiful the weather is today! I have absolutely no desire to study. And thank God for that—I can't stand math anyway. Tomorrow, that merciless math teacher is coming again. He hands out zeroes as easily as if he were giving out tens, without even opening the book. Istanbul is covered in green; when I look up at the clear blue sky, a voice rises within me, whispering countless words I cannot fully express but somehow understand. My heart encourages me—it urges me toward something good.

The school is cheerful today; the breeze is cool and sweet. Everyone is laughing at everything. Only the wretched math teacher's face remains frozen and grim. Honestly, would it kill him to relax a little and get along with the rest of us? Sometimes I wonder—could this man possibly be married? And if he is—poor woman! For a man like him, every action must be governed by a set of principles. If, for instance, he were legally required to love his wife, I am sure there would have to be a set of regulations for that as well. This operation—let's say—would have to take place between such-and-such an hour and such-and-such a time, and there would no doubt be specific condi-

191 Sühā: The name of a star. It is the smallest and faintest star in the Great Bear constellation, visible only to those with the sharpest eyesight.

192 No specific name for the school has been indicated within the novel.

tions to observe within that period... and so on. If the night monitor comes by, there's nothing to be done but to blow out the candle and hide under the covers. But I'm not sleepy at all. How can anyone force themselves to sleep? Sleep just won't come. The candle on top of the cupboard is burning down steadily, swaying and trembling with weariness.

I don't know how to explain it, but I feel a strange shift within myself. I think I am finally saying farewell to that cheerful childhood. In two years, school will be over. All of us—friends who have shared so much—will scatter and go our separate ways. But honestly, I am still amazed at Yavuz. Today, during literature class, we read one of his verses:

"While lions tremble beneath the wrath of my claws,

Fate has undone me with the gaze of a single gazelle's eyes."[193]

I can't quite grasp this kind of love—the kind that leaves you so defenseless. Why does a person love someone? Surely to run together through meadows and fields, to celebrate among birds and flowers. That's what love is about, isn't it? Let me finish school first. Once my wings are free, I will open them wide to the air and fly wherever I wish.

TWO YEARS LATER

Exams have begun. Soon I will be free of these high walls, this barren garden. But where will I go—and to whom? Sometimes, when I grow tired of my lessons, I wait for the day of freedom like everyone else. But before even a minute passes, my eyes cloud over. Month by month, day by day, I feel myself changing. That sadness, which wrapped itself around my

---

193 Yavuz Sultan Selim (r. 1512-1520). The orginal poem: "Şirler pençe-i kahrımdan olurken lerzan / Beni bir gözleri ahuya zebun etti felek."

heart when I was still a child, has started creeping toward me once again. But really—does laughter, does hope suit an orphan like me? I receive letters now and then from my nanny and Zeliha. After seven years, I will finally return to the farm I have not seen since childhood. This year, school is not as strict as it used to be. We can go to dances and the cinema during the week if we wish. After the weekend, all the other girls return with stacks of love letters tucked into their pockets. It amazes me—how many Leylā's they have, how many hearts they possess!

But I feel nothing but melancholy. Especially when I am alone, I sense a terrible loneliness. Sometimes, even in the middle of a lively night—filled with the sound of laughter and chatter—I suddenly find tears collecting in my eyes. I don't know where they come from. I tell myself perhaps I've laughed too much. So I laugh with the others—loudly, carelessly—hiding my heart and my feelings beneath the noise. But I grow weary in places of pleasure and entertainment. There is nothing there but deceit and disloyalty. As I said, this year we have freedom in every sense—even when it comes to mocking our teachers. When we are bored and restless, we amuse ourselves by teasing them. The classroom where we once trembled with fear during lectures—we now sit there during study hour and sing waltzes in unison.

JUNE 15

That Celāl—how he has charmed me. In the past year, my entire outlook has changed. I find myself increasingly drawn toward beauty and higher things. Celāl's spirit, always inclined toward poetry and elevated love, draws me more and more with each passing day.

JUNE 18

Last night, Celâl and I went for a walk in the park. We sat on a bench facing the sea. Both of us were quiet. The air was as still as we were. I was holding a bunch of fresh lilacs I had bought earlier from a street vendor. A thin layer of mist covered the city, making it seem lost in thought. Suddenly, across from us, that beautiful girl arrived again with her Arab maid. She sat down on an empty chair. For the past few evenings, we had encountered her often—and each time, watching her filled me with deep pleasure. My eyes lingered on her short skirt, her fiery lips. How I wish I could love such a beautiful girl! I thought to myself. I started building fantasies in my mind—pure, innocent dreams. I imagined offering her the flowers in my hand. She would blush and accept them shyly, and from those first glances, a love would begin to grow. I carried my fantasy further: I imagined us far away, living alone in a small cottage, unaware of the world—seeing nothing but each other.

So convinced was I by these thoughts that I suddenly decided to act. I would give her the lilacs. Rising with boldness, I didn't say a word to Celâl. I approached them directly and said to the Arab servant:

—"Pardon me... I would like to offer these lilacs to the young lady. Would she accept them?"

I was stammering. My eyes searched hers for an answer, still lost in the light of my own illusions. The beautiful girl suddenly looked startled. Then her gaze turned cold—contemptuous even. She surveyed me with an expression of distaste. I could see her biting her lip to keep from laughing. After a moment, she composed herself, smiled politely but distantly, and said,

—"Merci."

I was humiliated. It felt as though ice water had been poured over my head. I regretted coming over. But I had already offered the flowers, so I had no choice but to hand them over. As I turned away, I stumbled over a stone and nearly fell. I did not go to the park tonight. I will not go again. But Celâl went. He told me that the wilted lilac stems were still there on the bench, not yet swept away. Now I am sitting in a quiet corner of the garden, far from the noise of the other children. Someone is playing a Chopin waltz on the piano. I don't know why, but the sound burns my heart.

I bury my face in the earth and sob until my whole body shakes. The moon is pale—completely white. Not a trace of color on its face. I feel broken by everything. All I have left are the tears in my eyes.

JULY 12

Zeliha and my nanny arrived today. They had planned to surprise me. Zeliha has grown so much since I last saw her. Her delicate face looks a little pale, and her figure has taken on the shape of a young woman. But the two long braids of honey-colored hair that used to fall down her back—those have been cut. My heart sank when I saw it. How could they cut off the silken hair that carried the delicate beauty of womanhood? She threw her arms around me, trembling with the wild affection of twelve years apart. I kissed her soft, innocent eyes with my racing heart beneath my lips. My nanny's hair had turned completely white. Her face was lined and tired. She held me like a child. The other children gathered around us, watching with curiosity. I felt proud to have a sister—someone of my own blood. Zeliha has gone to the farm now. I will follow her in a week. There, just like before, I will fall asleep to the sound of summer insects singing lullabies among the roses.

JULY 13

It was past midnight when Celâl and I were still walking along the shore. Near the fishermen's huts, we came across a little girl—about ten years old—sitting on a mat. An old fishing boat lay half-buried in the sand, rocking slightly with the tide. Who knows why the girl was still awake at that hour? As we passed, I noticed that one of her eyes was blind. My heart ached for her. I turned back and looked at her with compassion. But just as we passed her, she stood up and suddenly shouted triumphantly:

—"Ohhh… how nice it feels to wipe my muddy hands on his coat!"

I looked down—my coat was smeared with mud. My God—had I not just pitied her? Had I not thought her deserving of mercy? But now I understand—nature gives each person the fate they are suited for. We have no right to question that. Still… why is it that I always expect betrayal from everyone? Celâl gave me a book a few months ago—I cannot recall the title—but in it, I read the following words:

—"If you feel betrayed by everyone, you must search for the source of that betrayal within yourself."

Perhaps it is true. Ah—Celâl! I am drawn toward the sacred beauty I see in him. How will I ever separate from him? The thought tears at my soul, as though a piece of my very being will be torn away.

JULY 14

Childhood is strange. Our headmaster likes to say that we still smell of milk—but I don't think that's true anymore. I think back to how I was three or four years ago—what were those days? I remember sitting with a physics book in front of me, attempting to calculate heat and light… but I never believed what the book said. And those grand ambitions I had—to become a physicist, or the greatest explorer in the world. But today, I know that even the greatest scientist, the most brilliant mind, carries burdens of his own. Nothing in this world is truly lasting. Even the most sacred altars eventually crumble into dust. Even the most radiant beauties—one day, the worms will feast on their eyes. Pompeii…And how many other lands, built over centuries with sacrifice and the blood of millions, have vanished in an instant beneath ashes and fire?

JULY 15

Today, Celāl and I spoke at length about the day I lost my father. Ever since childhood, deprived of a mother's tenderness, my soul had always carried a quiet loneliness—but that day, I was left utterly broken, like a bird with a shattered wing. That day, my father had collapsed suddenly from heart failure at the farm. The workers carried his body to the village and laid him upon a marble bench. The air was heavy with the scent of ether. My nanny pulled me into her arms and dragged my frozen, shocked body toward the garden. Zeliha was just learning to walk then. Our neighbor, Fatıma Hanım, was there too. Everyone loved and respected her; they sought her blessings and prayers. But for some reason, I could never warm to her. She would tell me countless stories—stories that left a deep impression on me—but I rarely listened. More often than not, I would run away. That day, to distract me, she began telling me a new story. But this one was different from anything I had heard before. It was so sweet, so captivating:

—"There was once a young man—a happy and carefree soul—who fell in love with a young girl, a mermaid with long flowing hair. But the mermaid was promised to the King of the Seas. One morning, the young man saw her bathing on the shore. He was about to wrap his arms around her fragrant body when suddenly a deer of fire appeared. The deer sprang forward and branded the boy's innocent forehead with its burning tongue: 'From now on, you shall know only hardship and suffering."

Stories are strange things. Even those that seem absurd often contain profound truths. These figures that seem unreal are, more often than not, nothing but meaningful symbols. Love, desire, virtue… love and virtue—countless symbols wrapped in the guise of living or lifeless forms. I remember that story well—I had never heard it before. And just then, a boy—strong and beautiful—leapt through the hedge. It was Celâl. Seeing him lifted my heart. Celâl's eyes were always slightly downcast, as though weighed down by a quiet sorrow. His pale face carried the traces of some deep, unspoken emotion. Yet he was always lively and hardworking. His eyes held the dangerous clarity of calm seas. Though we were the same age, he was taller, broader in the chest. We had grown up together. There had always been small sparks between us. Sometimes we would quarrel over something trivial—a leaf, a feather. And it was always my fault.

Celâl had many friends. All the village boys followed him like satellites. When he was with them, he would change—he would forget about me. He would stand at the center of a laughing circle, half-turn his head toward me as if to invite me into their games. When I remained silent, he would drift away with the others, surrounded by their lively chatter. And in those moments, I would lash out at the flowers and leaves with a stick, tearing them apart, crying. Afterward, I would stop speaking to Celâl—sometimes for days. But Celâl always had forgiving, gentle eyes. He would stroke my hair, quietly coaxing me back with his tenderness. And now… this boy, my only friend, held my hand. We walked without speaking toward a magnolia tree where my father had once given us evening lessons. The air was filled with the delicate scent of magnolias and the deep crimson of fallen leaves. Birdsong floated through the branches—but now those songs sounded like elegies for time forever lost.

Once, Celāl and I had built a small fire pit there from stones. It was gone now—collapsed by the wind. The soft fragrance of jasmine clung to Celāl's hair and hands. His mother must have applied it that morning. For a moment, it reminded me of the feel of my mother's silk hair brushing against my face, of her warm gaze filling my heart. Yes, jasmine grew on my grandmother's grave in Istanbul. I had once knelt down and breathed in their scent. The golden shadows darkened. The birds trembled and fell silent. On the wing of the storm, a sorrowful woman seemed to rise from a distant land—she pulled me into her clean, wind-washed chest and held me there. That night, by the dim light of a flickering candle, Zeliha and I lay in her wide bed. She slept soundly and quietly. The house was wrapped in silence and mystery. The sky and earth seemed to be infused with a sacred stillness. All day, I had listened to the sounds of crying and lamentation—but I could not fully believe that my father was gone. My nanny's face was flushed; her breath was shallow. She lay perfectly still in bed, weeping. Green stars floated through the air. Slowly, with tired breaths, sleep crept over us. My nanny laid us down in our beds.

That night, I dreamed: "I was lying on burning sands. The sun, like a hellish flower, scorched the desert. Caravans passed by. One of the camels stepped on my shoulders. I screamed, I begged—but I could neither die nor be saved." I woke up. The morning sun had warmed my face. My forehead was damp with sweat, and my eyes ached slightly from the brightness. The house was once again filled with turmoil. The sound of crying reached even the farthest corners of the house. Zeliha kept asking for her father. Even my nanny, without giving us our milk, hurried us out into the street. The earth was cool, washed by the morning breeze. We arrived at the station. It was hot—unbearably hot. The leaves had thickened into deep green groves, and the blue sky had become strikingly profound.

By evening, we had reached my aunt's house in Rumeli Hisarı. I hadn't been there in over a year and a half, and I had longed to see it again. But the heaviness in my chest dimmed any sense of joy. I couldn't throw my arms around my aunt's neck as I used to—not even though I loved her as dearly as my own mother. The last time I had seen her was when little Zehrā was born. Since then, I had not seen my aunt at all. My aunt— the beautiful woman everyone loved with a kind of stunned devotion. What was it about her? I still don't know. But surely they had brought me here because they knew how much I loved her.

I will never forget that day. A distinguished guest came to visit us. I had seen Yusuf Cemāl Bey many times at the farm. He was a distant relative of my uncle, so we knew him well. My father, who was a proud man by nature, treated him with the greatest respect—though Yusuf Cemāl was younger, my father would kiss his hand and sit at his feet. As for me—I loved him. His voice fascinated me. Every time I saw him, I felt an unexplainable relief, an elevation of spirit. I often saw him in my dreams. But now—things are different. Even Celāl, who saw him at the farm, seemed to admire him too much, and I resented Celāl for it. Once, my aunt left her family for him. She abandoned her child to be with him. Poor Zehrā now lives with a distant relative.

Where was I? That summer, my aunt, Zehrā, and I slept every night in the lemon house. My uncle was in Antalya. The lemon house was cool and pleasant in the summer heat. The air was thick with the scent of lemons. A pale purple lantern hung from the ceiling, casting a drowsy light over the room. When we lay down at night, we could see blue stars drifting above our heads. Some would burn out before they could reach their lover, dissolving in midair. When I crawled into bed, I would play with little Zehrā for a while, and then my eyes would close on their own.

***

Two years passed. One summer night, I had fallen asleep once again beneath those gilded stars. But at midnight, I woke suddenly. Zehrā was still sleeping beside me. Then—Fatıma Hanım's story came back to me. Ah… surely this girl was my beloved, the mermaid! I sat up. I was about to wrap my arms around her with all my strength when Zehrā stirred. In the dark, her small hand reached toward my face. I was confused. I lay back down, and Zehrā fell asleep again, her tiny hand stroking my face. But I could not sleep. In my mind, the fiery deer returned. Its burning tongue seared into my forehead: "You shall suffer hardship and sorrow." The fire warned me that the love I had given to the Sea King's favorite would bring me torment and longing. But isn't that the nature of love? Does anyone ever find peace after loving someone? I fear love (*muhabbet*).

JULY 17

Last night's performance became, in truth, a farewell gathering. There were twenty-one of us graduating. We were all dressed in different costumes—some as Chinese, some as Arabs, others as Caucasians. Each of us was also performing a custom or ritual from the faith or culture we represented. I became a Hindu (or Buddhist). I wrapped my waist and shoulders in sacred, earth-toned fabrics of soft texture. In my hand, I held a distinctive set of flat and rounded prayer beads. Two small children played the roles of my disciples. One carried a large fan made from date palm leaves and waved it gently over my head. Celāl was dressed as a Burmese woman. He had tied a fringed loincloth at his side, a mark of his adopted identity. He wore a loose floral shirt, unbuttoned at the collar. A wig sat on his head, and he gathered the long strands of hair at the crown, binding them beneath a headband. He bowed before me, paying his respects. Then he lit one of those thick Burmese cigars, and we sat together, smoking calmly amid the thick coils of fragrant smoke.

The audience loved me the most. The teachers made me repeat the ritual several times. Celāl was in high spirits. His lightheartedness on this night of partying filled me with sadness. My thoughts drifted back to a night a year ago: It had been a rainy, cold evening in October. He had just arrived at the school. We were gathered in the study hall—everyone had retreated into small groups, either working or whispering poetry in quiet corners. I was immersed in my books. Then I saw Celāl. He was leaning his head against the piano in the dark, his face turned toward the ground. He wasn't moving. I went over to him.

— "Are you feeling unwell, Celāl?" I asked.

He lifted his head. His eyes were red and wet. There was a warmth in those tears that drew me toward him. Hesitantly, he said,

—"No."

In that moment, I felt as though I had known him forever—as though our souls had touched in some unseen realm long before. I took his hand with the tenderness of that ancient familiarity. It was cold—ice cold. I tried to warm it with the full heat of my affection. And now—on this last night—Celāl was like a bird who had at last found his long-lost freedom. He seemed ready to take flight on green wings of joy. Yet, just like when we were children at the farm, I suddenly felt the irrational urge to weep—to sob uncontrollably over something small and unspoken. I pleaded with him:

—"Please, Celāl—just surrender yourself to me."

He laughed—a little confused. I took his arm and pulled him toward the piano. With my own hand, I gently rested his head against it and closed his eyes.

JULY 18, BEYLERBEYİ

Who knows how many times the sun has left Bülbüldere with that crimson smile? Ahmet and I are walking side by side, striking our canes against the stones, scattering yellow dust as we go. Neither of us speaks. We seem as though we belong to separate worlds, lost in thought. Celāl is not with us—he had a headache. I wish he were here. By my feet, next to a thicket, a white lamb bleats. A young shepherd is running after it. I catch the little creature and hold it still. The shepherd, with his warm, dark Anatolian face, approaches me and smiles, showing polished white teeth. I ask him,

—"Why are you chasing it?"

—"The Russian girls asked for it," he answers, nodding toward the other side of the plane tree.

Suddenly, a fresh young voice calls out to me in Russian:

—"Bravo, beautiful hero! Bring it here—quickly!"

The loose stones beneath my feet shift and scatter. Colorful insects flutter around us. I walk through the bright reeds and wild thorns, the struggling lamb in my arms, its cries never ceasing. On a rock, a blonde girl in a lavender dress is plucking mountain violets. Her friend sits nearby, seated on the green grass, threading wildflowers into a string across her white skirt. The girl in lavender lets the flowers in her hand slip to the ground. I blush and hand her the lamb. Its soft white wool brushes against her cheek, which is faintly shadowed by the trembling crimson light.

—"What's your name?" she asks in Russian.

—"Sühā."

—"How harmonious! Mine is Milica."

Her small, curved lips look as though they've been stained with some fiery mixture of blood and flame. I close my eyes to avoid seeing that vivid, living red. Lavender light. A soft, sky-blue fragrance seems to fill the entire world. The leaves shimmer in a pale blue haze. Everything seems to be searching for something. Night has fallen. The moon has cast its spell over Bülbüldere, transforming it into a blue paradise. Milica's warm, slender arms are wrapped around my neck. My chest and lips are burning. A nightingale sings with fluid, sacred melodies—an act of devotion to love and beauty. Ahmet has drifted away with Milica's friend, the one in the white dress. Cemāl is unwell. I hear voices—sometimes I think it's the rustling leaves of the forest expressing hidden thoughts. Sometimes I remember them—other times, I don't understand a word. A strange breath seems to carry them from some far-away place.

It feels as though countless minutes are passing. We are walking through measureless distances. We stop at the edge of a stream. Milica holds out her small pink palm and lets me drink from it. The water is cool—so cool. I murmur, "It's like healing…" It feels as though I'm drinking from the eye of heaven itself. I think to myself—if I could remember this white water as I die, surely I would be reborn. But I don't know why I'm still burning. My lips grow hotter; my palms are blistering. My soul is on fire with longing—I am frantic with the need to embrace my beloved with the full madness of my love. My body is no longer enough to worship her.

I am in the sea. Silver shadows swirl around me. I am collapsing, falling away from my god. A deep, aching emptiness spreads through my heart. It feels as though I have walked through thousands of worlds in a single night—through thousands of miles. I search for my bracelet—the one Zeliha had woven with golden hair and embroidered with rubies—but my arm feels bare. I search for Milica, but she is gone. My God— if only I had been a poor shepherd with no gold, no jewels to steal… I had thought that the tears, the blood, the small, fragile heart of a lover were the only treasures one could offer.

—"Tell me, Milica—for God's sake, tell me—did not even a drop of mercy stir in your heart?"

You have left me with a wound that will bleed for eternity. Can you not soothe this torment with another sip from your beautiful hand? I am afraid of the emptiness in my soul. I search for something to cover it, to warm it—but I cannot find her chest to rest upon. I am caught in the wild dance of cold waves. I will lose myself, dissolve into the clouds, into the water. I fear this dark sea—this silent abyss. Even the small, white-winged birds fill me with dread. We come ashore at Beylerbeyi, stepping onto the sands in front of a white mansion. Ahmet pays the boatman. With eyes dull and fogged, he says:

—"Mine took ten liras from me too."

His pale face looks utterly drained of blood, of life. He walks like a dead man, shrouded in silence. I see Celāl at the pier. Relief floods through me. Ahmet and I part ways. Celāl and I walk down a road lined with green trees. A gentle sea breeze rustles through the leaves, carrying the scent of acacia blossoms. My heart feels washed clean by the cool air. The garden lies ahead of us, vast and deep like a green ocean. Petals from fevered roses fall to the earth. In the clear waters of the fountain, brightly colored fish glide beneath the surface. We stop beneath a stone lion's head, where water flows from its mouth. A dark-skinned boy, perhaps nine years old, is sitting among the flowers, dozing. A jug rests at the fountain's edge, spilling white foam over the ground. The soil glistens with thin streams of water. Celāl taps the boy's curly head gently with his cane and calls out:

—"Bilal! Bilal! The ground is flooding."

The boy leaps up, rubs his eyes, and gazes at us in sleepy confusion. When he sees Celāl, he cries out with delight and runs toward the mansion. A cloud of dust rises from the heels of his little shoes as he disappears from sight.

JULY 19, BEYLERBEYİ

After spending this night here, tomorrow I will finally go to the farm. If Celāl had been with me the day before yesterday, none of this would have happened. He instinctively guides me. I couldn't help but follow whatever he told me to do. I still can't believe it. I thought that woman loved me. We parted from each other in tears. I thought this night, which passed within the grove until morning, was the first chapter of a love story. Oh, this childlike heart of mine that believes in everything! As long as I live among these people with this heart, I am certain that I will never escape disappointment.

"Haven't you learned your lesson yet, Sühā?" you are still searching for honey among these poisonous flowers. How many times have you burned your tongue, how many times have you been poisoned? And yet, you still haven't learned. Look—listen to the pure, divine sound of the waters stretching out in this beautiful night. Does it resemble the confused language of your sorrow? Do you hear how this peaceful, natural sound rises far above the heavy groans of agony—the restless murmurs that are nothing more than the sound of a dying breath? Next to the candle, a moth is slowly stirring its fragile horn. There is an endless need for love—not for that tainted storm I endured in the grove, but for true love. From time to time, the breeze drifting in through the open window brings me hope from afar.

Surely there are extraordinary people in this world, just as Celāl believes. Isn't Celāl himself one of them? Is he not a body that carries the scent of such people? To my parched lips, Celāl is like water dripping from a height so lofty that it will not crack or burn me. He soothes me, enough that I will not be consumed. Could the whole world really be made up of the people I have known and seen? No, what I have seen—those are not people.

There must be a true being, one worthy of the name human. Even an otter grieves and cries when its offspring dies. Sometimes it cannot bear the pain and dies from longing. A dog does not hesitate to sacrifice its life for its owner. Are there not animals greater than many of the people I have encountered? If the whole universe is truly the world I have seen, then what is this hidden and manifest worship of beauty and greatness within souls? How deceived I was by appearances! Beneath a body so beautiful that I couldn't even bear to look at it, I discovered such repulsive and sickening meanings. No matter how perfect and beautiful the cover of a book may be, once I open it and feel disgusted by its contents—what then?

Must I return once again to these people? By the end of this summer, I will have to come back here to complete my higher education. I still haven't decided which career to pursue. Part of me thinks I should study literature. After all, I have enough wealth to live comfortably without having to work. But working the land doesn't seem so bad either. Would it be so wrong to converse every day with the earth from which I was created?

FIVE YEARS LATER

JUNE 1, THE FARM

My notebook! Today, I found it among the discarded books piled in the corner. That last entry—where my thoughts dissolved into longing for love—left me troubled. These five years of schooling have taught me many painful lessons. Yet, after all, how could I have understood the essence of life without first tasting its bitterness? Now, I breathe alongside the birds and flowers, inhaling the clear breath of warm mountains. I kiss the fragrant earth alongside the swallows. The farm seems to be lost in quiet contemplation—wrapped in the serenity of unbroken peace. Everywhere glows with the soft light of green. My song is love, my feeling is love, even the water I drink tastes of love. Here, there are flowers woven from light and angels spun from the melody of radiance. The house in (…) is watched over by a villager.

On the farm, it's just Zeliha, my nanny, a few servants, and the old steward. Veli Ağa still stands tall—he has not yet weakened. His body is as strong as iron. He can still lift Zeliha into his arms and carry her with ease. Sometimes Zeliha goes down to the village with my nanny or travels to Istanbul for a few days. Occasionally, she returns with a few friends. And when she does, the farm seems to smile. Laughter blooms among the laurel and reeds like scattered blossoms. I have become a joyful, restless soul—always in motion. Under the scorching sun, I throw open my chest and lift my head to the sky, running like the birds, like the wind, singing as I go. I've started neglecting Zeliha, my nanny… all of them, really. But I have my nameless flowers, my bright and still sanctuaries, my open skies to speak with. Zeliha sits on Veli Ağa's knee, telling him stories about our father. Truly—I never think of him anymore.

JUNE 15

I was playing my flute (kaval) on the lakeshore. Sunset was near. The surface of the Silver Lake had begun to flush red in places. I grew thirsty and went to drink from the "Traveler's Fountain." An old village woman was there, filling her jug. She wore a white headscarf and a faded shawl. In a soft, deep voice, she said:

— "Come here, beautiful boy. Where are you coming from?"

—"From the lakeshore."

—"Why are you walking alone? Don't you have a sweetheart?"

My heart pounded. I wanted to stop her words from reaching me. I was afraid of being poisoned again. The woman leaned against the weathered, crimson-streaked stones of the fountain. In a strange and commanding tone, she said:

—"Can youth really pass by without thirst?"

Only then did I remember my thirst. I pulled the jug from the fountain and drank deeply from my cupped hands. I splashed water on my face and head, but the burning in my chest refused to subside.

—"Grandmother," I said, "there is a heart of fire here, wrapped in flames and the searing rays of the sun. The water of the Traveler's Fountain will not be enough to cool it."

The village woman suddenly laughed—an unforgettable, meaningful laugh that revealed her pearly teeth. Even the mountains seemed to echo her laughter softly. She gazed at me with such intensity that I had to lift my eyes from the ground. Her gaze reached into the depths of my soul.

—"Son, do not fear love—fear emptiness of the heart."

She picked up her jug and walked away. Her parting words drifted toward me on the wind:

—"May God protect you. May He grant your heart's desire. May your brow remain unstained, my child."

JULY 9

I am so at peace that I could weep from happiness. I feel more in need of these burning yellow fields and these flaming skies than of my own eyes. The soft cries of the seagulls pierce me as though they carry the accumulated longing of centuries. Even the small black flashes of light beneath the wings of the larks fill me with a quiet sense of loss.

JULY 18

I am sitting at the foot of my father's grave. Thorny brambles grow all around me. I pull my knees to my chest and sit quietly. I cannot even touch a single leaf. I am afraid to breathe in the scent of the pink carnations. I feel as though my father, forgotten for so many years, will not forgive my sins. The wild roses sway in the breeze, scattering their pale petals over the smooth white stone of the grave. From deep within the bright green thickets, the sound of insects rises—wearied and fading. Even they sound exhausted now. The sunlight, freed from the thin shelter of the clouds, burns my knees and hands. On the distant lake, a hesitant silver tremor ripples across the water. Between the reeds and the rocks, two crimson starflowers sway gently. The scent of the roses dulls my senses. The pale wildflowers bow toward one another, as though whispering the story of death (*hikāye-i mevti*). Their breath is so faint, so quiet, as if they fear disturbing this fragile peace.

I cannot bring myself to touch the insects and the wild plants that have fed on the dust of my father's bones. I recoil even from my own body. Boiling rays pour down from the sky. The sun—a copper disk of blazing light—the ground, streaked with burning sparks... All the things I have loved and worshipped. Yet they are not enough. I need another miracle—something greater, a *Suzān* (burning) that will consume me completely. But I cannot reach what I seek. Silver shadows melt away into another realm. The insects fall silent. The sun trembles and slowly sinks into the haze. A strange coolness settles over the evening, replacing the joyous spring warmth. The cold dampness of the gravestones seeps into my bones. I sit there, still and forgotten, unable to move.

Suddenly, the enchanted flowers around me tremble as though startled. Shapeless, shadowy figures dart through the dark. I want to flee through the cypress trees, but these strange, shifting forms seem to cling to my feet. From the depths of the darkness, clouds of fire erupt—red flames spewing forth an uncountable number of eyes. White shapes of fire rise from the earth like restless spirits. And in that moment, I lose myself completely. By morning, I awaken as though I have died and been reborn—as though I have returned from the realm of spirits (*ālem-i ervāh*). The fever of last night's hell has burned out. The morning breeze washes over my body. The flowers' damp, innocent faces glisten with light. The grave seems to sigh, sinking back into its old, silent ruin.

I stumble. It's as if I've forgotten how to walk. The world around me feels faintly familiar, like a dream half-remembered. For the first time in years, I pass through the village. The old villagers seem vaguely familiar. But the younger ones—they must have changed a great deal… They all look at me like I'm a stranger. How strange—this village once seemed so vast to me, filled with countless people. But now I see how small and empty it truly is. Ah… tell me, little travelers—there used to be a brown-haired boy with a clear and innocent face here. Where is he now? I can't hear the sound of his mare's hooves or the echo of his bright laughter. In front of the fishermen's houses, a thin woman sits sewing a torn net. A boy in a red dress crouches on the sunlit earth, his shaven head dark and shining. A crooked black sign hangs on the door of the post office: "For Rent."

And there—there are the iron bars of the house we used to live in. Celâl and I used to run back and forth on that stone wall. How many games did we play there? I walk slowly toward the house. It's deathly still. The old steward must have gone somewhere. I sit down on the bricks of the terrace wall. My God—is there nothing on earth that is not fleeting? I gaze at the garden for a long time. The pool, once bright with colorful fish, now floats with rotting leaves. The trees have been swallowed by waist-high weeds. Even the ivy has wrapped itself around the old double chestnut trees. Where is the magnolia tree beneath which we used to sit and study? It should be behind the climbing rose—but it's gone. Cut down. Even the silverberry tree at the gate seems to have moved. Its thin branches and pale, dull leaves used to brush against the windows. Now it leans toward the roof of the silver house, pressing its chest against the eaves.

Strange Greeks now look at me from the windows of Celâl's house. The wooden latticework is gone. The bay windows have been removed. Brightly colored laundry flutters where the goddess of the house once stood. Where have they gone? An unbearable sense of fatigue floods through me. I feel as though I'm dying. My vision blurs. Tears burn my cheeks. I am without truth (*hakikatsiz*), without a temple (*mabetsiz*), without an idol (*putsuzum*). All the roads blur together—I lose my way. It's not until the afternoon that I finally find the farm.

When Veli Ağa sees me in the garden, he cries like a child and throws his arms around my neck. His tears stream down his weathered beard. I find Zeliha lying on her bed, still dressed in her white garden gown. When she hears my voice, she jumps up and runs toward me. I don't tell anyone where I was last night. But Zeliha studies my face with careful, fearful attention, as if afraid to come too close. It's true—I no longer know how to belong among people. I am no longer ashamed. I feel no pity. I only shrug my shoulders. Veli Ağa lifts his trembling, veined hands to the sky and prays for a long time. The next morning, my head aches. Zeliha begs me to stay home, to rest. That evening, she sets up a chair beneath the jasmine arbor and strokes my hair as she sits me down. She has softened the chair with pillows and cushions, but sitting there feels like torture. I long to lie down on the grass. Yet I no longer have the strength to refuse even her smallest request. We talked with Veli Ağa until evening. The poor man—how many burdens he had been carrying! Someone from his hometown in İzmit had arrived—his only surviving relative. But even that child was in a terrible state—stricken with consumption.

—"Go, Veli Ağa," I said. "Don't lose any time. Bring the boy here. But first, find someone to watch over the farm temporarily…"

The simple-hearted old man kissed my hands with joy. The sun had already set, but Zeliha had not yet returned. I sat in the wicker chair, slowly rocking back and forth, smoking a cigarette. The air was so still that the blue swirls of smoke gathered around me, hovering in place. I passed my hand through them, scattering the haze. In the distance, Veli Ağa appeared like a dark bird in the middle of the cornfields. He stood in front of the watchman's hut, gesturing toward the fields as he gave instructions to one of the servants inside. Suddenly, two small, soft hands covered my eyes. I recognized Zeliha's touch immediately and grasped her wrists. I kissed her cool cheeks.

—"You're cold, Zeliha," I said. "Come, let me wrap you in my coat. Where is my nanny?"

—"They're coming."

—"They? Who?"

I looked toward the narrow road, which was growing darker by the minute. Two shadowy figures were approaching quickly. Zeliha drew closer, curling into the folds of her large coat. She lowered her head and whispered:

—"Don't be upset, brother, please! If you keep turning away from me like this, I'll die. There's barely any life left in me—less than our poor canary's! Please, don't be angry. I brought Zehrā. We won't laugh too much, I promise."

—"Zehrā? Who is that?"

—"Don't you know Tamburī Faik Bey from the village? She's from his carriage. Her father died somewhere, I don't know where. She has no one left. So they brought her to the village."

Poor Zeliha—how terribly she misunderstood me.

—"Why would I be angry?" I said. "How could I not love you? Do you think I'm as selfish as that? If you laugh, I feel consoled."

Her soft blue eyes glowed faintly in the dark. She pressed closer to me and rested her head against my chest. In a voice that seemed to rise from the depths of her heart, she said:

— "Brother... why have you changed so much? The letters you wrote to me from Athens were so beautiful. Back then, you loved me. Tell me—what have I done wrong? Brother—have mercy on me."

Her voice broke. I held her chin gently and turned her face toward the moonlight. Her cheeks were wet with tears. Her eyelashes trembled. I couldn't find the words to answer her.

— "Brother—have mercy on me."

Those were the only words of complaint I heard.

JULY 22

Zeliha is already deeply attached to her new friend. At this rate, she won't let her go for months. I hadn't paid much attention last night in the dark, but this morning I ran into her in the garden. When she saw me, she blushed and darted behind the fig saplings. Zehrā—what a lovely child. Her hair is golden—so bright and pale, even lighter and more luminous than Zeliha's. Late in the morning, Zeliha came into my room. She seemed surprised to find me there. Truthfully, I was a little surprised too—I had been home for two days now, which was unusual. I told myself it was because of my lingering headache.

— "What is it?" I asked. "How's your guest?"

She lit up with joy that I had asked. Stroking the flowers in the small pot on the table, she smiled:

— "Oh, brother—you wouldn't believe how sweet and beautiful she is! My heart races just thinking about her. I wish she would come with us to Ayazma."

I didn't want to disappoint her, so I said,

—"Alright."

We had lunch under the walnut tree. Afterward, I played with them. We made garlands from mountain flowers. Later, we were picking grapes in the vineyard. The air was hot—the sun seemed to burn through our blood. I came up with a game: Zeliha and Zehrā would each try to find the biggest bunch of grapes. Whoever picked the smaller one would have to accept whatever punishment I decided. They both darted between the vines. I was secretly hoping the little one would lose. Zeliha sang as she ran through the rows. Now and then, Zehrā would lift a bunch of grapes toward the sunlight, examining it carefully.

Suddenly, Zeliha dashed ahead, laughing:

— Mine's bigger! Mine's bigger!" she shouted.

Zehrā followed more slowly, looking uncertain. She was clutching her bunch tightly in her small, pale hand. I took hold of her slender fingers. She resisted at first, unwilling to open her hand. I had to pry her fingers apart—perhaps a little too roughly, leaving a faint mark on her delicate skin. Her bunch was much smaller than Zeliha's. With the cruel authority of a king, I declared:

— "Well, 'little lady,' it seems you've lost. Now you'll have to feed me each grape, one by one—straight from your lips."

Her face flushed a deep crimson. She couldn't do it. No matter how much I coaxed or pleaded, she simply couldn't do it. My lips burned with the imagined heat of an unrealized pleasure.

JULY 27

At noon, I was lying beneath the shade of the hazelnut trees. The only sound around me was the quiet hum of insects. Soft, restless clouds drifted lazily across the sky. I was thinking to myself: Even the tenderness of the mountains, the flowers, and the gentle winds can only hold a person's attention for so long. These mountains, this fragrant earth, these crystal waters and springs… But this beauty is not enough for me. I cannot understand the language they speak. It's like listening to a foreign woman with an extraordinarily beautiful voice reciting a poem in her own language—I might be enchanted by the harmony of her soft voice, but I wouldn't understand the true meaning of the words. I had sunk deep into my thoughts when I heard Zeliha's voice:

— "Shall we sit here?"

I saw the laurel bushes shifting in front of me. They couldn't see me. They sat down beneath a tree close to where I was lying.

— "Zeliha, can I ask you something?" Zehrā's voice was quiet, uncertain. "Do you love this world?"

— "Of course I do. Don't you?"

— No. Nothing gives me joy.

Could it be that Zehrā loves someone? Of course—it's possible. She's no longer a child. But for some reason, the thought fills me with an inexplicable sadness.

— "Zeliha, look at those doves."

Two doves were circling in the sky. They landed on a tree along the hillside, pressing their beaks together as if to sanctify their love. The small spring beside them trembled. The old almond tree sighed and shed a leaf. A caterpillar crawling on a sapling suddenly fell to the ground.

JULY 28

What an astonishing thing! Zehrā—it turns out she's our Zehrā. My aunt's daughter, little Zehrā!

Were we asleep all this time? When I told Zehrā about our family ties, she was stunned. Then her face lit up with joy. Finding a surviving relative—a connection, a lifeline—was a profound comfort for this orphaned girl. Yet at the same time, her eyes filled with tears. The memory of her sorrows seemed to resurface—the chapters of her life reopening all at once. Poor Zehrā... The way she and Zeliha embraced, as if they were meeting for the first time, brought tears to my eyes. I returned to the farm a little while ago. As I made my way through the garden, a flickering lantern's light floated toward me like a restless spirit. Then suddenly, I saw Veli Ağa's smiling, weathered face. He set the lantern down on the damp earth, resting it on the broad melon leaves that lay flattened beneath the darkness.

— "I've come, my boy—thank God I lived to see this day." He clasped my hands and kissed my face. Tears rolled down from his beard. I asked about the boy. — "He's sleeping," he said. Then he led me to the room, opening the door with practiced care. I looked around for the child. I spotted him beneath a heavy, dark-colored blanket. Only his head was visible—a thin, dark face, fragile as a skeleton. I leaned down instinctively to listen to his breath. He didn't look like a fourteen-year-old boy. He looked like a mummified corpse, preserved at the fragile age of ten or twelve. And yet, Veli Ağa said he was seventeen. I forced myself to sound cheerful so as not to disturb him:

— "Well, Veli Ağa," I said lightly, "Is this child an Arab?"

Veli Ağa shook his strong, weathered head.

— "No, sir... it's the sun—and the sickness. That's why."

I can't bear to stand before a life whose strength is slowly draining away. This land of fire and love—now abandoned by the weary soldiers of life's end. Fearfully, I listen to the night. I brace myself for the sound of a frail, troubled cough. But the seconds and minutes pass, and nothing comes. A thin green light from the lampshade leaves soft patterns on my hands. A small moth has fallen onto the lantern's glass. Its wings have rubbed away their gold dust onto the paper. Now it lies motionless. The sight reminds me of a night in Istanbul—ashes, soil, the grey breath of dawn. I want to sleep—but I can't. I listen to the night... Suddenly, like sunlight breaking through clouded skies, a sharp need pierces my soul. I search for Zehrā's breath. I search for her eyes. I cannot extinguish the light. In the darkness, I try to see the shape of her heart with my eyes.

AUGUST 13

My suspicions were unfounded. Süleyman isn't coughing. I had feared he might poison the air—feared that the very act of breathing beside him might be dangerous. For two nights, I had resisted taking a breath near him, waiting for dawn so I could slip away unnoticed. But it turns out he's just a harmless boy. He never disturbs anyone. With his sweet Abyssinian features and small, dark eyes, he drifts about like a shadow. He is so small, so fragile, that you wouldn't believe he was seventeen. In the mornings, he lies beneath the shade of the mulberry tree, stretched out on the straw mat. Today, as I passed by, I asked him:

— Why do you always lie there, Süleyman? Do you like it so much?"

He was gazing at the sky. He didn't move. He curled his lip slightly, as if half-understanding my words—or perhaps as if I already knew the whole story of his past.

— "I used to work as an apprentice at the coffeehouse in the village," he said. "I'd lie like this on the mat in front of the coffeehouse."

AUGUST 14

The other night, Zeliha played the *tambur* for a while. Zehrā loves the Hicaz peşrev—she said so herself. Since that night, Zeliha has played Hicaz nearly every evening.

AUGUST 24

I'm returning to the farm at midnight under the moonlight. From a distance, I can see Zehrā's shining head among the ta-flans. Zeliha has fallen asleep in her wicker chair. Her braid rests in small loops on her knees. Her face is turned toward the moon, and it looks as though thin streams of light are dripping from the ends of her hair. Zehrā and my nanny are sitting on the ground, heads close together, speaking in slow, quiet breaths. They're so immersed in their conversation that they don't even hear my footsteps. I approach them. My nanny says:

— "Children, at least go for a walk. What kind of young people are you? In our youth, this place used to echo with our laughter. You don't know how to enjoy the world and these beautiful surroundings."

Zeliha uses her sleepiness as an excuse and heads inside to bed. This is the first time Zehrā and I have been alone together at night. The air is stifling—like we're breathing fire. Neither the trees nor the sky shows any movement. Only our hearts are beating. From a distance, a flock is approaching us. The landscape is so open and bright that it dazzles the eyes. I can't believe that such beauty exists. The sheep seem to be gliding over water, like a delicate, ghostly procession. We walk toward them. In this delicate and otherworldly night, how I wish I could see into Zehrā's heart, nestled inside her beautiful body. There's something so familiar about her, a connection so intimate that it almost feels as though we share the same essence. That's what captivates me about her—that sense of deep familiarity, as if a part of her belongs to me. And yet, she carries a sadness—a waiting, a quiet melancholy—as if she's longing for someone. I keep inventing games, trying to amuse her, but she remains distant, detached. She seems to be waiting for something or someone, unable to engage with anything I do.

I care about her entirely—her health, her sleep, her happiness. And yet, all I sense from her is indifference. There's nothing more I can do. The other day, I asked her:

— "What has been the happiest day of your life, Zehrā?"

She didn't answer. Could it be that she's afraid of being loved? That she's resisting it? The flock surrounds us. We sit down carefully on the grass so as not to startle them. The sound of the sheep grazing and their soft breathing fills the air. The shepherd stands nearby, holding his staff and whistling a mournful tune. There's something in the sound that touches the heart—a sadness so deep it could pierce stone. The sheep's devoted obedience to that sound is so touching. Zehrā doesn't say a word. She seems entranced—lost. Oh, God—how much I need to truly love someone! What am I to do? I've realized that nothing but love will ever satisfy me. My soul won't rest. All the adventures I've had so far were childish, illusions rather than real experiences. The only thing that's real—the only thing that remains—is disappointment.

Suddenly, I hear the sound of quiet sobbing. Zehrā has laid her head on her knees and is crying uncontrollably. I'm shocked and deeply moved. Why is she crying? The scene before us is so beautiful, so divine—it's natural to be affected by it. But what has shaken her so deeply? What does she want? Zehrā's sadness lasts the entire night. Her eyes remain full of tears, her expression mournful and expectant—as though she's waiting for something. That night, Zehrā talks about my aunt for the first time:

— "My father was still alive," she begins. "It was an autumn evening. My mother was lying down as usual, resting her head on a red pillow. She had embroidered that pillow herself when she was at school—with little blue dolls and flowers. I loved those so much, I couldn't even bear to look at them. That evening, she wasn't talking to me. She was distracted, twisting strands of her hair, the way she always did when she was deep in thought. I waited, like I always did, for her to fall asleep. I put my toys away, afraid to make any noise. I even held my breath. After a while, she closed her eyes. I thought she had fallen asleep. I tried to cover her with a blanket, but she pushed me away without opening her eyes. I fell onto the rug and began to cry silently. At midnight, I woke up. She was gone from the bed. The candle had burned out. Faint red shadows flickered on the walls. I was terrified. I jumped out of bed and prayed to God. Then I saw her standing by the stove. Her pink dress was glowing red in the light of the fire. I ran to her, crying, and wrapped myself around her legs, begging her to move away before she got burned. But she said coldly, 'Let go. Go back to bed.' By then, the heat was searing my face. On the oilcloth on the floor, a stack of papers was curling and twisting in the fire. I pleaded, 'Mother, please put it out! It's a waste!' But then—I don't know why—I began to feel drawn to the fire, as if I were watching the moon. My bare feet were freezing, but I stood there quietly, watching the bright, colorful flames. The papers burned so quickly, you wouldn't believe it. Suddenly, there was a loud crackling sound. My mother had thrown all her memories—all her past—into that fire. She had set her whole body, her whole world, ablaze. Among the blackened ash and thin, golden embers, small glittering worms began to creep through the ruins. And then—it was over. My mother's entire history turned to ashes. That night, we lay down together. When I was little, I would often fall asleep holding her cheeks in my hands. That night, for the first time in two years, she let me sleep beside her like that. Early in the morning, before the dawn prayer, I woke up. My nanny, Servet, opened the door and drifted toward me in her red dress covered with large white roses. She pushed me aside. I didn't complain about the smell of oil on her clothes like I usually did. I just asked where my mother was. 'She went out,' Servet said. A cold pain filled my chest. Later, I learned the truth. My mother had run away— to be with him. It's been five years. I've never seen her since. I've heard they're still together. They went far away—to Arabia. No one knows what secret lies between them."

My heart aches as I picture the imposing figure of Yusuf Cemāl, his commanding gaze. Poor Suzān... Zehra lifts her face to mine and says:

—"I'm just like my mother. I'm nothing more than a life reborn in her shadow."

I laugh and tease her:

—"Are you in love with him too?"

She says nothing. She seems like a mysterious inscription of love etched high upon a tablet. My heart races. A soft star fades in the dark mist of the horizon before it can reach its mate. We head toward the lake. I watch Zehrā. On the clear surface of the silver lake, thin (*rakik*) white clouds gather and thicken. Then, as though illuminated by the light of an unknown sun, they melt and part. I see a figure, like a vision of the prophet of Israel—shining, pale, and beautiful, half-naked, smiling. And then I see Zehrā—our little Zehrā—kneeling before this radiant figure, worshipping it like a divine being. I open my eyes. It was a dream. Zehrā stands beside me, unaware. She says softly:

— "I'm cold," she says.

I take her hand and lead her toward the "Fire Rock" (*ateş kaya*). This is a small rock, just past the village road that leads from the farm. A lone pine tree stands over it, swaying sadly against the wind every day.

— "Look, Zehrā! I've brought you to the Fire Rock. Are you still cold?" I ask. "Do you know why they call this place Fire Rock? It's a bit of a dark story, but I'll tell you."

— "There were once two young villagers—a shepherd and a milkmaid—who fell in love. They were still very young, so their parents laughed at them. Every day, they would meet here, release their flocks into the hills, and sit together talking for hours. But when the milkmaid's uncle learned about their meetings, he was furious. He was a harsh and severe man. He swore, 'Even if I knew she'd die, I wouldn't give her to that shepherd!' One night, the two young lovers built a large fire right here. They embraced one another, and together, they threw themselves into the flames. Since then, the villagers have called this place Fire Rock."

Zehrā looked frightened. I regretted telling her the story and helped her down from the rock. The night air was damp and sharp. Worried she might catch cold, I took off my jacket and wrapped it around her shoulders. The moon hung low on the horizon, drifting listlessly. Its pale face was washed white, like a piece of water splashed up from the earth, veiled in soft white mist.

AUGUST 28

Süleyman has been keeping me quite busy lately. In the evenings, I've started giving him lessons for about an hour each day. His mind is so sharp and quick that at this pace, he'll have acquired quite a bit of knowledge within a year. He's already beginning to read and write, though it's only been a short time since we started. He's a mischievous boy, but there's the soul of a poet in him. His speech, which used to have a slight Rumelian accent, is improving rapidly. If you spoke to him now, you'd think he was a well-mannered boy from Istanbul. Still, the poor boy sometimes slips up in class and mispronounces a word in that peculiar accent. When this happens, Zeliha and the others can't help but laugh. His mind works so quickly (*faal muhayyilesi*) that it often reshapes words and phrases without his realizing it. Sometimes, when writing, he'll spontaneously insert completely unrelated sentences. He's a bit absent-minded! But when I pose more complex scientific problems (ilmī mümarese) to him, I'm often surprised at his understanding. He approaches them with the insight and reasoning of someone far more educated than he actually is.

AUGUST 29

Zeliha found some of Yusuf Cemāl Bey's compositions and played them for us on the violin. They were truly masterpieces. While listening, Zehrā began to sob uncontrollably. I kept my head bowed, eyes closed — almost as if I were asleep. But it was the kind of sleep brought on by the rapture of those melodies — a fusion of body and soul, a harmonious blending of meaning and sound. It was impossible not to be entranced. The notes seemed to dissolve the boundary between the material and the spiritual, weaving them together so seamlessly that they became one.

AUGUST 30, NOON

Not a single rooster is crowing, nor is there the sound of a bird. Though the sun is up, it feels like night — everything is pitch dark. The weather has turned suddenly dreadful. What happened to that beautiful sky? Outside, the rain is falling incessantly. It feels as though the heavens are melting and pouring down upon us. I've closed the curtains to avoid seeing the lightning. Other than the mournful rhythm of the rain, there isn't a single sound across the whole farm. I want to open my chest to the roads, to walk and breathe in the rain — but instead, I've fallen into a state of deep listlessness. The storm and the lightning fill me with dread. Ah… will I have to see that green, flower-filled world of mine darkened and extinguished like this? I had thought that bright heavens were eternal, unchanging.

This morning, at dawn, I wandered through the abandoned ruins of the farm. Even it has its desolate, sorrowful corners. In the small worker's room behind the stables, I could almost hear the echo of the laughter from the games Celāl and I used to play there. On the ruined walls, perhaps the same rusty nails we once climbed on were still hanging. Between the broken floorboards, I saw a small, dented garden pail stuck there. Dirty red putty still ran down the edges of the shattered glass panes. I remembered how we would chase each other, breathless with excitement, smearing that red paste all over ourselves. Back then, my grandmother was still alive. We used to come here from the village by carriage, overflowing with joy, hope, and excitement. Our happiness would fill the fields, the sky — it seemed to encompass the entire world. Now, faces from the past drift before my eyes — the young faces of the neighborhood girls. Over there, just by that library, I see Celāl's bright eyes and beautiful face, surrounded by a crowd of laughing children. Some have golden hair, others dark.

Each one carries the promise of a different life. But suddenly, with pale lips and an expectant look of disappointment, they retreat into the corners and fade. Now, I see nothing at all. The library sits there with its slightly dusty glass and dark books, as if still immersed in my father's thoughts. That large walnut grandfather clock has stopped. It hasn't worked since my father died. It frightens me. Its pitiless silence feels like reproach, like quiet disdain. But soon, it too will shatter — and its fragments will mingle with the earth, the sky, and the dust of mankind.

Ah... So Zehrā is gone. Who knows how long it will be until I see her again — maybe I never will. Yet I had grown so used to her presence. Since yesterday, I still can't believe that she's really gone. Any moment now, I expect the door to swing open and for her to come in, smiling with those green eyes of hers. I'm waiting... Two days ago, Faik Bey had come to the farm. How much he has changed! His back has curved, his stature has shrunk, and the brilliance of his eyes has faded. His face is lined with deep wrinkles. Zehrā was more pleased to see him than I had expected. She threw her arms around his neck and kissed his cheeks. Yet it's so strange — not once had she ever mentioned her uncle to me. Poor Faik Bey adored her. He watched her constantly with tearful, loving eyes. He even swore that if he had a daughter, he could not have loved her more than Zehrā. But his wife never liked Zehrā for some reason. This upset Faik Bey deeply. He was relieved when Zehrā stayed with us for a while. Apparently, Zeliha had gone to Faik Bey's wife that day, when he wasn't home, and asked for permission to bring Zehrā to the farm. His wife had allowed it, but they were surprised that we had lived unaware of each other for so long.

That night, we sat beneath the chestnut trees. There was something about sitting with artists that gave me deep pleasure.

Beneath the dark folds of his black coat, Faik Bey's small, pale yellow eyes trembled with endless tenderness. They reminded me of the pure stillness of heavenly skies. His white hair, resting neatly on his thin shoulders, commanded reverence. His quiet, delicate expression seemed to preserve traces of a deeper youth beneath the surface:

—"I have loved three things in my life," he said, his voice trembling with nostalgia. "Women, wine, and the tambur. They burned me for years like a fire in my soul. I loved, and I was loved in return. "But time passed... my warmth, my color, my strength — all of it is gone now. I now play my tambur within the stillness of my youth's grave. Ah... old age!"

He stopped speaking and fell into thought. I sat there peeling chestnuts, the husks falling at my feet. Zehrā, sitting on a swing, let the hem of her dress flutter through the piles of green leaves. Amidst this sorrowful reflection, I couldn't imagine her wilting in this world of dreams.

Here he was — one of the greatest artists in the world! A man who had loved and been loved, who had been cheered and celebrated, had reached the highest heights of fame and admiration. Now, stooped and trembling before me, he was bidding farewell to the world, to glory, to the fire of youth. The admirers who had once worshipped him would soon vanish. Even those who still admired him could only accompany him as far as his grave. No one could stop him from parting ways with the lovers and the music of his youth. Faik Bey sighed and looked up at the moon:

— "You were still so young then. Zeliha wasn't even born yet. It was beneath this very moon that I left for the village of (...). My cheeks were as pink as yours, and my hair shone under the light. This moon was just as enchanting then — it made promises and whispered poetry to me! But now... look at me — I'm spent. Don't you see? The moon is still so bright and mesmerizing, while I've withered... What was I saying? Ah, yes. You were very young — only old enough to know your grandmother's affection. I went to that village after a beautiful girl. I stayed for two years, but the girl I loved left for Egypt. So I returned to the noisy, glittering cities, to the lively, bustling places. I have seen many cities, many women. I have drunk from the most ornate goblets. But time passed. I turned my back on youth, bearing the heavy burden of life on my shoulders. When I returned, I was utterly alone. No one stood beside me. My eyes grew sunken, my hair fell and turned white. All that remained of the burning days I left behind was exhaustion. The moon was bright and magnificent once again this month. I searched for the old songs he used to recite to me on the village roads — but I couldn't find them..."

Zeliha lay a little further away, as if asleep among the grass. Zehra, gliding over her, was soaring toward the stars and the moon...After a while, I asked Faik Bey:

—"Which artist do you admire most? Do you like Yusuf Cemāl Bey?"

— "Yusuf Cemāl? To me, he is more than just a composer — he is a true 'human being' (*insān*). In the fullest sense of the word, a human... Of course, I adore his compositions with deep reverence. But that is not the only reason I admire him. Without a doubt, he is the extraordinary human being that Socrates and many other philosophers tried to describe. I see in him the virtues they spoke of: compassion, grace, loyalty... and more. Do you know how many poor people he clothes, feeds, and shelters? But beyond all this, I am in awe of the perfection and beauty I see in him. In history, I would liken his beauty to that of the prophets of the Children of Israel...Many men and women love him. But I am certain that even the women are in love with his soul. He cannot be loved with a base, selfish passion..."

Confronted with such ecstatic admiration, I was left bewildered. Since it was already midnight, we stood up to go inside the house. We were walking along a narrow path covered with small green saplings. Zehra and Zeliha were walking ahead of us. Suddenly, Zehra leaned toward Zeliha. Out of curiosity, I quietly moved closer to them. Zehra said to Zeliha:

— "Look, Zeliha! Doesn't the moon up there look like the 'Prophet of Love'? All the stars seem small and pale beside it, as though they're worshipping it."

The moon was a thin, silver crescent, sharp and delicate, glinting like a dagger in the clear sky. It was buried among the fine veils of thin clouds, resting softly against the dark expanse of the heavens. I was jealous — jealous of everything about Zehrā. Even her quiet devotion to the moon stirred something dark in me. Arm in arm, Zehrā and Zeliha stood there, lost in admiration for that pale, regal ruler of the night sky.

SEPTEMBER 1

Yesterday, I said to Zehrā:

— "So you're really leaving? But won't you come back to visit Zeliha?"

— "Of course I will… but maybe I won't," she said.

— "Why not? Faik Bey will let you. And even if he doesn't, it's not that far," I said, joking. "You could sneak away."

She frowned:

— "You can't visit secretly," I was going to say that I was joking, but her voice suddenly changed. Her green eyes smiled softly at me. Then, in a quiet, trembling voice, she said:

—"I want to ask you for something. Won't you give me anything tonight?"

—"How do you mean?" I asked. "Something?" (What could I possibly give her now?) "Would you like my heart, Zehrā?"

She pursed her red lips and closed her bright, emerald eyes. Slowly, dreamily, she said:

— "I was going to pin a sprig of wallflower to your chest."

She stopped speaking. Then she took a small branch from her hand and slipped it into the buttonhole of my jacket. She pulled two strands of her hair from behind her ear and tucked them next to the branch. I smiled, confused but happy. I pulled out a small wallflower from the path, wrapped my own hair around it, and gave it to her. She seemed surprised but pleased. I laughed and asked:

—"What will you do with it, Zehrā?"

She blushed, then answered weakly and distantly:

— "Nothing. I'll keep it."

She fell silent. I could tell she had something else on her mind.

—"Please, Zehrā," I said, trying to sound lighthearted. "Be honest. What will you really do with it? Is a sprig of wallflower more precious than my heart?"

Suddenly, a strong wind rose. Beneath the silver dawn light, I saw the clouds gathering. Rain began to fall. The flowers bent their tiny heads beneath the weight of the raindrops. Zehrā said:

—"I'm going to show it to Hikmet, my uncle's son… But he doesn't love me," she added softly.

Then she ran off, holding her hair to keep it from getting wet. I stood there, stunned and miserable. How foolish I was! I told myself. Zehrā is still just a child. The world around me was fading — the flowers had lost all color, the leaves had drained of their green. The wind that had scattered the flowers from my hand was now whipping through my hair.

SEPTEMBER 2

This evening, Veli Ağa came to me at dusk. He was holding a sickle, which he swung against the dried branches of a rose bush:

—"Little master," he said, "the sheep are dying. Three more died today."

Death! Oh, how I didn't want to think about it. I shook my shoulders and walked away. In the dark, I tripped over something at my feet. It must be the clay statue Süleyman has been working on for days, I thought. I struck a match and held it up to the object. It was the figure of a woman — the lines smooth and graceful. The talent of this village boy amazes me. Beneath that frail body of his lies a deep and noble heart. I can't help but admire him.

SEPTEMBER 25

An astonishing piece of news! Yesterday, I received a letter from my uncle. Yusuf Cemāl Bey, my aunt, and my uncle — all three of them — are coming here in the spring! The postmark was faded and hard to read, but I'm sure it was sent from Arabia. When I read the letter, I was shocked. I've come to believe now that nothing is impossible in this world. But how? Why are they coming here? And how could my uncle be with them? My uncle — who was always so knowledgeable, so serious, so clever. He had studied for many years in Germany, completed his education there, married there, and had become the director of a large factory. He had gained a reputation and was respected for his economic and scientific articles.

What business could he possibly have in the deserts of Arabia? Now I picture the sandy yard of the school, where we used to gather on Saturday evenings, slipping quietly between the trees to avoid being noticed. We would pull novels and newspapers from our pockets and read them in secret. Sometimes we would even gather for these secret meetings during study hours. And then we would exchange letters — the faint scent of violets still lingering in the paper — or sometimes a lock of hair folded into a note. We would share our stories and laugh or cry over them. Ah, if that sandy yard could speak, how many tears, how many bursts of laughter, how many moments of longing it would reveal!

Sometimes a few of us would pull away from the group and sit alone in a corner. Celāl was always among us. For us, Yusuf Cemāl was an ideal. But Celāl thought of him differently from the rest of us. He used to say:

— "I fear their harsh judgments; I am jealous of his beauty, even from these indifferent people — even from you."

We never understood what he meant. He would grow quiet and make us fall silent too. But sometimes, when we were alone, he would tell me about him. Everyone knew Yusuf Cemāl. He was admired for his books on music and his compositions. He had once taught music lessons, and people of every social class — learned men and illiterate villagers alike, men and women — had attended his classes. Celāl had started attending his classes too during the summer holidays. After that, his admiration for him grew even stronger. He would talk to me endlessly about the beauty of Yusuf Cemāl's voice. And then Celāl left for Cambridge. In his letters from there, he would write about Yusuf Cemāl with intense affection. I even received one letter that was stained with tears. In it, Celāl said that he wanted to travel as far as Arabia just to find him. He wrote of him as an "idol of love" (*aşk mabedi*). Isn't that the nature of love — a force that burns through every heart, hidden or revealed, consuming everything in its path?

OCTOBER 2

New preparations have begun at the farm. Veli Ağa is constantly restless, giving hurried and agitated orders to the servants with his strong hands and his well-worn, black-and-white rodingot. Even the dried branches of the trees are being pruned. Veli Ağa saw him when he went to İzmit — he loves him so much that a glowing flush, a purplish hue, has appeared on his weathered face. It's as if the dream of reunion is shimmering there. My nanny, with her delicate taste, is preparing Yusuf Cemāl's room and bed. Heavy, gold-embroidered curtains are being hung at the windows, and richly colored carpets, untouched for years, are being laid on the floor. Then Zeliha's small, affectionate hands are moving over the silk coverlets on the bed. She brings out small baskets of artificial grapes, bouquets of roses and tulips, and pomegranate blossoms from the cabinet — the little keepsakes left by her grandmother — and carefully places them on the velvet-covered table. All the finest, most adorned objects in the house have been brought into this room. But all these changes — the bright colors, the vibrant air — fill me with a strange and bitter sadness. I feel as though my peace is about to be shattered. Soon, I fear I'll be standing before ruins. Or maybe… maybe I don't know anything at all. Perhaps I am simply running from shadows, dreading nothing.

From inside, I hear Zeliha playing the tambur. Each note flows lightly, gently. Ah, Hicaz! It burns my heart like a blissful sun. Two doves are wandering among the dry acacia leaves above the low pergola whose branches brush against my head. Their damp feathers glisten. The female nestles against the male. They merge together; the male covers her with his wing, hiding her head beneath his neck. He closes his dark eyes and surveys the sky — and me — from beneath his half-closed lids. I search for Zehrā. How I long for her sweet green eyes.

OCTOBER 27

Yesterday, Zeliha had taken Zehrā to the village again. I remember the night only through a haze of fear and unease. It was cold — so cold that it felt as though snow was falling outside. For a while, I watched the stars through the dry leaves at the window, gazing at the cloudy sky. The heavens were so clear, so open, that a strange and wild brightness seemed to spill over the dense trees of the farm. But for the first time, I hated this beautiful place. Apart from Süleyman, a few servants, and an old dog, there was no one else at home. Zeliha, Veli Ağa, and my nanny were all gone. The sound of a bat's fluttering wings and the croaking of a frog made my heart race. Even the dry leaves falling to the ground felt sinister and cursed. I was afraid, like a small child. The chill seemed to seep into my bones, burning my lips and cheeks.

Suddenly, an owl let out a sharp, mournful cry. Trembling, I closed all the windows, drew the heavy curtains shut, and made sure not even a single star could be seen. I lit the fire in the stove and, trying to drown out the dreadful sounds, I covered my ears and lay down on the small green rug. The blue, red, and green flames leapt and scattered with fierce intensity. The golden glow among the roses shimmered and blinded my eyes. In the darkness, pink reflections slid across the polished surface of the oilcloth. The fire hissed and cracked; it seemed as though someone was striking the dying flames with a poker. And I imagined that I could see his beard turning red from the heat once again. It was as if the walnut doors were swinging open and veiled, bashful maidservants in long skirts were entering the room, standing respectfully before withdrawing to the corners of the walls and kneeling. The dogs were howling again. Even after all these years, I felt as though I was sick once more. A thin hand — my grandmother's delicate hand — caressed my forehead and hair.

The howling of the dogs echoed in my ears and reverberated through my fevered brain, swelling with deep, layered echoes. The world seemed to be collapsing around me. It felt as though all life on earth had withered away, leaving behind only these dreadful, haunting cries. The lingering warmth of past fevered days still burned within my soul. I climbed into bed, but I couldn't sleep. I drifted off for a moment, only to wake again. My entire life — every scene, every chapter — unfolded before my eyes, and I wondered: "Had I truly lived through all of this?" And I asked myself the same question over and over again: "What have I gained in this world until now? Nothing."

Days were slipping by, one after the other, drawing me ever closer to old age. The roosters crowed. I heard the sound of bells from our sheep. The dawn was breaking. At last, I heard the footsteps of the shepherd coming to gather the sheep. I got out of bed, dressed, and washed my face. Suddenly, the door burst open, and Zeliha rushed in.

—"Brother! Brother! I brought Zehrā back! Faik Bey, Remziye Hanım, and Hikmet Bey have left. They almost took Zehrā with them — but they've left her here with us! Did you know? It was so sudden! Faik Bey sent you a letter. Let me read it to you."

"My dear son,

I am leaving Zehrā with you for a short time. I am doing this partly for her comfort and partly to keep Remziye happy. Take good care of her — she is very much in need of care. Treat her as you would a helpless orphan. Perhaps I may never return. We are going to Mersin to look after some property. Please don't forget this request from an old man. Farewell, my son. I had hoped to see you before we left, but our departure was sudden. Farewell again."

28 OCTOBER

Yesterday, one of our old neighbors, a landowner, took us to his farm behind the village. Our bodies, worn out from the jostling of the migrant cart, were exhausted from the long journey. We were all thirsty, but as luck would have it, the water from the fountain on the road had stopped running, so we couldn't drink. The landowner's two small children were crying incessantly. Their mother was sweating as she tried to quiet them. Zeliha was helping the poor woman. Zehrā and I sat down on the ground. Just then, a girl wearing blue şalvar and a red yemeni was passing by on the road. For fun, I called out to her. She showed her white teeth, giving us a languid, coquettish look. She made a playful little bow and climbed up the hill. Then she approached us, dropped the bundle hanging from her arm onto the ground, and sat down in front of us. We were both eyeing her teasingly, yet pleased. With casual familiarity, she pressed her injured, dark hand on Zehrā's knee and said playfully:

— "Make a wish, pretty lady. What's your name?"

Zehrā pulled away slightly. The girl didn't care. Rattling the yellow beads around her neck, she spread her broad beans, blue beads, and charms across the cloth in front of her. Then, tilting her head, half-closing her eyes, and swaying flirtatiously, she began to speak:

— "Your star is bright, your heart is big. You're a lady. You have a wish in your heart... but I can't say if it's a matter of love or something else. But don't worry about it. Just place a few petals from a 'seven-bloom rose' under your pillow at night."

At this, we both burst into laughter and asked:

— "Why?"

The gypsy girl, holding one of her bare feet with one hand and running the other over the beans and beads scattered on the ground, frowned and said:

— "Oh… It's a charm. But do as you wish!"

Then, adding the phrase that's often customary in these kinds of fortunes, she said:

— "And you have a traveler coming from across the sea!"

Zehrā smiled bitterly:

— "I have no one. You're just making it up for nothing," she said.

The girl laughed again. She took her hand off her foot and rubbed her shining black eyes. Then she gathered her things, swung the bundle over her shoulder, put her hand on her hip in that famous gypsy way, and walked away. At that moment, I leaned toward Zehrā's ear and said:

—"Your aunt is coming."

Her face turned pale. It was as if a long-forgotten, neglected part of her soul had suddenly been revived—half distressed, half joyful.

29 OCTOBER

Tonight, we were sitting by the fountain. The weather, which had started to cool down significantly, granted us a rare and pleasant evening—so mild and sweet that it almost felt like spring. The three of us were half-asleep in our chairs. At one point, thinking I was asleep, Zehrā pulled her chair next to Zeliha's. I took advantage of her assumption and stayed completely still. Zehrā said:

"Zeliha, I have something to tell you. I feel such an extraordinary sensation within myself… This morning, which is unusual for me, I woke up at dawn. From the stillness of the air, I could hear the faint sound of the ezan coming from the village minaret. It felt as though my heart was being cleansed at the edge of a divine sea, preparing itself for a great love. All of the waking heavens were singing of love to me. Ancient melodies, as though from a heavenly guitar, were pouring out and calling to my heart. I wonder who is playing this guitar of love? I sense an extraordinariness in my hands, my eyes—especially in my heart, which seems to have caught a newly kindled fire. And I find myself bowing in reverence to this fire, crying in surrender."

Ah, Zehrā—if only you were mine!…

6 JANUARY

The whole farm is buried under snow. The ice chandeliers hanging from the trees are so beautiful. This morning, the sun peeking through the clouds was shining brilliantly. A dazzling light gave the cotton-white landscape a new kind of beauty. The three of us, caught up in a big snowball fight, managed to knock poor Süleyman to the ground. After nearly a month and a half without sunlight, today's sunshine brought us a little extra joy. Toward evening, we grabbed our coats and headed toward the pine woods. We stayed outside until quite late, making the most of the brightness reflected off the snow, and only returned home well after dark. For the past two months, our days have passed in a monotonous rhythm—either playing chess or reading books. But I'm not complaining. Even if I'm not in Zehrā's heart, at least I'm by her side. Everything is white. Every day, as I watch the snow falling in handfuls, I feel as though spring will never come again.

APRIL 1

They have arrived…

APRIL 15

It was the first of April. A light rain had fallen. A fresh, delicate fragrance filled the entire farm.

Everything had been washed clean. Small streams were flowing down from the mountains, and the soft sound of trickling water could be heard everywhere. When I saw him standing before me, I couldn't collect myself. It was as though I had been reborn, as though I had never witnessed any trace of existence on earth before and was opening my eyes for the first time. For a moment, I was intoxicated. Only after some time did I begin to awaken from this stupor and truly see my surroundings. His divine eyes, commanding with infinite grandeur, and his majestic figure, towering above everyone else—he seemed as though he had been created to be the qibla of love (*aşkın kıblesi*).

APRIL 18

I've been watching Zehrā grow more pale and withered day by day over the past eighteen days.

There is a truth I'm afraid to admit to myself: I fear that he will take Zehrā away from me. My aunt has changed so much. She is almost a shadow of herself. Yet love—and especially love of this intensity—instills in a person the feeling of reverence, compelling one to bow in worship. There is such purity and divinity in her affection that I no longer dare to recall any of my previous notions of devotion. My mind cannot grasp the mystery of it.

I said, "She's like a shadow of him."

Yes, because there isn't even a trace of selfishness or *beşeriyet* in her love. She exists entirely within the beloved. In her, there is nothing but the name, the qualities, and the image of the one she worships. As for my uncle, I can't believe my eyes. What has become of the pride of this majestic man? Yet perhaps, only now, he has truly approached humanity. What was that greatness before! He was certainly a knowledgeable man, but that knowledge had been carved into stone. Zehrā was nowhere to be seen that day. We started to worry. For a while, Zeliha and I couldn't even think where Zehrā might have gone. My aunt, too, upon arriving at the farm, first concerned herself with Yusuf Cemāl's comfort. About fifteen minutes later, she asked about Zehrā. I checked her room. She wasn't there. We searched all the rooms in the house and the courtyards, but she was nowhere to be found.

At last, I thought of asking Bibi where she might be. The old dog led us forward. It stopped in front of the gardener's hut among the bushes in the garden. It wagged its tail and reared up impatiently, as if trying to turn the handle of the door. I opened the door. They were both kneeling on the ground in the hay. Zehrā had her hands covering her face and was crying. Her friend was sitting beside her, trying to console her. Zeliha saw us, jumped up, and threw herself around my aunt's neck. Zehrā also stood up. There was a pale, tragic expression on her face. Her delicate cheeks were wet with tears. I had never seen her so shattered, so distressed. She still stood apart, like a stranger. My aunt walked toward her and stroked her hair. Zehrā, her eyes closed, kept weeping silently. My aunt was her usual self—so natural, so composed, it was almost astonishing. There was no space left within her for another affection; she was completely consumed by this one.

That evening, a few people from the village, upon hearing that the Prophet of Love (yes, that's what they're calling him now—Zehrā and Zeliha gave him this name. My aunt had scolded them for it. But now everyone says it. Even I slipped and said it once, though I had been avoiding it), came to visit him.

Among them was a mayor from Istanbul who had known him years ago. Three of them were officers from Istanbul who had known him since their school days. In total, there were five people. But the most remarkable visitor was a gardener woman. Because this poor woman had only seen him once—fifteen years ago, when she was a child in the village. One day, as he passed by, he had said to her, "How are you, beautiful gardener?" That was all. Yet for fifteen years, this woman had carried his love in her heart. For fifteen years, she had been unable to forget the person who once asked after her well-being. She said with such innocence that she had been longing ever since and could no longer bear it, so she finally came to see him.

Her bare feet were in tattered shoes, her dress was torn. But love bestowed a kind of holiness upon all of it. Oh, great and life-giving love; what ruins and what palaces you create. How many of the dead you bring to life in an instant. When the Prophet of Love appeared, she ran toward him, forgetting herself, and threw her arms around his neck. Tears were flowing from her eyes. She cried so beautifully that it made us cry as well.

Ah, here I am speaking of him again. Yet I am afraid of him. Zehrā's cheeks grow paler by the day.

True, Zehrā behaves coldly toward him. But this coldness is not as intense as it was in the early days. And I see the true meaning of surrender in this very coldness. It is enough that she once called him the Prophet of Love. But that gardener woman drew my attention. To be so grateful and devoted for a single "How are you?"—how remarkable. One of the reasons why Yusuf Cemāl binds people to himself with such devotion is because this attachment is extraordinarily genuine and profound.

Let me describe the state of the gardener woman and the reverence she evoked in us through a sublime metaphor by the

Italian poet D'Annunzio[194]. D'Annunzio is not handsome, yet women love him with a devotion akin to worship. In this context, D'Annunzio compares love to a king. When this king is forced to spend the night in a poor hut while traveling through his realm, suddenly this humble hut gains significance and becomes a place of pilgrimage. But are the visitors coming to see the hut, or are they coming for the king who stayed there? Likewise, what we revere in this poor gardener is not her worn shoes or her tattered jacket, but rather the King of Love who resides within her.

APRIL 19

My flute (*kaval*) lies on the ground, resting its head against the grass, exhausted and weary. I don't know why it seems so sorrowful. I try to play it, but it refuses to sing. A little while ago, I had taken down the Rubaiyyat of Omar Khayyam[195] from the library—it's lying there, too. After five years of weariness with reading, I find myself turning to it again. I need something to distract myself. But Khayyam speaks to me of such distant things. He speaks of things as if a great, magnificent fire had been lit in the middle of the world— its reflection cast out in every direction. And Khayyam tries to speak to me of these reflections. But if you put your hand on these shadows, your palm will not burn.

---

194 Gabriele D'Annunzio (1863–1938) was an Italian poet, playwright, and novelist, known for his influential role in Italian literature and politics. A leading figure in the Decadent movement, his works combined sensuality, nationalism, and aestheticism.

195 The *Rubaiyyat* is a collection of quatrains (four-line verses) attributed to the Persian poet, mathematician, and astronomer Omar Khayyam (1048–1131). Khayyam's poetry reflects themes of love, mortality, and the fleeting nature of life, often with a philosophical and sometimes skeptical tone.

Yes, color is the form of the universe's shape and order—but where is the majestic heat of the original fire? Where are these dim heavens? Wine, the cup, eternity—they are beautiful. But where can I find them, and how? And according to what I have only recently come to understand— Oh Khayyam, it is not as you say! "What am I?" you say. "Nothing!" But you are not nothing. How can a being become nothing? You don't yet grasp the true meaning of existence.

I slam the book shut with force. I pick up my flute again. My flute—my companion of seven years— speak to me. But it will not sing what I seek. After a few breaths, I throw it into the grass— my companion for so long— and I stomp on it and break it beneath my feet. Then I wander alone among the trees, agitated.

MAY 2

The living being that made me break my flute (*kaval*) and tear Khayyam's book to shreds—it was him. There's such a power in his voice, in his gaze—whether it's a stone or a human being, whatever he touches, he sets it aflame. Then I start to notice—he neglects no one. He's so involved with everyone, so intimately connected— I can't comprehend how a single being can care so deeply, so genuinely, about so many people. Yet he's most engaged with me. And at the same time, he never forgets Süleyman's cough from across the room. I take pleasure in speaking with him. After every conversation, I feel as though I have learned something new.

MAY 13

The wedding was before dawn; Yusuf Cemāl, Zehrā, Zeliha, and I went all the way to the forest.

We stood beneath the trees blooming in the spring. The Prophet of Love began playing on the violin a waltz of his own composition— The Birth of Love. At times, he also sang. Truly, it was an extraordinary voice. Had he kept singing, we would all have fainted. The sun was just beginning to rise, slowly appearing at the point where the clouds met. The Birth of Love had ended. But the scene and the melody were so perfectly in harmony— we were all utterly entranced. I was lost in my own thoughts when a sudden sob broke the silence, jolting me awake. Beside me, I felt a sudden movement— Zehrā, sobbing, had thrown herself at the feet of the Prophet of Love. With her whole being, Zehrā had now declared her love. I turned my head away and closed my eyes. I walked away from the scene toward the mansion— alone, utterly alone.

I will not write another word in this notebook.

Perhaps I will even burn it.

But isn't it strange? Now a voice from my heart asks: What did you ever see in the Prophet of Love besides beauty? Tell me— Didn't he fill your path with armfuls of flowers and offer you their fragrance? Wasn't it from him that we learned perfection? Didn't he teach us that beauty and virtue exist in this world? What more do you want?

It was a warm July night in the East—Under the broad, radiant sky, a small gathering of four or five people sat around the large fountain. The Prophet of Love sat beside a small, beautiful girl with green eyes on the same couch. From a gilded green cup in his hand, he would occasionally take a sip of lemon balm sherbet, then slowly lift the cup to the lips of the fair-haired girl, whispering as he let her drink. Four others sat nearby, all seated on the ground. Zeliha was resting her elbow on the marble edge of the fountain, staring at the full, still circle of the moon. Silent white swans floated by, sometimes scattering the golden reflection. Then, for a moment, the rippling water would shimmer with small golden flashes, and the moon would appear fractured, trembling as if it were melting. Sühā was there too, his pale, undefined gaze lost in the distance. He sat quietly on the flowerbed, as though he were asleep. The Prophet of Love was lost in thought. He had wrapped his arm around Zehrā's slender waist and slowly whispered into her ear:

— "Will you leave? Where will you go? I came for you."

— "You came for me? That's as impossible as this magnificent sun descending to the earth!"

His breath was burning the young girl's face. Zehrā wanted to pull away, to escape— but he held her by the waist, grasping her hands. The Prophet of Love was so powerful tonight!

— "So, you want to leave the Prophet of Love? Then who will bring me my sherbet?"

— "My mother used to bring it before. From now on, Zeliha will bring it."

— "No, Zehrā, no. I am not as disloyal (*vefasız*) as you think."

***

The Prophet of Love had been born in a village in Rumelia, on the delicate soil where songs are eternally composed. Yet, his temperament was like that of a desert child— fiery and unyielding. He was such a reckless troublemaker that no one could control him. But because he was so charming and lovable, people had no choice but to endure his mischief and give in to him. He could not be contained within the narrow confines of a house— he would wander through the open air, and through these wanderings, he managed to torment half the village with his mischief.

And yet, there were many who would stand at their doors each morning, waiting for him with bowed heads, as though they were in need of his presence. The village girls, especially the older ones, fell in love with him— they longed to lead him to secluded places. The Prophet of Love stayed in that village until he was nine years old. Then his father, an Istanbul native, brought him to Istanbul to attend school. His school years in Istanbul were long. The Prophet of Love was adored by his classmates. There were those who endured his many cruelties without complaint. He was met with longing wherever he went— he was always met with love.

Love had emerged into existence just to behold him, and in doing so, had become captivated by him. The Prophet of Love sat on an invisible throne, woven from the hearts of those enamored with him, and he wore a crown forged from the fire of love.

It was a "Navy Night."[196] All the neighbors from the farm had gathered, and they had organized a grand festivity at the farm, primarily in honor of the esteemed composer. Colorful fireworks and çarhı felek (spinning wheels of light) were igniting in the garden. The musicians played, sometimes national melodies and songs, sometimes beautiful waltzes. The shapes of the Japanese lanterns glowing among the trees made the farm resemble a dreamland. Boats decorated with flowers floated on the lake. Zehrā was sitting alone on the balcony. The sky was clear and cloudless. Even the clouds (*sahābe*) were visible above. She was indifferent to all these lights and melodies. She was thinking about her mother. Why was she so sorrowful again?

There she was—lying on the cushion, playing with the hair on her forehead. But the blue-embroidered red pillow was not under her head this time. Suddenly, the balcony door opened. Suzān entered with her thoughtful gaze, her eyes fixed on Zehrā:

— "Why are you sitting there all alone?" she said. "Go sit with the Prophet of Love."

— "Mother, let me be. I can see everything so beautifully from here."

— "No. Go upstairs and watch from there. Go on!"

Zehrā lowered her head. She went to the hall. She had no desire to go upstairs. A small, faint lantern was burning in the hallway. Shadows curled on the heavy curtains and the walls. Her body was weary. She lay down on the couch there. The sound of the fireworks and the overall commotion was blending with the sound of a violin:

"There is no desire left for love in that bright dawn,
There is another life on this pale, moonlit earth,
The dew and the nightingales remain in their old place,

------

196 Celebrations held with flags, lights, and fireworks on festive days.

While gray hair scatters sunlight upon my love."[197]

The music seeped through the floorboards and spread throughout her entire body. She heard footsteps again on the soft carpet. Her mother was coming. A moment later, Suzān commanded her with a stern and forceful gaze:

— "Zehrā, go upstairs immediately."

Everyone in the house had either gathered by the windows or gone out into the garden, or lined the side of the road. There was no one else around. They climbed the stairs together in the dark. The Prophet of Love, the large and imposing figure, was sitting by the window. Zeliha was beside him. When Zehrā saw Zeliha, she insisted on leaving. But it was one of The Prophet of Love's most intense and fervent nights. Sometimes he would wake, fiddling with the prayer beads in his hand; other times, he would gently stroke Zehrā's hair.

The music stopped for a moment. From afar, the sound of a tambur filled the air—intoxicated, restless. The majestic and powerful strains of love, with a searing star burning above it, seemed to kiss the fresh lips of a young girl and drip love into her, note by note. Suddenly, The Prophet of Love gripped Zehrā's shoulder.

— "Do you like this peşrev?" he asked.

It was as if she answered, "I was living within its melodies. I am composed of its songs, of its essence." They walked toward the pavilion, as far as the lake. Along the path, under the tired glow of the fireworks and the moonlight, the Prophet of Love whispered to the young girl:

— "You are the star of my heart!"

The fountain was still cascading with colorful waters. The *sabā* star was still rising toward the sky. The next morning, a

---

197 "Yoktur emeli aşkın o parlak seherinde, Var başka hayat arzın o solgun kamerinde/Şebnemleri, bülbülleri hep eski yerinde, Kır saçları sevdama güneşler saçıyorken" Composer: Nasibin Mehmet Yürü (d. 1953)

cold autumn sun shyly entered Zehrā and Zeliha's disheveled room. Both of them were half-naked—one was rubbing her eyes in bed, while the other was brushing her hair in front of the mirror. Zeliha got out of bed, rubbing her eyes:

— "Zehrā, I saw The Prophet of Love in my dream," she said. "He repeated what he told me last night—and he pinned a fragrant flower to my chest, one I've never seen before."

Zehrā curled her lips. She lifted the ribbon of her gown, which had slipped from her round, pink shoulder.

— "What did he say last night?" she asked.

— "Nothing… nothing important! He said, 'You are the star of my heart."

Zehrā blushed and brushed her hair a bit too harshly. Strands of golden hair fell onto the marble floor. At that moment, Zeliha began singing as she opened the shutters. The wind scattered her hair in every direction. A sparrow perched in the window, chirping to its mate, suddenly flew away. Zeliha continued singing as she watered the violets. They went out into the garden. The sun had risen high. Dew shimmered on the damp soil; clear, pure droplets trembled on the evening primroses.

The Prophet of Love's windows were tightly shut. The curtains were still drawn, even though every morning, he would wake them by throwing pebbles at the window. Suddenly, there was a faint movement behind one of the green curtains. Zehrā's heart began to pound painfully. She left Zeliha behind and ran off, disappearing into the laurel bushes. From that incident onward, Zehrā began to stay close to The Prophet of Love. Yet, she seemed more distant and withdrawn than before, as if she were trying to hide herself from everyone at the estate. It was one evening. The ferryman, Ahmed Ağa, who always awaited the orders of The Prophet of Love was growing impatient.

Even though the moon had risen high in the sky, no one had arrived yet. Why were they late tonight? Ahmed Ağa's dark purple clothes blended in with the cushions of the boat so well that he was almost indistinguishable from the seating. He sat motionless for a while, watching the round ripples made by the fish diving and surfacing in the calm waters. Still, there was no one in sight. Ahmed Ağa took off his cap and embroidered jacket and laid them on the boat's cushions. He rolled up his sleeves and began washing the boat with water from the stream. When he sat down again, a group of ducks had gathered around the boat. He pulled a piece of bread from his small pouch, crumbled it, and tossed it to the ducks. Then, he started rowing idly along the stream. This matter of military service was troubling. If he left, what would happen to his wife and children? Finally, he spotted Behice coming toward him, holding a bouquet of flowers in her arms.

— "Where are they?" he asked.

— "Only one person is coming tonight," Behice said.

Ahmed Ağa felt disappointed. What had happened to the beautiful couple he had rowed across the water so many times? He took a long drink of water from his pitcher. Behice handed him the bouquet.

— "Put these somewhere nice," she said.

Ahmed Ağa took the bouquet and decorated the boat with the flowers. That night, the Prophet of Love rowed alone. As for Zehrā—she stayed in her room, clutching her chest and secretly weeping. The roses were fading. Zehrā could no longer hide her state of mind. The whole world seemed to burn with the love of the Prophet of Love. Everything except him seemed to be dissolving at an alarming speed. Zehrā knew that if she didn't see him, she would not be able to go on. It was another night. About twenty minutes away from the estate, the waves of the sea were gently lapping at the shore, caressing the sand under the delicate glow of the moonlight. The deep sound of the water hitting the sand seemed to echo an eternal hymn of love in peaceful reverence. A young girl wrapped in a shawl wandered timidly along the shore, not even feeling the cool waves lapping at her feet. She seemed to be waiting for someone. Five minutes later, a handsome figure approached her with quick strides. His luminous face shone so brightly that it seemed as though he was casting light toward the hills. The young girl walked toward him. The young man took her hands in his, bringing his face close to hers:

— "My love," he said, "I came for you."

The young girl wavered, twice overcome by the scent of roses and the burning heat of his breath. They walked a few steps further. A small white sailboat was resting nearby on the calm sea, bathed in the soft light of the moon, as if it too were intoxicated with love. The Prophet of Love took Zehrā's hand and helped her into the boat. They sat side by side. The Prophet of Love placed his arm around Zehrā's shoulder. Slowly, the boat drifted away from the shore. The village lights faded one by one, and the quiet sea stretched wide and open beneath them.

— "My dear Zehrā," he said, "have you figured out who played that heavenly guitar, the one calling you to love?"

Zehrā, still in awe, replied, — "How did you know about that?"

He smiled.

— "Is there no connection between your heart and mine?" he said. "I heard it from you."

The Prophet of Love held Zehrā's heart with the kind of gentle authority that only love could give.

Zehrā was completely intoxicated that night. The spring breeze, the sound of the water, the moonlight, and the sea—all of them whispered of his love.

— "The moon looks so pale tonight," she said.

— "Why, my dear Zehrā? I don't know why," he answered.

But Zehrā knew. Since the moment she had seen The Prophet of Love's beautiful face, the moon had paled and lost its brilliance. Yet she couldn't say it out loud. Then, a moment arrived when love completely overtook the small white sailboat, leaving no corner untouched by its fire. The Prophet of Love released the rudder. The boat, now surrendered entirely to love, drifted toward the boundless horizon on its own.

-4-

ZEHRĀ'S DIARY

Why do you keep circling around me like this? What are you looking for here with that burning voice of yours? Where did you come from with the divine fire in your eyes? Sometimes I find myself lost in the distance, seeing nothing but you. Sometimes I feel my heart trembling with agitation. I try to distract myself by turning my eyes toward the moon, toward the delicate stream descending from the mountains, toward the blue stars scattered across the sky. But my heart refuses to listen. It finds the moon dull and lifeless, the rose blooming in spring flawed and imperfect, the rushing stream beneath me unworthy of even a glance. And when I look within myself, I find my heart disturbed by the thought of you. All of existence—the heavens and the earth—speaks to me of you in a burning language. The breeze that comes at dawn is filled with the scent of you, heavy with the fullness of your love.

Since the moment I saw you, the world has lost its color. I can no longer look at the rising sun or the stars that light up the night. Because I have breathed the sacred air touched by your breath, the air that was enflamed by the heat of your body, made entirely of love. I can no longer smell the rose that blooms in spring. Everywhere I turn, I feel that burning sensation again. And when you leave my side, my hands, my eyes—every atom of my body— burns. I almost believe that I, myself, am turning into fire. Ah, it is fire indeed. Let those who doubt it touch it just once.

I can no longer find Zehrā in the light of your love. You are the scent of her soul. You are her body and her essence. You are the fragrance of her love. What remains of me now, my love? Take all of me. Leave nothing behind that could attach me to anything but you. Ah, but leave this heart untouched—because you reside there. The shepherd? Yes, I love the shepherd. Because in some way, he resembles the one I love. When I see him tending his flock at night beneath the delicate light of the crescent moon, my heart trembles. I imagine my beloved standing at the head of the flock of love, resembling the moon itself. Just now, I opened my journal to read about that sacred night, the night of the festival when we first touched. I knelt with reverence and began to read. How much I have changed since then. I was so strong back then.

Listen, listen—there is nothing left for me in this world but you. In the room where we met, I lit the candle again just now. As I approached the bed, I was filled with the hope that I might see you there. For a while, I stood and stared. When I could not see you, I blew out the candle and tried to see you through the darkness, without sight. Why, why did you not appear before my eyes as clearly as you appear in my heart? What happened to the moon tonight? Why is there only one star beside it? What happened to the magnificent moon that every night used to be surrounded by thousands of beautiful stars? Tonight, there is only a single star at its side. The whole sky is filled with light. Deep in the heavens, all the other stars have gone dark. Only those two, lost in their own world, have surrendered to love.

***

Sühā had gone down to Istanbul one morning to handle some orders from Zehrā and Zeliha. On the second day of her arrival, after wandering through several shops, she was walking toward the train station, exhausted. On the way, she ran into Fahri, one of her old high school friends. Back then, he had been pale and thin—a frail figure. But now, the man standing in front of Sühā was completely transformed—a well-dressed, stout man with a solid presence. The difference between the sickly boy she remembered and this self-assured figure was striking. Yet Fahri thought that Sühā had not changed at all. Indeed, the pure and carefree innocence in Sühā's eyes had not yet faded.

They walked together for a while. The sky was dark, and a fierce wind was blowing. Clouds of dust rose from the street, and brittle yellow leaves spun constantly in the air. Everyone was running, urged on by the storm, trying to avoid getting caught in the rain. Fahri mentioned that he was working in commerce now. His manner had gained a sense of control and confidence. He no longer had the quiet, hesitant demeanor of his youth. Money and the comforts of life had likely softened and pleased him.

As they were reminiscing about the past, a small memory involving Celāl came up. One day, the three of them had skipped their geography class together. But they had been caught behind the water barrels. The punishment they received at the time had felt so bitter. However, Fahri's tone when he spoke about Celāl was slightly different—there was a note of doubt, almost hesitation in his voice. Sühā began to wonder if Celāl had fallen ill. Curious, he asked about him. But Fahri's gaze was distracted, following the fluttering hem of a dark-haired woman's coat as it caught the wind, revealing glimpses of her legs. He answered absentmindedly, almost without thinking:

— "Celāl died of heart failure on a ship voyage about a week ago."

Sühā was stunned—shocked into disbelief, paralyzed by grief and horror. His mind spun. He couldn't accept it. Dear

God! They had spent so much of their lives together. The warmth of their blood had mingled over the years. How could Celāl suddenly be torn away from life? It felt as though half of his soul had been ripped away. His own voice sounded foreign—distant and strange—as he asked:

— "Fahri, can you tell me more?"

Fahri was now guiding him toward a candy shop. Sühā looked at him with surprise:

— "What are we going to do here?" he asked.

Fahri was eyeing the sweets in the glass display case:

— "Don't you feel the cold? The wind is about to blow us away. Let's sit down here—we can talk and have something to eat."

This response upset Sühā even more. He stood still, but Fahri took his arm and gently pulled him toward the door. He forced him inside. Sühā felt a deep sense of disgust toward Fahri — his eyes, his mouth, his body repulsed him. Outside, the sea was raging and foaming, darkened by rebellion. The rain hovered in the sky, gathering like tears that well up in moments of sorrow but never fall. Fahri sat there, eating candy while recounting the story:

— "We were traveling together on the Medaniye. It was around midnight. I had just drifted off to sleep after struggling to fall asleep because of the storm and the shaking of the ship. Suddenly, someone started pounding on the door. I opened it — a worker was standing there, telling me that Celāl was ill. I rushed to his cabin. His heart was failing. He lasted only about half an hour. The next day, we buried him in a cemetery near Medaniye."

Fahri suddenly remembered something and paused:

— "Oh, it's really good that I ran into you. Celāl had entrusted me with a message for you just before he died. While he was dying, he said — wait, let me get this right — yes, he said:

— "If you see Sühā, tell him that if I die without ever meeting Yusuf Cemāl Bey, my eyes will remain open even in death. Tell him not to remove me from his heart. By the way, Sühā, who is this Yusuf Cemāl Bey anyway? What a strange kid."

The story of Celāl's death, told between mouthfuls of candy and while ogling a woman's legs exposed by the wind, pierced Sühā's heart like an arrow. It was as though he had been pulled back into childhood. The school, the garden, the sandpit — all of it came rushing back, burning his eyes. Yet now, he could no longer bear the weight of those distant memories — the relics of days long past. Half of those memories had already been swallowed by death. That day was a heavy, bitter one for Sühā. When he returned to the farm, his eyes were swollen and red from tears, and his heart felt weak, as though it had grown weary from beating. After dinner that evening, the Prophet of Love summoned Sühā. He was standing beneath the arbor, bathed in moonlight. That night, his figure seemed taller than ever. His body stood erect with an almost regal grandeur. In his eyes shone the divine sun — the sun that ruled over splendor and enchantment. He was wearing a long black cloak that flowed behind him. His face was almost too brilliant to behold. He stood motionless. In his presence, one could not help but feel diminished — as if afraid of being consumed by his radiance. And Sühā — poor, broken Sühā — was already weighed down by the bleakness and grief of that terrible day. The tasteless recounting of Celāl's death — told while eating candy and distractedly eyeing a woman — had left his soul in tatters.

Now, standing before this great prophet of love, whose heart seemed to radiate warmth and light, Sühā could not imagine anything more sacred than the devotion that poured from his heart. The Prophet of Love knew all of Sühā's sorrow and fragility. He was tender and compassionate. With his soft, comforting hand, he gently stroked Sühā's hair. Then, with his always measured and profound voice — a voice that seemed to speak directly to the soul — he said:

— "Sühā," Then, lowering his beautiful voice, filling it with a trembling harmony that resonated deep within the heart, he repeated:— "Sühā?"

Sühā remained calm, yet the weight of Celāl's death still pressed upon him. The Prophet of Love suggested they take a walk together. The sky was entirely blanketed with heavy clouds. Lightning flashed frequently, and the sky roared with thunder. The trees creaked under the force of the wind. All of this fury — this intensity of the elements — mirrored the turmoil that Sühā felt inside over Celāl's death. And yet, amidst the storm, the Prophet of Love stood even more strikingly beautiful. His magnificence became more pronounced, his grandeur more radiant. Sühā held an electric lantern in his hand as they walked side by side, talking aimlessly as they wandered toward "Kör Irmak" — the Blind Stream. It was quite a distance from the farm, nestled between two small hills. Long ago, the stream had flowed freely, but now it resembled a dry cave. The rocks, once shaped and hollowed by the stream's relentless flow, bore such intricate patterns and delicate forms that even the most gifted artist might have spent years trying to recreate them.

The Prophet of Love was captivated by the place.

— "How beautiful! How beautiful!" he murmured.

The moon had freed itself from the clouds, casting its golden net over the earth once again. The storm had softened; some of the clouds had become so thin that they seemed on the verge of dissolving into the night sky. One feared even to disturb these delicate carvings, these intricate patterns, with their gaze.

— "What is this place, Sühā?"

"The villagers call it Kör Irmak (*blind stream*)," Sühā replied. "There used to be a stream here once — it dried up."

The Prophet of Love suddenly interrupted him.

— "Listen, Sühā, listen! … A sound — can you hear it?"

Indeed, a sound could be heard — the gentle trickling of water. They moved toward the direction of the sound. Tiny drops of water were seeping through the rocks, one by one. Sühā gazed from the water to the Prophet of Love, whose imposing figure seemed beloved not only by the mountains but also by the heavens themselves. My God, Sühā thought. Could it be that this water, reviving the Blind Stream, was responding to the touch of his fiery, vibrant presence — his love itself? Sühā had never seen anything so beautiful. But this grace, this enchantment, wasn't confined to his physical beauty alone. Where did this fire come from? It couldn't be merely the beauty of his form. There was such an extraordinary force in him that it pulled one away from earthly sensations, washing their face and eyes with the waters of a divine waterfall, casting them into the fiery horizons of an undiscovered, sacred valley.

— "What beautiful water — so clear, so vibrant!"

They stood there for a while longer, listening to the delicate melody of the water. Its soft sound was irresistible. The Prophet of Love said:

— "Water… What a beautiful thing! We've been listening to its sound for a while now — have we grown tired of it?"

They left the cave. But instead of taking the usual path, they decided to cut across the mountain for a shorter route. Halfway through, a cliff appeared before them. The Prophet of Love crossed the cliff in a single leap and reached out his hand to Sühā. But Sühā's pride was wounded — he couldn't bring himself to accept the outstretched hand. Instead, he jumped on his own. His foot caught in a bundle of thorns. He barely managed to grab hold of a rock. He nearly fell all the way down. The Prophet of Love took him by the hand and pulled him up. But Sühā struggled to stand because his knee was badly injured.

***

A few weeks had passed since then. Sühā sat on the Fire Rock. A cold wind mixed with rain blew through the air, and the sound of the 'Traveler's Fountain' drifted toward him. Ah, military service! So Sühā was going to serve in the military. He was deeply unsettled by this departure, whose end was uncertain. It had already been three days since they had left. A deep silence and mourning had settled over the land. And Zehrā... Zehrā now seemed to have lost much of the commanding influence of her identity. Though they shared a spiritual familiarity, she had become merely a shadow of herself. Sühā sat alone, lost in thought. The women he had loved — or rather, the women he had aspired to love — seemed to flicker and fade like sparks of light, vanishing as quickly as they appeared. Even Zehrā, whom he had felt closest to, had left much of his heart empty without even realizing it. He was bound to her by an indescribable affection, a profound sense of closeness — yet it didn't quite resemble love.

Why was he so sorrowful tonight? There was a difficult-to-define pain in his heart — a wound. But where had this wound been inflicted? For a moment, he felt an urge to go as far as the "Kör Irmak." Why did he feel this? Why wasn't he even aware of it? If only the Prophet of Love hadn't left! He was surprised to hear himself say this aloud, in the silence of his surroundings. But the desire that arose from his heart was impossible to resist.

If only he hadn't left! There was something in his voice, his words, his face that soothed Sühā, that cleansed his soul. But now he felt utterly alone. He had no one. Slowly, he stood up.

Hoping to find some comfort, he decided to visit Zeliha's room. He found Zeliha sitting by the window, perched on a chair. Her face was pale — it was clear that she hadn't been able to sleep. Sühā knew, deep down, that Zeliha had given her heart to the Prophet of Love.

Why?

Why does everyone love him so much?

From what Sühā had heard, there were many people who loved him with such passion. At that moment, his eyes fell upon Zehrā's bed. It lay in the corner, covered. In this room, filled with so many memories, it was perhaps Zeliha's eyes — silently speaking of the most vivid memory of all — that stood out the most. Without looking back, Sühā left the room. The next day, Sühā was on his way to Istanbul, with his papers in his pocket. As he passed by the Traveler's Fountain (*yolcu çeşmesi*), his steps slowed. He half-expected to see that dark-clothed peasant woman with the lightning-patterned shawl again — and he could almost hear her old words repeating in his mind. The weather was cold — bitterly cold. The clouds sometimes parted, allowing thin streams of light to filter through, but rain still fell intermittently. Sühā pulled up the collar of his coat. An old street dog followed him, sometimes lagging behind, sometimes rushing ahead. Its fur was soaked, the dust and dirt on its coat now mixed into muddy streaks. Its tongue hung out, and its eyes looked weak and tired. Where was it going? Why was it running like this?

As Sühā crossed the Çağlayan Bridge, he slipped his hands into his pockets. Suddenly, his fingers brushed against something cold and smooth — it was an envelope. He pulled it out and examined it. But just as he did, a strong gust of wind swept the envelope from his hand and flung it into the water. Sühā rushed toward the shore. The envelope had lodged itself against a rock. He waded into the shallow water, pushing down his walking stick for support, and retrieved the envelope. The writing on it had bled and blurred, the ink washed away. He sat down on a moss-covered rock at the base of a tree and pinned the envelope to the stone to dry.

His mind began to wander.

Death?

He had never truly examined the idea of death before. It seemed impossible. No… Sühā couldn't die. How could someone who was alive, who could feel, who could love — simply die? It was impossible. After all, his heart was still beating. His eyes could see the flow of the water, the trembling leaves falling from the trees. Death was nothing more than an unreachable mirage. As he was lost in these thoughts, his hand began to dig into the wet dirt at his feet. His finger caught on a shard of glass, cutting him. Blood dripped onto the ground. He dipped his hand into the water, washing the wound, and then wrapped his finger with a handkerchief. When he reached the front of the office, an old man was sweeping away the muddy streams and fallen leaves. He paused as Sühā passed by, almost as if he were waiting for something. Then, without saying a word, he resumed sweeping, splattering Sühā's coat with mud. Inside, men in tattered uniforms hurried up and down the staircase. Sühā remained indifferent. On the second floor, the hallway outside the commander's office was crowded with people. A weak electric light flickered above them, casting a dim glow down the dark corridor. Sühā approached the crowd.

A steward sat behind the door, yawning as he wound his watch. He stood there for a while — nearly half an hour — waiting. Finally, he was called inside. He handed the envelope to the pasha sitting at the desk. The man was large-bodied and somewhat casual in his manner. His pale yellow eyes studied Sühā carefully. He seemed like a good man — there was no trace of military harshness in his demeanor. With the care of a jeweler handling fine gems, he adjusted his glasses. He tore open the envelope with his plump fingers and began to examine the writing. A fly buzzed near his ear. He slapped it dead with a casual flick of his hand. Tossing his cap to the back of his head, he thought for a moment. Then, placing the paper down on the green felt of the desk, he gave Sühä a detached, almost indifferent look — glancing at him from head to toe. He lit a cigarette. Sühä stood silently, absentmindedly kicking at the dust gathered at the foot of the iron stove. In a week, he would be deployed to the Erzurum front. The restless, agitated crowd outside was growing more impatient. They were now knocking at the door. At that moment, large snowflakes began to fall. Two stray birds landed outside on the window ledge. The commander, as if suddenly reminded of a more pressing matter, slipped the paper into a drawer. Adjusting his glasses once more, he called toward the door:

— "Come in."

Of course, that also meant: "You may leave."

When Sühä found himself back on the street, everything was covered in white. The air had thickened with snow. Snowflakes stung his eyes. It was so cold that the wind burned his face and hands. It was over now. In a day or two, he would become a soldier — completely. Perhaps he would never return. His former lightness of spirit was entirely gone. It was as though he had emerged from beneath the ruins of a collapsed building, newly born into a life of pain after a long, unconscious slumber. His whole body ached; his soul was steeped in melancholy.

Ah, the world was unbearably harsh and cruel.

The lights from the shop windows scattered strange reflections on the snow-covered roads. His face and wrists were covered in melting, icy snow. He kept walking for a while like this. Without realizing it, he had arrived at Karaköy. It was getting late; it was time to find a place to sleep. The closest place was Beyoğlu. He boarded the funicular. Inside, a white-haired woman dressed in mourning attire was shaking the snow from her hat. Beside her, a blond, irritable boy was throwing a tantrum, demanding that the windows be opened. He stepped out of the funicular, shivering. Among the quiet flow of people passing in front of the grand shop windows, he began to walk as well. He was unaware of the glances from women drawn to his gentle features. The presence of these unfamiliar bodies made him feel suffocated, and he instinctively pulled away from them. Only the chrysanthemums and carnations, drooping with pale faces in the shop windows, seemed to call out to him longingly. From time to time, automobiles and carriages would pass by, carrying young couples dressed in fine clothes — gazing into each other's eyes, searching in vain for something they had yet to find.

That night, there was a strange and wild transformation stirring in Sühā's soul. He was not the type to wander among such aimless crowds unless absolutely forced to. And yet, now, he passed in front of several hotels but could not bring himself to go inside. The idea of being alone terrified him. At one point, he turned down a narrow and gloomy street. Here, there was a row of taverns, each one reeking of alcohol like the breath of a drunkard. His feet wobbled, slipping into muddy puddles. He stopped on the sidewalk. A dim light was spilling out from a tavern across the street. He stood there, peering inside for a while. At one of the tables, a group of men in hats were playing cards. At another table, two Turkish youths were flirting with a Greek girl. None of them seemed troubled or hesitant — they were carefree and at ease.

A moment later, a young woman with well-defined features appeared at the window. Her blouse was made of fine, sea-green fabric, and her dyed, voluminous hair framed her face. Seeing

Sühā, she gestured toward him with her lips and hands. Sühā shivered. A dark and foreign wind swept through his heart. He walked toward the door. As he opened it, a wave of warmth hit his face. He sensed a few pairs of eyes briefly turning toward him before losing interest. Without looking around, he sat down at the table near the stove. He shook the snow from his shoulders. Then he said to the drunken girl in the sea-green blouse, who was wiping the dust off the table with a rag under her arm:

— "Wine!"

***

When he opened his eyes, it was morning. He was lying in a filthy bed. He rubbed his eyes so hard it hurt, unable to believe the state he was in. It was a small, whitewashed room with bare floors. A few pieces of women's clothing and a sea-green blouse were carelessly thrown over a chest in the corner. He sat up. Whose blouse was that? A bitter, hazy scene — he could not tell if it was real or imagined — floated before his eyes. He looked back at the bed. There was no one beside him, but there was a dirty indentation on the pillow. It was not from just one or two nights; who knew how many hungry and corrupted heads had pressed into that spot?

Dear God, what was Sühā doing here?

He got out of bed. He couldn't even bear to touch his clothes — they felt filthy. From outside came the sound of men and women laughing, the clinking of plates and cutlery. Beyond that, the air was thick with a suffocating, vile smell. Sühā was trying to figure out why he had come here. How had he ended up in such a place? Was it despair, or was it some excess of pain that had dragged him here? It was a small mercy that, under the influence of the wine, the drunken girl from the night before had simply laid him down to sleep. The night had passed in a dreamless haze, and he had been spared from anything worse. Sühā was deeply shaken. At that moment, he saw the Prophet of Love standing before him. His radiant gaze seemed to pierce through Sühā's soul.

Sühā couldn't hold himself back any longer. He collapsed to the floor, sobbing uncontrollably. It was as if divine help had arrived — the Prophet of Love had prevented him from doing what he had nearly done. After some time, he pulled himself together. He rose suddenly, dressed quickly, and stepped into the dark corridor. But he froze in shock at the sight in front of him. In the middle of the hallway, two half-naked bodies lay entwined. The woman was the same girl who had climbed into Sühā's bed the night before. The man was a large, heavy-set Greek. The woman wore nothing but a thin nightgown. Like dogs, lying in the open like that...

My God, where is humanity?

The woman laughed shamelessly and glanced at Sühā with a brazen smile. She seemed to expect a curse or insult from him. Sühā turned away sharply, disgusted. He ran down the stairs, nearly stumbling as he reached the door. When he stepped outside, everything was frozen. Large icicles hung from the eaves; the smoke from the chimneys disappeared almost instantly into the crisp white air. It was still early. There were few travelers on the street. The ones who passed by had frost in their mustaches and beards. Sühā thought to himself:

— "Ah, Celāl, you should have seen this night. How furious you would have been! How you would have scolded me."

The cherished memory of Celāl filled his eyes with tears. After getting off the train, he was caught in a violent snow-storm in the mountains near the farm. He could barely see a step ahead of him. He was terrified of losing his way. At any moment, he could slip on a stone or fall into a ravine. From time to time, the sound of jackals howling in the distance filled his ears. His courage was fading. He barely kept himself from collapsing into the snow. This was the kind of weather that could not be crossed without a carriage — but Sühā's mind was not clear. After about fifteen or twenty minutes, the storm began to ease. But now the sky was darkening, and night was closing in. The snow had finally stopped falling. The trees of the farm appeared ahead, standing like white orbs in the distance. When he reached the farm gate, Süleyman greeted him:

— "Zeliha has fallen ill," Süleyman said.

Sühā took off his wet clothes and rushed to Zeliha's side. Her eyes were burning with fever as she lay in bed:

— "How are you feeling, Zeliha? What happened?"

— "It's nothing," Zeliha said. "Just a bit of a headache."

This was not a triumph. Ah, this Prophet of Love!

Zeliha forgot about her own illness as soon as she saw Sühā shivering. She tucked warm flannel into his back and chest, brewed him linden tea, and laid him down in a lounge chair by the fireplace. She adjusted the lounge chair [a portable seat with a cloth stretched over a frame for reclining] and wiped her forehead, stressed and sweating. Poor Behice was running back and forth, trying to warm Sühā and care for Zeliha at the same time. Sühā sat there, gazing into the flickering flames of the fireplace, lost in thought. How could he leave Zeliha here all alone? True, Behice and Veli Ağa would still be there — but could they really take the place of a mother, a father, or a sibling?

Zeliha was genuinely ill.

A week later, the bitter cold persisted, but the snowfall had finally stopped. The two siblings walked as far as the hyacinth field. The ground crunched beneath their feet. The icicles hanging from the branches and the roof of the barn resembled the salt caves beneath the earth's surface that never see sunlight. The trees, the farmhouse, and the clouds were all dazzling white:

— "Zeliha, look over there!" Sühā said. "I've never found this place so melancholy before. But make sure you don't catch a cold — wrap the scarf tightly around your neck!"

This was the most beautiful spot on the farm, nestled where two mountains met by the riverbank. The Prophet of Love had always loved this place. Zeliha looked around absentmindedly, as if searching for someone. The river was frozen solid. A thick layer of snow now covered the hyacinth field — as if the snow had jealously tried to conceal it. Then, uncharacteristically sharp and intense, Zeliha suddenly said:

— "Ah, Sühā — if only I could go to Erzurum in your place!"

Sühā did not respond. They walked on silently for a while, crossing the river's bridge. Lost in their thoughts, they climbed the slope toward the mountain's peak. Then Zeliha said:

— "Sühā, I'm going to tell you something. But first, let me say this — don't bother objecting. My mind is made up. You won't be able to change my decision, so don't waste your energy."

Sühā stopped walking. His face darkened.

— "What decision?"

— "You're leaving in ten days. I've found a place for myself to go."

— "Where?"

— "It doesn't matter. A school in a distant village — I'm going to take a teaching position. Everything is already arranged. You don't need to do anything or worry about me. I took the petition myself the other day."

She spoke with quiet resolve.

— "Within a few days — maybe even tomorrow — it'll be confirmed. I told them I'd accept any location, so there's no reason it won't be approved. Why are you so surprised? There's nothing strange about it. When you leave, I don't want to be left here alone. That's all."

Sühā pulled himself together.

— "Zeliha, my dear sister — don't I have any right, as your brother, to talk to you about this?"

— "What's there to talk about? There's nothing to discuss. When you leave, I'll be left alone — that's all there is to it."

Zeliha didn't want to talk; she even avoided looking into Sühā's eyes. For two days, Sühā tried with all his strength to dissuade his sister from this decision. How could her delicate body endure such hardship? Surely, loneliness and the unforeseen trials of living in a foreign place would overwhelm her. Would Zeliha be able to withstand all of this? But Zeliha wouldn't listen. She met his words with a quiet smile, and more often than not, didn't respond at all. Over these two days, she had visibly paled and wasted away. Finally, the assignment order arrived. Sühā realized he wouldn't be able to change her mind. Neither the promise of future days they could spend together once his brief military service ended, nor the possibility of the Prophet of Love returning to the farm one day, could persuade her to abandon her plan.

Veli Ağa cried on one side, and Behice on the other, while Süleyman begged:

— "Please, let me go with the young lady!"

But Zeliha didn't want to take him along. She packed her suitcase. Together, Sühā, Süleyman, the poor Veli Ağa, and Behice accompanied the two siblings to Istanbul to see Zeliha off. Everyone was crying on the way — everyone except Zeliha. Sühā's eyes were constantly wet; he could barely hold himself together. His deployment was imminent, too. On the deck of the ferry, as they waited for departure, Sühā said:

— "Look, my dear Zeliha. You're going to ruin yourself. Do you really think that kind of lonely life will be easy? You're still a child; you don't understand what you're getting yourself into. I will return soon, God willing. And then my aunt, Zehrā, and the Prophet of Love will definitely come next summer. They won't leave us. Really, how much time is left until then? Can't you just be patient until we're all together again?"

Zeliha was distant. Even though she had spent the last two days smiling, she now seemed withdrawn. She listened to his words distractedly, as if only pretending to hear. Sühā still held on to hope that she might change her mind and come back with them. He prayed to himself:

— "My God, please protect this child."

He began to blame himself:

— "I should have insisted more. I should have found a way to stop her."

The ferry sounded its final whistle. They began to pull up the gangway. Zeliha bit her pale lips and looked at Sühā with an expression of deep sorrow. They all stood up.

— "Sühā, don't write to me," she said. "I'll learn about your health from the farm through a brief telegram or two."

— "Why not, Zeliha? Do you want to cut yourself off from the world completely? Why shouldn't I write? And I'm sure my military service will be over soon, God willing. Then we'll both return to the farm together."

Zeliha received Sühā's final words with a sense of quiet despair, as if he were speaking of a dream that had already been shattered beyond repair, with no hope of ever being restored. Her silence was heavy with resignation. The steward came. It was time to separate — the last gangway was about to be lifted. The deckhands were shouting orders. Zeliha threw her arms around Sühā's neck. Veli Ağa and Behice were waiting in the boat. Behice had rested her head on her knees. Sühā descended the staircase and jumped into the boat. The rising sea sent sprays of foam crashing over them. Zeliha leaned against the iron railings of the deck, watching them drift away. Sühā couldn't bear the sight of her standing there alone. He couldn't bring himself to lift his gaze toward her. Foam swirled and sprayed upward. The boat began to pull away slowly, then gained speed, cutting through the sea as it drifted farther and farther. The waves rocked the boat violently. Sühā covered his face with his hands.

It was Victory Day. Beautiful Istanbul was adorned like a bride, with flowers, flags, and intoxicating scents. Everyone was smiling and joyful. The weather, which for so long had seemed restless and stormy, had suddenly softened into a gentle smile—flowers bloomed on its breast, and fresh fragrances filled the air. The marching songs of the soldiers intertwined with the songs of the sparrows and swallows. The roads were decorated with triumphal arches adorned with spring flowers. A few clouds stood still in the emotional blue horizon, inhaling the scent of the heavens, listening to the melodies, and drifting off as they watched the bright, sweet colors…

A pale-faced young soldier with weary eyes was descending the wide steps of the station. He leaned heavily on his crutch as he walked with difficulty. The left leg of his pants was pinned up. His clothes were worn, and his hair was overgrown. Yet, there was a noble sorrow in his expression. Under the large clock, a little girl stood with furrowed brows, watching him with curiosity. Children were running around with flags in their hands. Everywhere was bursting with color and scent. It was as if all the flowers from every garden had been scattered onto the streets. The young man was looking around. He had no one waiting for him—no mother, no father, no sibling. And who knows—was his elderly uncle Veli Ağa even alive or well? If only there had been someone waiting for him, a mother, a sibling—how he longed for that simple comfort! His soul could not shake off these childlike feelings. How much he longed for a mother's affection.

The veterans who had disembarked from the train with him had already been embraced and taken away by their mothers, fathers, and lovers. But no one even turned to look at him. This triumphant parade celebrating victory was completely oblivious to him. And yet, this victory had claimed his leg as a sacrifice, draining the color from his face. Amid this passionate parade, there was a selfish ingratitude. Sometimes, elegantly dressed women with fluttering hearts would pass by him. Some would brush against his shoulder, others would nudge his cane with the tips of their shoes, leaving behind a trail of delicate perfume as they disappeared. Among all this cheer and excitement, he could only see the trampled lilacs and violets beneath their feet, the burnt ruins of buildings destroyed nine years earlier, and the cold, imposing facades of the new foreign buildings that had replaced the coffeehouses and shops whose shadows he had passed by countless times before.

For a moment, his gaze caught his reflection in a shop window. His entire body shuddered. Who was this hollow-eyed, pale-faced, half-ill figure with thinning hair? Poor Süleyman! No—that Süleyman had died long ago.

Yet the harsh sound of his crude cane, jarring and grating, echoed unpleasantly amid this paradise of color, scent, and light. Suddenly, he broke into a sweat. It was as if the whole world had stopped, every sound silenced. The entire universe seemed to be listening to the dull thuds of his cane striking the pavement. He searched for a path on the side of the road where the earth was softer and would absorb the sound. Slowly, with chronic and sorrowful resignation, he began to walk along the narrow strip of soil at the edge of the street... The stream shimmered, faintly adorned with diamond-like reflections from the stars... There was no moon, but the sky was so clear that the stars illuminated the earth with a strong, radiant glow. By the bank of the stream, Süleyman saw a crimson light. He remembered that there had once been a fisherman's hut there.

As he approached, he saw two small children — one blond and the other with chestnut hair — crouched around a large heath fire, warming themselves. An elderly migrant woman with furrowed brows was busy throwing twigs and branches into the flames. A little further away, a beautiful girl of about eleven or twelve sat with her legs stretched out toward the riverbed. Her hair was jet black and reached down to her knees. She had loosened one of her braids and was combing it while watching the flow of the water, singing a folk song to herself. Süleyman stopped involuntarily. He found it strange at first to see such foreign people living on familiar soil. The small children warming themselves by the fire glanced at him sideways, giggling mischievously and letting out teasing laughs. At one point, the chestnut-haired girl leaned toward the blond boy, shaking her dangling earrings and her short, tangled curls as she whispered, seemingly quietly:

— "What happened to his leg?"

The boy replied with an inaudible, secretive answer. Then he nudged his sister with his knee and sent her tumbling to the ground in a fit of laughter. Süleyman saw all of this. He himself was puzzled as to why he was still standing there — but he was simply too tired, and his nerves were weak and frayed. The young girl by the river bent down, splashing the water with her hands as she washed them. Then she stood up. Her bare wrists were delicate, and her figure was graceful...

The village woman turned to Süleyman and said casually:

— "Son, why don't you go on your way?"

— "The road is too dark, grandmother... And it's far. I said to myself I'd rest here for a while."

— "Ah, well then, come stay with us tonight. We have enough blankets and soup to share."

— "I can't… I'm returning from a journey. I'm going to reunite with my loved ones."

— "Oh? Well, may it be a blessed reunion. At least rest for a bit before you go."

As he approached, the old woman pulled out a sheepskin rug from the hut and threw it in front of him. Then she returned to her work. Her furrowed face had softened into a slight smile. Süleyman sat down.

— "May God bless her—you have a beautiful daughter!" he said.

The woman frowned and snapped a twig between her strong hands. While continuing her work, she replied casually:

— "Take her if you want!"

Süleyman laughed, thinking she was joking.

— "I'm serious. If you want her, take her—there she is!"

Blushing, the woman walked toward the girl hiding behind the hut. She took hold of the girl's arm and lifted her onto her lap. Süleyman said:

— "Grandmother, we have nothing left to make our girls smile anymore."

The village woman put her hands on her hips and said, as if angry:

— "What? I am raising these girls, I swear by my God, for brave men like you!"

Süleyman sat the girl on his healthy knee and began stroking her hair. Her hair was extraordinarily soft and sweet-smelling. But the little girl seemed to be searching for a way to escape. She had even abandoned her shyness; she pulled her beaded, pink wrist away from his face with visible displeasure. At one point, her foot touched Süleyman's cane. Her face changed instantly, as if she had touched something frightening. She suddenly stirred, clearly preparing to run. Süleyman let her delicate body slip from his lap. The girl darted off toward the riverbank like a startled gazelle. Süleyman already knew he was out of place there. He picked up his cane and, despite the old woman's insistence, said his goodbyes. The village woman, in a voice that showed she meant her promise, said:

—"You're engaged now, right, son? You'll come back, won't you?"

—"Ah, grandmother, don't say that. Your generosity has already warmed my heart enough. But love—it comes from a noble soul. I wouldn't be so selfish as to tie your beautiful daughter to a flawed man like me and make her spend her life in sorrow. Even if her body were mine, her soul never would be. Farewell, grandmother."

In the distance, a few scattered lights flickered faintly in the transparent, pure air of V... village, as if a soft breeze might extinguish them at any moment. Though it was the second night of the Victory Festival, the village was quiet, without much celebration. Occasionally, a tired firework would rise toward the sky and disappear. He walked along the riverbank, his feet pressing into the sand. It was so quiet and still that the sound of insect wings could be heard. Only the dull sound of his cane striking the ground disturbed the mountains, wrapping around them like a throbbing ache. His exhaustion weighed so heavily on his frail body that he felt as if he might collapse with a single blow. The stream... That clear stream, shimmering here and there like silver—what it must have witnessed. In his mind's eye, Süleyman imagined the Prophet of Love with his arm around a young, beautiful girl's neck, gliding away on a flower-decked boat.

How beautiful this place had been back then. Wherever the Prophet of Love had passed, there had always been a brightness, a light. Why, my God? What was this divine beauty, this innocent magic that resided in him? Süleyman's heart had not remained untouched by his love. Because if a human heart, even with the smallest capacity for love, encountered him—it would be impossible not to burn. Whether man or woman—it made no difference. Yes, even if it was a man. Because this was not the love of the flesh. There was such purity and innocence in him that only he could make one believe in love and beauty. Süleyman kept walking, lost in thought. There was no sound—no movement. Aside from the burning stars in the sky and the silent majesty of the mountains submerged in their sacred stillness, there was nothing else. Süleyman found himself repeating something Sühā had once said: "I did not believe in the love that created and revealed this world until I saw him." Now, he felt as though he could see his exalted image standing before him. He imagined him walking through these hills, caressing this gentle paradise where he and Zehra had once known the heaven of their love...

This place had been the cause of so many affections! Zehra's, Sühā's, Zeliha's, and Süleyman's... But it was Zeliha who had truly suffered in this love.

Sühā... Süleyman was thinking of Sühā now. My God, how much he has changed! A figure with whitened hair, eyes swollen shut from crying — how strange this worn and aged image seemed next to the bright young vision Süleyman had left behind here. Yet, Süleyman felt a deep respect and admiration toward him.

He was approaching the vineyards of the farm. His feet were sinking into small potholes. The light from the vast sky and the abundance of stars was not enough to illuminate his way. He took out his electric lantern.

There it was — the house was now visible. But no lights were shining in the windows. Perhaps they were in the back room — in Behice's room. Had Zeliha come back from Konya? If she had, what would she say now? Wouldn't they ask him about Sühā? What would they do when they saw that Sühā was not with him? How would he tell them about the abandoned, blind, and ruined master he had left behind on the road?

Süleyman's heart, filled with loyalty and kindness, was overwhelmed with anxiety. He had reached the gate of the garden. He hesitated for a moment. He wanted to ring the bell — but it was broken. It wouldn't ring. Seeing this gate and this garden, which he had not seen for seven years, made him tremble inside. He pushed the gate open gently and stepped inside. At first glance, a chaotic scene unfolded before him. He walked through broken flower beds and withered rose bushes. A heap of old furniture was piled in front of the glass door. He climbed the stairs and knocked on the inner door, his heart pounding. He knocked once, twice — his hand trembling.

After a while, hesitant footsteps approached the door.

— "Who's there?"

Behice's voice!

— "It's me," Süleyman said.

The door opened. Behice's voice was weak from emotion — she could only throw her arms around Süleyman's neck. Süleyman held her too. But suddenly, he came to his senses and, with a mother's desperation, half-mad, he cried out:

— "Where is Sühā? Süleyman, where is Sühā?"

The poor woman seemed to have lost her mind.

— "Nothing happened to Sühā. I'll tell you everything soon…" But then she collapsed in front of the door, sobbing uncontrollably…

ZELİHA'S TELEGRAM TO SÜLEYMAN

Süleyman,

I heard you have returned to the farm. I'm very worried about Sühā. My dear Süleyman, please write to me truthfully and tell me everything. Why didn't Sühā return? You can imagine how happy I am about your return. I know that you will try as much as possible to avoid being distressed over something that has been sacrificed for such a sacred cause.

Zeliha

SÜLEYMAN'S LETTER TO ZELİHA

My dear little lady,

Are you still not coming back? Isn't it a shame for you? Please, why don't you return already? But my dear little lady, please don't worry about little master. There's nothing to pity him for or to be deeply upset about. In fact, I wish I could have been in his place. I envy him. We had been stationed at the camp for five years. When I first saw him, I was quite surprised. His face looked almost faded. But somehow, in his eyes—eyes I had never thought to look at so closely before—I now sense a captivating transformation. Even when he calls me Süleyman, I feel a mournful undertone, a quiet complaint.

Before meeting me, little master had fallen in love with a Circassian girl named Nihal. He even ran away from the camp twice because of her. Fortunately, the commander liked him very much and forgave him. The girl was truly beautiful and seemed to show great affection toward little master—at least outwardly. But it seems that she was a little too fond of money. Little master sold his rings and his watch. A sheep merchant, knowing that he was wealthy, loaned him some money for a while. But when the roads were cut off, the merchant grew afraid and stopped giving him money. This deeply affected Sühā.

Then, one evening, that cunning Circassian woman slammed the door in Sühā's face as he tried to enter in secret. Three days later, she ran off with a factory worker to an unknown place. That's all I know from hearsay… but what came after, no one knows except for me. I can never forget the kindness of that commander. He showed great affection toward Sühā, granting him exceptional privileges, and excused his absences by saying Sühā was unwell. One night, Sühā went out again. He had developed a habit of wandering. On cold nights, no matter how much I or anyone else tried to stop him, he would walk alone in the mountains opposite the camp. That night, I wrapped my coat around me and followed him. I found him at a mountain pass. I had run to catch up, and I was sweating from the effort.

He saw me but didn't seem bothered.

— "Is that you, Süleyman?" he said. Then he added, "Come, sit here," and pointed to a rock.

It was after 11 o'clock. The intense cold was burning my face and the back of my neck.

— "But why should we sit here in this freezing weather?" I said.

— "Come on, Sühā, let's go back to the camp. If you like, we don't have to sleep—we can sit and talk instead."

But it was no use—he wouldn't listen. He insisted so much that I finally sat down beside him. There was no other choice. I couldn't bring myself to leave him alone on that mountaintop. We both wrapped ourselves in our coats.

He said:

— "Süleyman! You, like everyone else, don't know why I wander alone in these mountains or why I sometimes cry at night, do you? I can't share even a fraction of my pain with anyone. But you have a pure heart. After all, that day—he stroked your hair, remember?"

He stroked my hair. Sühā was talking about the Prophet of Love. I was stunned. I had expected him to talk about the Circassian beauty.

— "You know, don't you?" he continued. "That affair with that vulgar woman, whose name I don't even want to mention now—you've heard about it. But since my love was sincere and well-intentioned, I respect her for that. After all, could anything be as great and instructive as misfortune?"

It was during those bleak days. Nihal had left about fifteen days earlier. The commander was giving me more freedom. Sometimes he would sit me down and talk to me at length, trying to comfort me. They gave me fifteen days of leave. I was staying at a boarding house. In those lonely days, I was completely lost in myself, becoming even more disheartened. Nihal's betrayal had drained my heart of any attachment to the world. One morning, I was walking along the train tracks. The passengers were dispersing after disembarking from the wagons. A traveler with a small suitcase was walking toward me. His collar was turned up, and his face was hard to see from a distance. But when he got closer, I shouted:

— "The Prophet of Love!"

Yes, Süleyman, we spent a whole week together. Ah, those nights… We would sit and talk until morning. I would tell him about my life, and he would listen. Then he would tell me about beautiful events. Sometimes he would play the guitar—pieces from his own compositions—and sing one or two waltzes. He said he had left Zehrā and my aunt behind but didn't tell me where. He said he had only come to see me for a day—but he stayed for a week. He understood me so well that I barely had time to be amazed at how quickly we connected. Until then, I had never found peace in any woman's company. But this was pure, spiritual love. I loved him with the devotion of a student toward a master, the love of a child for a father. I couldn't bear to be apart from him for even half an hour. It felt as if we had been together for not just years, but centuries. The past and my life before him were completely erased. I was focused only on him.

To him, nothing else existed but love. My old ways of thinking no longer mattered. I thought only as he thought, lived only as he lived. For him, there was nothing in the world besides love. Finally, the time came for us to part. I was devastated. I felt as though my soul was leaving my body. Time passed, and I heard no news of the Prophet of Love. My heart was dark, void of light. With each passing month, I felt more hopeless. Life's bitterness was eating away at me. My very humanity was unraveling. I felt no different from an animal. Rumors began circulating about our deployment to the front. But I couldn't wait. One day, I fled to the riverbank behind the mountains where I would often go to pour out my troubles. Many times, I had looked at those rushing waters and imagined throwing myself into them. I would think: "If I let myself sink beneath the waves, what would happen? The water would ripple for a moment, then the current would return to its usual rhythm, as if nothing had ever happened." That day, I was sitting at the riverbank again. My heart, so at odds with the blossoming spring, was empty of desire, hope, and longing. I took off my jacket and shirt. I was about to enter the water when someone seized my wrist.

— "Where are you going?"

I turned around and saw him.

— "The Prophet of Love!"

My voice echoed through the mountains. He said only:

— "Sühā, I came today for you."

I was completely intoxicated by his voice. I held his hand. But then he said:

— "Zehrā and Suzān are waiting for me on the train. Goodbye, Sühā."

He quickly walked away. I stood there, repeating to myself:

— "Where are you going?"

One day, while speaking with Sühā, I said:

— "Suha, surely some people will be surprised to see how much you love the Prophet of Love, won't they?"

She interrupted me, speaking with excitement:

"Ah, those who know nothing of love may think so. But those who reduce love to physical passion—how wrong they are! I am in love with his soul, with his virtue and sublimity. My love for him resembles more the affection a disciple feels for their teacher. I did not believe in the divine love that created this universe until I saw him. Some may see him and feel nothing. But doesn't fire ignite everything capable of burning? Would that diminish the fire's power?"

Months passed. Suha grew more distant with each day. She could no longer talk to me. She would go off alone for hours, disappearing into the distance. The army was preparing to go to the front. But at that time, Suha was discharged from military service after a medical examination because a thin veil had formed over her eyes—she was half-blind.

Ah, little lady, she couldn't sleep at night. She cried for hours.

Within a few months, her hair had turned white. Everyone was moved by her condition and respected her love. From young children to the elderly, everyone held her in reverence.

One morning, we were talking about her eyes. Suha was neglecting the baths prescribed by the doctor. I was annoyed with her and scolded her. Suha said to me, almost casually:

— "Süleyman, these tears have restored my humanity. They have shown me the path to my humanity. I do not regret the tears I have shed for him."

Sühā often wandered around the pension where she and the Prophet of Love had met.

Finally, little lady, the day arrived when we were to be sent to the front. Dawn had just broken. We were already marching in the square in front of the camp. There was a strange light of hope on her face. She said to me:

— "Süleyman, I'm leaving."

— "Where to?"

— "To Arabia. I can't endure it anymore. I'm going to search for him."

I was shocked and said:

— "Absolutely not! I will take you back to the pension. Two months from now, you and Ahmed Çavuş will return to Istanbul. He promised me you would come back together."

Sühā didn't even answer.

— "How can I let you go, half-blind, with nothing but a cane in your hand?"

Yes, all she had was a cane. How could she possibly go anywhere in that state? She gazed toward the light of dawn and said:

— "Isn't the love in my heart enough?"

That day, little lady, I left Suha behind on the road. Just think—Erzurum and Arabia—how far apart they are! Later that day, I found nothing but a piece of paper in her cabinet. I still have it. It says:

"Oh evening breeze, carry my greeting and my devotion—my faith, which is love—to the God of Love! Oh wind that brings the peaceful, pure scents of the mountains, I no longer have the strength to inhale you, no matter how gentle you are. Go, brush against his knees once more, and return to me filled with his essence—for any other fragrance, even for a single second, would poison me. Go, and come back filled with him. Oh colors, scents, and sounds that surrounded me during those long nights apart from my beloved—I am burning. Come, bring me his fire in your hands, and approach me with your palms full of it. Rivers flow into seas, stars meet stars—does my longing truly have no end?"

Please, little lady, let me go just once. Let me stay for a week. Then I will return. I would tell you so much more.

I kiss your hands and hem many times.

Süleyman

Semiha Cemāl
September 1923

Afterword

NAVIGATING THE "THIRD SPACE": SUFI AND PHILOSOPHER, TRADITIONAL AND MODERN

One of the central insights that emerges from Semiha Cemāl's story is how she managed to navigate a "third space" between what might seem like two disparate or even opposing orbits: the world of Sufi devotion and the world of modern philosophical reason. Her life exemplifies a historical and textual strategy of inhabiting the in-between – a liminal space where religious tradition and secular learning could co-exist and even enrich each other. This concept of a third space, in the sense used by cultural theorists to describe hybrid or interstitial identities, is vividly applicable to Semiha Cemāl. She neither rejected modern education in favor of mysticism nor did she abandon her spiritual heritage for the sake of Westernization. Instead, she embraced both, crafting an identity that was not two-faced but rather double-faceted – a synthesis greater than the sum of its parts.

Historically, Semiha Cemāl's milieu made such a synthesis both challenging and urgent. The early Turkish Republic of the 1920s and 30s was characterized by radical secular reforms: the caliphate was abolished, Sufi orders and lodges were outlawed in 1925, and a vehemently positivist, Western-facing ethos permeated official cultural policy. To openly be a practitioner of Sufism in those years, or to espouse mystical ideas, risked being labeled reactionary or outdated. Conversely, to be a woman pursuing higher education and intellectual work was an embodiment of the Republic's progressive ideals – yet those ideals were premised on a break with the Ottoman-Islamic past. On one hand, she was exactly the kind of "new woman" the Republic aimed to cultivate: educated, intellectually active, contributing to the nation's literary and philosophical output. On the other hand, the content of her intellectual passion – Sufi metaphysics and ethics – drew from the deep well of Islamic mysticism that the new state was trying to relegate to the private sphere. Rather than experiencing these allegiances as irreconcilable, Semiha Cemāl found a way to reconcile them in her own work and persona. She effectively carved out a cultural third space where fidelity to a spiritual tradition could coincide with engagement in modern scholarly and literary life. In doing so, she quietly subverted the rigid secular/religious binary of her time.

The support of her Sufi mentor, Ken'ān Rifā'ī, was instrumental in this negotiation of identities. Rifā'ī himself was a reformist mystic who believed Sufism could be modernized and aligned with the Republic's aims, who welcomed Western cultural forms. Under his guidance, Semiha and her female peers were encouraged to pursue higher education and public roles, in parallel with their spiritual training. In Semiha's case, Rifā'ī's influence is said to have inspired her to return to academia and become the first female scholar of philosophy in the early Turkish Republic. It was under Rifā'ī's wing that she translated Plato and Marcus Aurelius into Turkish – tasks perfectly in line with the Republican project of knowledge transfer – and simultaneously deepened her Sufi practice of *sohbet* (spiritual conversation) and *irfan* (gnosis). Semiha Cemāl's writings, as examined in this volume, consciously reflect this fusion of Sufi and philosophical paradigms. Perhaps the clearest example is her propensity to draw explicit parallels between ancient Greek thought and Sufi Islamic thought. As a student of philosophy, she was well-versed in the idealist philosophers like Plato, and as a Sufi adept, she was steeped in Islamic teachings of ethics and transcendence. In her analysis, these were not antagonistic sources of wisdom but deeply resonant ones. She observed, for instance, that Plato's elevation of virtue and the notion of an eternal realm of truth "overlaps greatly" with the moral vision of Islam that would emerge centuries later. She also interwove Stoic philosophy into this tapestry: the Stoics' emphasis on the fleeting nature of the material world and the pursuit of inner goodness aligns neatly with the Sufi view of worldly life as transient and the need to focus on the eternal, bringing together Plato's idealism and Stoicism. This comparative philosophical maneuver is not merely an academic exercise – it is Semiha actively fashioning a conceptual third space where East and West, past and present, mystic and rationalist, speak to each other. It exemplifies her literary-historiographic methodology, to borrow a term: she frames texts and ideas as meeting points across ideological and historical thresholds. The novel *Aşk Peygamberi* itself becomes a site of such synthesis – a narrative where a modern genre, the novel, is used as a vessel for age-old Sufi wisdom and classical philosophy.

THE PROPHET OF LOVE:
AN ARCHIVE OF LONGING AND A SUFI ALLEGORY

At the heart of Semiha Cemāl's legacy is her novel *Aşk Peygamberi,* presented in this volume in full English translation. This text is many things at once: on one level, it is an affective archive – a repository of the author's emotional and intellectual world, preserving the traces of a unique moment in Turkish cultural history. On another level, it is a Sufi allegory or cosmology rendered in modern narrative form – a story that encodes metaphysical principles and mystical symbolism within the structure of a coming-of-age tale. Reading *Aşk Peygamberi* with the benefit of the scholarly context provided, one appreciates how the novel serves as both archive and expression, document and poem. It is an archive in the sense that it captures, as between its covers, the confluence of ideas and influences that made Semiha Cemāl's outlook distinctive; and it is an affective expression in that it gives voice to an intensely felt longing for truth and transcendence, the kind of longing that is at the core of Sufi devotional literature.

Several thematic currents running through *Aşk Peygamberi* mark it as a distinctly metaphysical novel of longing. The protagonist, Sühā, is portrayed as a young man in search of an undefinable ideal – a quest that clearly mirrors the author's own spiritual yearnings. Sühā grows up orphaned in a boarding school, feeling a sense of alienation from ordinary life and an almost inchoate suspicion of worldly love. Early on, he deliberately shuns romantic attachments, fearing the turbulence that love might bring, yet paradoxically, he is also driven by a curiosity about the very nature of that tumult he avoids. The narrative unfolds largely through Sühā's notebook – effectively his inner archive of reflections – which the novel presents to the reader. Through these reflections, and through the events that follow his graduation, we witness the gradual crystallization of a mystical worldview. Sühā repeatedly confronts the ephemerality of the material world. This sentiment – the unbearable lightness of the finite, so to speak – encapsulates the novel's affective core: a state of wistful longing for a love and truth that do not die. The resonance with Sufi poetry and philosophy is clear: one hears echoes of Rūmī's couplets about the moth longing for the flame, or Yunus Emre's songs about the lover's heart aching for the Beloved. *Aşk Peygamberi* is, at its essence, a chronicle of a soul's yearning – an affective document of the author's own spiritual thirst, thinly disguised as fiction.

As an archive, the novel also meticulously preserves the intellectual and spiritual influences that shaped Semiha Cemāl's understanding of love. Within its pages, we find intertextual homage to the great Sufi masters and their archetypal relationships. Notably, the novel presents a transformative friendship between its characters that parallels the bond of Rumi and Shams, updating that legendary mentor-disciple relationship through fictional counterparts. This is not a coincidence: Semiha Cemāl was clearly inspired by the model of spiritual companionship epitomized by Rūmī and Shams – where one person becomes the catalyst for the other's enlightenment, a "prophet of love" guiding the seeker. In the novel, when Sühā encounters the figure of Yusuf Cemāl Bey – who indeed is the titular "prophet of love" in the story – their interaction is imbued with the same mystic electricity known from Mevlānā's encounter with Shams. Yusuf Cemāl has an almost otherworldly aura (the text describes his beautiful voice and charismatic presence that enchants those around him, and he leads Sühā toward revelations of the heart. By weaving this Rūmī-Shams allusion into modern prose, Semiha Cemāl is effectively linking her novel to the Sufi understanding of centuries past. In short, *Aşk Peygamberi* is a curation of spiritual thought, preserving in its fabric the heritage of Islamic mysticism as filtered through a young woman's pen. It stands as an archive of a lineage– connecting the reader to a chain of wisdom stretching from Plato to the Sufis, as noted earlier. Indeed, one contemporary commentator has highlighted that the novel's premise and its period of writing together make it a text of high symbolic value, signaling how it operates as a cultural artifact of layered meanings.

Semiha Cemāl wrote *Aşk Peygamberi* at the age of only 22, and as the product of a spiritually nurtured yet youthful imagination. We should remember that in 1927, to pen a novel that openly discusses spiritual love, the search for Truth (*hakikat*), and critiques the pull of worldly pleasures was an unusual endeavor, especially for a woman writer. Semiha Cemāl's very choice of subject constituted a bold and innovative act. And being a young woman author, she brought a distinctive sensibility to this metaphysical genre. Unlike many male Sufi writers of previous generations, Semiha's treatment of the longing for the divine is intimately tied to questions of personal identity and emotional vulnerability. Sühā's existential angst, his fear of and attraction to love's "soul-shaking" power, can be read as *a* reflection of the author's own psychological landscape – the cautious yet curious approach of someone who has not known love even from the margins but is nonetheless compelled to imagine its spiritual heights. In a way, Semiha Cemāl writes *around* her own gendered experience: she chooses a male protagonist, perhaps because a male seeker could more freely move in society and undergo certain experiences (like night-time excursions and intellectual conversations) in that era's norms. But through that male persona, she channels a deeply feminine intuition about love as something that is nurtured inwardly, a force that can be transformative without being overtly romantic or erotic. The love in *Aşk Peygamberi* is a cosmic force – an energetic pull toward the sublime – and its "prophet" is not a lover in the ordinary sense, but a guide to higher truth. One might say that Semiha Cemāl appropriates the male-dominated discourse of Sufi writing and subtly infuses it with a woman's interiority and empathy. Her authorship thus carries a quiet feminist significance: it asserts that a Muslim woman in the 1920s can be the author of a profound spiritual narrative, that she can envision and articulate *the path to God* with as much authority and insight as any man.

The novel's new English translation, provided in this book, underscores all these facets for a contemporary audience.

Readers in English are now able to witness how *Aşk Peygamberi* serves as a threshold text – one that bridges genres (mystical treatise and modern novel), bridges eras (invoking classical Sufi tales within a 20th-century context), and bridges sensibilities (rational inquiry and passionate faith). As an afterword, we can conclude that *Aşk Peygamberi* is both the product and proof of Semiha Cemāl's successful navigation of her in-between world. It is the creative trace of her third space: a novel that could only have been written by someone equally conversant in Rumi's *Masnavi* and the latest intellectual currents of her day, someone who was as much a dervish of love as she was a daughter of the Republic.

SUFI FEMINISM AND THE REFRAMING OF EARLY REPUBLICAN MODERNITY

Semiha Cemāl's life and work, as presented in this book, prompt a re-evaluation of women's roles in Turkish intellectual history – amounting to a major intervention in how we understand the interplay of gender, religion, and modernity in the early 20th century. In academic discourse, one might anachronistically call her stance (and that of her female peers) a form of "Sufi feminism." By this, we refer not to explicit political feminism – Semiha did not campaign publicly for women's rights – but to a mode of thought and practice where being a woman and being a spiritual-intellectual leader were mutually reinforcing rather than contradictory. The Sufi ethos within which Semiha operated was, somewhat surprisingly, enabling of female authority through which women's public participation was fueled through spiritual and intellectual synthesis, supported not by secularist ideology alone but by enlightened religious mentorship. In this way, she and her female counterparts in the Rifā'ī circle expanded the definition of what it meant to be a modern Turkish woman. They claimed space as philosophers, writers, translators – all the while embracing a spiritual identity. This dual claim was their innovation and can rightly be seen as a feminist act, carving out a legitimacy for women in domains (like philosophy or Sufi literature) that had traditionally been male dominated.

The book makes a timely intervention in intellectual history by insisting on the inclusion of figures like Cemāl in the genealogy of Turkish thought. This broader lens reveals the 1930s intellectual climate as more than a monolith of Kemalist positivism, exposing the often-overlooked undercurrents of mystically inclined scholarship that shaped the era's literary and philosophical production. Semiha Cemāl's translations of *Apology* and *Meditations*, for instance, were published around 1932 – the same era when the Turkish state was avidly translating Western classics to forge a new intellectual elite. Her work fits into that national project, yet her prefaces to those translations undoubtedly carried her own interpretive voice, likely inflected with ethical and spiritual reflections. Thus, she stands at an ideological threshold, loyal to the nation-building effort but simultaneously channeling the moral tenor of her faith tradition into it. Including her in the intellectual timeline highlights the fact that women, and particularly spiritually oriented women, were actors in the knowledge production of the time.

In sum, the portrait and translation of Semiha Cemāl presented here reposition a "marginalized" woman thinker back into the picture and, in doing so, expand the very boundaries of that inquiry. We are prompted to consider how many other liminal figures might be hovering at the margins of modern Turkish intellectual history, especially women and religiously grounded intellectuals whom later secular narratives overlooked. Future studies might explore this genre, tracing themes of metaphysical longing and transcendent love in other women's writings and thereby enrich the canon of modern Turkish literature with new voices as the case of Semiha Cemāl helps delineate a nascent *Sufi-feminist genealogy* in modern Turkish culture. Tracing such a genealogy would broaden our understanding of Muslim women's agency beyond the secular framework, highlighting continuity in ethical and esoteric knowledge transmission. Finally, Semiha Cemāl's dual role as a novelist and a translator draws attention to the *translation culture* of the late Ottoman and early Republican period, especially the often-unacknowledged part women played in it. Further research could examine how women like Semiha contributed to the massive project of translating and thus transforming the intellectual landscape of Türkiye – a project that not only imported Western ideas but also reframed Islamic classics for modern readers. In investigating these areas – gendered intellectual history, women's metaphysical literature, Sufi-feminist networks, and early Republican translation efforts – scholars will continue the work that this volume so admirably advances. The Portrait of the First Turkish Female Sufi Philosopher has opened a doorway on the threshold of multiple disciplines; stepping through it, we can look forward to a more inclusive, nuanced, and interconnected understanding of Türkiye's cultural and intellectual heritage.

APPENDIX

A Tribute to Semiha Cemāl:
In the Words of Her Brother,
Prof. Dr. Ziya Cemāl Büyükaksoy[198]
(1896–1953)

Nearly everyone who knew my sister, Semiha Cemāl, has asked me for an account of her life. But how could the history of her pure and honorable existence—a life that transcended the bounds of human experience—ever be confined to the narrow vessel of letters and words? It was too lofty, too vast for such containment. I still cannot bring myself to believe that this sublime child—so delicate a manifestation of spirit clothed in flesh—once lived a life among the people of this world. Semiha Cemāl departed this life at the age of thirty-one. She received her early education at Çelebi Mektebi, later graduating from Çamlıca High School and, in 1926, from the Philosophy Department of Dārülfünūn. For a brief time, she taught Philosophy and Psychology at İzmir Girls' High School, and from 1929

---

198 Ziya Cemāl Büyükaksoy (1896–1953) was a distinguished Turkish dentist and academic, recognized for his significant contributions to dentistry in Türkiye. He played a pivotal role in organizing the First National Dental Congress in 1932, which aimed to advance dental practices and education in the country. His efforts were instrumental in shaping modern dental health policies and practices in early Republican Türkiye.

to 1935, she distinguished herself as a Psychology instructor at Istanbul Girls' Teacher Training School. All her teachers spoke of her with pride, marveling at the strength of her intellect, the clarity of her judgment, and the force of her resolve. Everyone who knew her—among them the esteemed professors Şekib and Yusuf Ziya, as well as Professor Dr. Nurettin Ali, who was then serving as the dean of Dārülfünūn—praised her exceptional gifts with heartfelt admiration. In fact, at that time, Professor Yusuf Ziya once sent me the following lines about an article Semiha Cemāl had submitted to a journal under his editorship:

> "Your sister's latest writing is truly astonishing! I don't know if you've ever read the Psalms of David... If not, please do so sometime. You will plainly see that both draw from the same source of inspiration. As I was reading it, I thought to myself: if this girl were to stand up and say, 'I am inspired by God—these words are my proof,' I would unquestionably be her first believer. Such was the immense impact her words left upon me."

Beyond this, there are also many words of high praise from Professor Şekib[199] regarding her work.

Semiha Cemāl... a blazing talent, drawn with grace from the bosom of centuries...

Semiha Cemāl... the embodiment of perfected and absolute virtue...

---

199   Mustafa Şekip Tunç (1886–1958) was a prominent Turkish philosopher and psychologist, known for his contributions to the development of psychology and philosophy in early Republican Türkiye. Influenced by French thinkers such as Henri Bergson, he played a key role in introducing modern psychological and philosophical concepts to Turkish intellectual circles. He taught at Istanbul University, where he shaped the study of psychology as an academic discipline. His works explored topics like consciousness, intuition, and the nature of human thought, bridging Western philosophical ideas with Turkish intellectual traditions.

Semiha Cemāl... a rare gift, in whom human sentiment finds expression through eloquence and luminous clarity...

Semiha Cemāl... a divine gift, a pure and transcendent spirit; a blessing bestowed upon humanity from the unseen realm; a living manifestation of moral perfection...

Human measures, the limits of human comprehension, stand in awe before the boundless strength that this young soul managed to contain within the brief span of her life. Her life, steeped in knowledge and wisdom, resembles a miracle worthy of wonder. A marvel adorned by divine power—an inspired work that leaves humanity astonished.

It is as if, in creating her, God wished to proclaim and reveal His own divine qualities to the world through this extraordinary being—a majestic monument brought into existence by His will. Semiha Cemāl... a pure and perfected soul, untainted by the weariness of human ambition, untouched by the distractions of worldly desires, unsullied by the loss of time. The energy within her being was never scattered by base weaknesses or earthly cravings. All her strength and resolve flowed toward a single path, a single goal, with unwavering focus. She was never enslaved by anything other than divine power. Her pure and unblemished existence knew nothing of lowly dependencies. Semiha Cemāl did not see the individual worth of a being in its own right; rather, she perceived within it the imprint of the Creator's artistry, the divine hand that had shaped it. Semiha Cemāl... "Good and evil—these are not two separate concepts," she would say. "In everything, there is goodness. What we call 'evil' is nothing more than the misguided perception of someone who, in mistaking it for good, is worthy only of compassion." She knew how to descend into the viewpoint of any wrongdoer, to see the world through their eyes and understand them with mercy. She watched the grand spectacle of the world not from the stage, but from behind the curtain. And she understood the true nature of the players. Semiha Cemāl… in her professional life, she taught the discipline of spiritual refinement with complete mastery and success. You may wonder, "Does a person speak of their sister with such praise?" But to those who knew her, even these words would seem insufficient.

She sought, with humility, to temper the lyrical and powerful expression of her eternal works. For a painter, a sculptor, a poet—or any artist, for that matter—external influences and the beauty of nature must align with the artist's innate talent, helping to expand the reach of their aesthetic sense. But for Semiha Cemāl, the source of inspiration lay not outside herself. It sprang instead from the depths of her own soul—a soul that, with each breath, uncovered some new and hidden corner of its own mystery. At the Girls' Teacher Training School where she taught—and likewise at Yovakimion Greek Girls' High School and the Italian Girls' High School—there was no one who did not love her, no one who did not weep when she departed from this world. On the day she was entrusted to the mercy of the Most Compassionate, among the words spoken by the teachers and students of the Girls' Teacher Training School, I write down the words of Miss Sabiha Orhan, spoken through tears in tribute to her beloved teacher, as a gesture of blessing:

> "Our dear teacher… we were so happy, so expectant, thinking that soon we would see you again at your lectern. But then— what was this? What was that news we heard yesterday? Did we hear it? No, no—we did not hear it. We could not have heard it. And even if we had, we could not have believed it. How could it be that such a strong, sensitive soul, housed within a body of steel-like strength, could vanish from this world in so brief a time? How could our minds ever grasp such a thing?"

But the sorrow our other teachers could not conceal, the tears they could not hold back—it struck our minds like a terrible blow… Believe me, believe me, this is a bitter truth. And yet we still cannot believe it—because you had taught us not to. "Children," you would say, "The soul is eternal; matter is transient." And so, dear teacher, we now repeat your own words back to you. Your body has departed from among us; death, at last, has laid its grasp upon you. Has it truly torn you from us, as though tearing flesh from bone? Has it truly severed you from us? No—no, you have not died. On the contrary, you have ignited a spark within our hearts. That spark will grow and grow; its flame will set our hearts ablaze—and nothing, no material force, will ever extinguish that fire.

What will comfort us is the imprint of your spirit etched into the deepest corners of our hearts—the memory of your presence, the music of your name, your ever-smiling face tinged with warmth and color. Your lips, saying to us, "You are mistaken, children; I have not died." You will live on—in our hearts, in our minds, and in the depths of our being—as long as we ourselves have life. And your works—they will never perish. The children who drew strength from you now carry within them the power to sustain your legacy. Rest now—rest peacefully and at ease in your eternal bed. Let your students' sobs reach you; do not tell them to hold back the tears they shed for you. Let them weep—let them weep freely for their sacred dead…

Prof. Dr. Ziya Cemāl B. Aksoy

BIBLIOGRAPHY

ARCHIVES

Presidency of the Republic of Turkey, Directorate of State Archives. Ministry of National Education (General). Fonds Code 180-9-0-0. Box 89, File 431, Folder 14.

Presidential State Archives of the Republic of Turkey, Ministry of National Education (General), Fonds Code 180-9-0-0, Box 121, File 583, Folder 32.

SECONDARY SOURCES

Abu'l-Qasim al-Qushayri. *Al Risala Al-Qushayriyya Fi'ilm al-Tasawwuf.* Translated by Alexander D. Knysh. Reading: Garnet Publishing, 2007.

Adıvar, Halide Edib. *Sinekli Bakkal.* İstanbul: Can Yayınları, 2019.

Afacan, Şeyma. "Searching for the Soul in Shades of Grey: Modern Psychology's Spiritual Past in the Late Ottoman Empire." *European Journal of Turkish Studies*, no. 32 (2021).

Ahmad, Feroz. *The Making of Modern Turkey.* London: Routledge, 2002.

Akbatur, Arzu. "Turkish Women Writers in English Translation." *MonTI* 3 (2011): 161–79.

Altıntaş, Hayrani. *Mustafa Şekip Tunç.* Ankara: Kültür Bakanlığı Yayınları, 1989.

Andı, Fatih. "Türk Edebiyatında Roman: Cumhuriyet Devri." *TALID Türkiye Araştırmaları Literatürü Dergisi*, no. 8 (2006): 165–201.

Ansell-Pearson, Keith, and John Mullarkey, eds. *Henri Bergson Key Writings*. New York: Continuum, 2002.

Apaydın, Cem. "Belgeler Işığında Tekke, Zaviye ve Türbelerin Kapatılması Üzerine Bir Değerlendirme." *Yakın Dönem Türkiye Araştırmaları* 16, no. 32 (n.d.): 149–71.

Arslan, Tolga. "Darülfünun'dan İstanbul Üniversitesi'ne Felsefe Öğreniminin Yapılandırılması." *Ankara Üniversitesi Türk İnkılâp Tarihi Enstitüsü Atatürk Yolu Dergisi*, no. 61 (2017): 51–86.

Aydın, Mehmet S. "İnsân-ı Kâmil." *TDV İslâm Ansiklopedisi*. 22: 330-331. İstanbul: TDV Yayınları, 2000.

Aydıngün, Ayşegül, and İsmail Aydıngün. "The Role of Language in the Formation of Turkish National Identity and Turkishness." *Nationalism and Ethnic Politics*, no. 10 (2004): 415–32.

Aytürk, İlker. "Pious and Modern: Women's Islam in the Ayverdi Circle." *Journal of Turkish Studies/Türklük Bilgisi Araştırmaları* 51 (2019): 219–236.

Aytürk, İlker, and Laurent Mignon. "Paradoxes of a Cold War Sufi Woman: Samiha Ayverdi Between Islam, Nationalism, and Modernity." *New Perspectives on Turkey*, no. 49 (2013): 57–89.

Ayverdi, Semiha and Nezihe Araz, Safiye Erol, and Sofi Huri. *Ken'ān Rifāī ve Yirminci Asrın Işığında Müslümanlık*. Edited by Semiha Ayverdi. İstanbul: Kubbealtı Neşriyat, 2003.

Ayverdi, İlhan. *Misalli Büyük Türkçe Sözlük* (Tek Cilt). İstanbul: Kubbealtı Neşriyat, 2011.

Balcı, Meral and Mervenur Tuzak. "Cumhuriyet'in İlk Yıllarında Nezihe Muhiddin Özelinde Türk Kadınlarının Siyasi Hakları İçin Mücadelesi." *Marmara Üniversitesi Kadın ve Toplumsal Cinsiyet Araştırmaları Dergisi* 1, no. 1 (2017): 43-51.

Bayrak Akyıldız, Hülya. "Representation of Women in Early Republic Era Turkish Novels." In *Oriental Languages and Civilizations*, edited by Barbara Michalak-Pikulska, Tomasz Majtczak, and Marek Piela. Krakow: Jagiellonian University Press, 2020.

Bayraktar, Fulya. "Cumhuriyet Döneminin Öncü Bir Kadın Felsefecisi: Semiha Cemal Hanım." *Felsefe Dünyası*, no. 52 (2010): 116–25.

Bayraktar, Levent. "Darülfünun'da Bir Felsefe Hocası: Mehmet Emin Erişirgil." *Felsefe Dünyası*, no. 50 (2009): 64–80.

Bergson, Henri. *The Creative Mind: An Introduction to Metaphysics.* New York: Dover Publications, 2010.

Berktay, Fatmagül. *Kadın Olmak, Yaşamak, Yazmak.* İstanbul: Pencere Yayınları, 2000.

Bhabha, Homi K. *The Location of Culture.* London: Routledge, 1994.

Bobzien, Susanne. *Determinism and Freedom Is Stoic Philosophy.* Oxford: Clarendon Press, 2004.

Boulet, Bernard. "The Philosopher-King." *A Companion to Plutarch*, ed. Mark Beck. 449-462. Oxford: Blackwell Publication, 2014.

Brouwer, René. *The Stoics Sage: The Early Stoics on Wisdom, Sagehood and Socrates.* Cambridge: University of Cambridge Press, 2014.

Buğdaycı, Çiğdem. "Medicalization of Sufism: the Discourse of Psychiatry, Psychopathology, and Secularity in Karay's Kadınlar Tekkesi." *New Perspectives on Turkey* (2024): 1-20.

Burak Adli, Feyza. "Agent of Change or Guardian of Tradition?: Sufism, Gender, and Nationalism in Cold War Turkey." *Culture and Religion* 24, no. 2 (2024): 156–81.

——. "Trajectories of Modern Sufism: An Ethnohistorical Study of the Rifai Order and Social Change in Turkey." Ph.D. dissertation, Boston University, 2020.

——. "The Portrait of an Alla Franca Shaykh: Sufism, Modernity, and Class in Turkey." *International Journal of Middle East Studies* 56, no. 2 (2024): 207-226.

Cemāl, Semiha (Evrenos). *Apoloji (Methiye-Sokrates'in Savunması) ve Kriton (Vazife).* İstanbul: Devlet Matbaası, 1932.

——. *Aşk.* İstanbul: Devlet Basımevi, 1936.

——. *Aşk Budur.* İstanbul: Marifet Basımevi, 1938.

——. *Aşk Peygamberi.* İstanbul: Kitabhane-i Sudî, 1927.

——. *Aşk Peygamberi.* Edited by Nurcan Şen. Ankara: Çolpan Kitap, 2023.

——. "Canana Hitap." *Hilal Dergisi* 2, no. 1 (1958).

———. *Gül Demeti*. Edited by Siyami Boylu. İstanbul: Cağaloğlu Yayınevi, 2023.

———. *Gül Demeti*. İstanbul: İstanbul bilgi Basım ve Yayın Evi, 2023.

———. "Kleopatra." *Hayat Dergisi* 96, no. 4 (1928).

———. "Züleyha." *Güner Dergisi*, no. 2 (1927).

———. "Bahar ve Şifa." *Mihrap* 1, no. 1 (1924).

———. "Çölde Bir Secde." *Mihrap* 26, no. 2 (1925).

———. "Mihrak-ı Aşkı Sücuda Geldim!" *Mihrap* 17, no. 1 (1924).

———. "Pervane." *Mihrap* 12, no. 1 (1924).

———. "Sabah Ezanını Dinlerken." *Mihrap* 16, no. 15 (1924).

Chittick, William. *Sufism: A Beginner's Guide*. Oxford: Oneworld Book, 2000.

———. *Sufi Path of Knowledge: Ibn al-ʿArabī's Metaphysics of Imagination*. Albany: State University of New York Press, 1989.

Chovanec, Johanna. "Literature and the Legacy of Empire: Approaching Turkey's Post-Imperial Condition Through Ahmet Hamdi Tanpınar." *Philosophy & Social Criticism* 50, no. 4 (2024): 608-628.

Demirci, Mehmet. "Hakikat-i Muhammediye." *TDV İslâm Ansiklopedisi*. 15:179-180. İstanbul: TDV Yayınları, 1997.

Ebbersmeyer, Sabrina. "The Philosopher as a Lover: Renaissance Debates on Platonic Eros." In *Emotion and Cognitive Life in Medieval and Early Modern Philosophy*, edited by Martin Pickavé and Lisa Shapiro. Oxford: Oxford University Press, 2017.

Efeoğlu, Ahmet. "Modern Türk Diş Hekimliğinin Öncülerinden Prof. Dr. Dt. Ziya Cemāl Büyükaksoy (13 Eylül 1896-6 Ekim 1953)." *Dergi* (2021): 64-68.

Eflatun. *Apoloji (Methiye-Sokrates'in Savunması) ve Kriton (Vazife)*. Translated by Semiha Cemāl. İstanbul: Devlet Matbaası, 1932.

el-Kuşeyri. *Kuşeyri Risalesi*. İstanbul: Dergah Yayınları, 1981.

Epictetus. *Discourses and Selected Writings*. Translated by Robert Dobbin. London: Penguin Books, 2008.

Erbay, Erdoğan. "Mihrab." *TDV İslâm Ansiklopedisi*. 30:29-30. Ankara: TDV Yayınları, 2020.

Erickson, Edward J. *The Turkish War of Independence: A Military History, 1919-1923*. Santa Barbara: Bloomsbury Publication, 2021.

(Erişgil), Mehmed Emin. "Yeni Çıkan Kitaplar: Fedon, Ruhun Bekası; Mütercimi Dârülfünun Felsefe Şubesinden Mezun Semiha Cemâl Hanım." *Hayat Mecmuası* 81, no. 4 (1928).

Erol, Safiye. Ciğerdelen. İstanbul: Kubbealtı Neşriyat, 2008.

———. Ülker Fırtınası. İstanbul: Kubbealtı Neşriyat, 2006.

Frye, Northrop. *Anatomy of Criticism: Four Essays*. Princeton: Princeton University Press, 1957.

Godelek, Kamuran. "The Neoplatonist Roots of Sufi Philosophy." *The Paideia Archive: Twentieth World Congress of Philosophy*, no. 5 (1998).

Göknar, Erdağ. *Orhan Pamuk, Secularism and Blasphemy: The Politics of the Turkish Novel*. London: Routledge, 2013.

———. "Reading Occupied Istanbul: Turkish Subject-Formation from Historical Trauma to Literary Trope." *Culture, Theory and Critique* 55, no. 3 (2014): 321–41.

———. "Turkish-Islamic Feminism Confronts National Patriarchy: Halide Edib's Divided Self." *Journal of Middle East Women's Studies* 9, no. 2 (2013).

———. "The Novel in Turkish: Narrative Tradition to Nobel Prize." *The Cambridge History of Turkey, Volume 4: Turkey in the Modern World*, ed. Reşat Kasaba, 472–503. Cambridge: Cambridge University Press, 2008.

Guerlac, Suzanne. *Thinking in Time: An Introduction to Henri Bergson*. Cornell: Cornell University Press, 2006.

Güntekin, Reşat Nuri. *Miskinler Tekkesi*. İstanbul: İnkılap Kitapevi, 2000.

———. *Yeşil Gece*. İstanbul: İnkılap Kitapevi, 2000.

Hadot, Pierre. *Philosophy as a Way of Life: Spiritual Exercises from Socrates to Foucault*. Translated by Michael Chase. Blackwell: Oxford, 1995.

Hahm, David E. "The Stoic Theory of Change." *The Southern Journal of Philosophy*, no. 23 (1985): 39–56.

Hanioğlu, M. Şükrü. *A Brief History of the Late Ottoman Empire*. Princeton: Princeton University Press, 2008.

Hız, Gürbey. "The Making of the 'New Woman': Narratives in the Popular Illustrated Press from the Ottoman Empire to the New Republic (1890-1920s)." *Early Popular Visual Culture* 17, no. 2 (2019): 156–77.

Huri, Sofi. *Hz. Mevlâna ve Yakınları*. Edited by Ayten Lermioğlu. İstanbul: Redhouse Yayınevi, 1969.

———. *İslâm Âleminde İlk Kadın Sufi Olarak Tanınan Râbiat-Ül Adeviye*. İstanbul: Redhouse Yayinevi, 1970.

İrem, Nazım. "Turkish Conservative Modernism: Birth of a Nationalist Quest for Cultural Renewal." *International Journal of Middle East Studies* 34, no. 1 (2002): 87–112.

———. "Undercurrents of European Modernity and the Foundations of Modern Turkish Conservatism: Bergsonism in Retrospect." *Middle Eastern Studies*, no. 40 (2004).

Irzık, Gürol. "Hans Reichenbach in Istanbul." *Synthese* 181, no. 1(2011): 157-180.

Izutsu, Toshihiko. *Sufism and Taoism: A Comparative Study of Key Philosophical Concepts*. Berkeley: University of California Press, 1983.

Kafadar, Osman. "Felsefe Öğretiminin Türk Eğitim Sistemine Girişi ve Tarihi Gelişimi." *Ankara Üniversitesi Eğitim Bilimleri Fakültesi Dergisi* 27, no. 1 (1994): 279–88.

Kara, İsmail. *Cumhuriyet Türkiye'sinde Bir Mesele Olarak İslam*. İstanbul: Dergâh Yayınları, 2016.

———. "Cumhuriyet Türkiyesi'nde Tarîkatlar." In *Türkiye'de Tarikatlar: Tarih-Kültür*, edited by Semih Ceyhan, 103–11. İstanbul: İSAM Yayınları, 2015.

Kara, Mustafa. "Hikmet." *TDV İslâm Ansiklopedisi*. 17:518-519. İstanbul: TDV Yayınları, 1998.

Karaosmanoğlu, Yakup Kadri. *Nur Baba*. İstanbul: İletişim Yayınları, 2023.

————. *Nur Baba: A Sufi Novel of Late Ottoman Istanbul*. Edited by M. Brett Wilson. London: Routledge, 2024.

————. *Yaban*. İstanbul: İletişim Yayınları, 2017.

Karay, Refik Halid. *Kadınlar Tekkesi*. İstanbul: İnkılap Kitapevi, 2010.

Karimi, Ahmad and Akbar Shahiditabar, and Farhad Morsali Pavarsi. "Narratological Re-reading of Prophet Yusuf and Zulaikha Story." *Interdisciplinary Studies of Quran & Hadith* 1, no. 1 (2023): 90-108.

Karpat, Kemal H. "Social Themes in Contemporary Turkish Literature: Part I." *Middle East Journal* 14, no. 1 (1960): 29–44.

Kenny, Anthony. *Ancient Philosophy: A New History of Western Philosophy*, Volume 1. Oxford: Oxford University Press, 2004.

Ken'ān Rifāī. *Sohbetler*. İstanbul: Kubbealtı Neşriyat, 2000.

Köse, Elifhan. "Muhafazakar Bir Kadın Portresi Olarak Semiha Ayverdi: Muhafazakarlık Düşüncesinde Kadınlara İlişkin Bir Hat Çizebilmek." *Fe Dergi* 1 (2009): 11-20.

Krentz, Edgar M. "ΠΑΘΗ and ΑΠΑΘΕΙΑ in Early Roman Empire Stoics." In *Passions and Moral Progress in Greco-Roman Thought*, edited by John T. Fitzgerald. London: Routledge, 2008.

Kürük Erçetin, Nur Zeynep. "Halide Edip Adıvar: The Forgotten (Self-) Translator Behing the Writer." *Nesir: Edebiyat Araştırmaları Dergisi*, no. 7 (2024): 123–37.

Knysh, Alexander. *Islamic Mysticism: A Short History*. Leiden: Brill, 2000.

Levend, Agāh Sırrı. *Türk Dilinde Gelişme ve Sadeleşme Evreleri*. Ankara: Türk Tarih Kurumu Basımevi, 1972.

Lewisohn, Leonard. "The Sacred Music of Islam: Samā' in the Persian Sufi Tradition." *British Journal of Ethnomusicology* 6, no. 1 (1997): 1–33.

Loisel, Gustav. *Kendime: Marcus Aurelius Antonius'un Düşünceleri*. Translated by Semiha Cemāl. İstanbul: Devlet Matbaası, 1932.

MacArthur, Daniel-Joseph, and Gizem Tongo. "Representing Occupied Istanbul: Documents, Objects and Memory." *YILLIK: Annual of Istanbul Studies*, no. 4 (2002): 91–98.

Marmodoro, Anna. *Forms and Structure in Plato's Metaphysics.* Oxford: Oxford University Press, 2021.

Massignon, Louis. *The Passion of al-Hallaj: Mystic and Martyr of Islam.* Translated by Herbert Mason, vol. 1. Princeton: Princeton University Press, 1982.

Milani, Milad. "Mysticism in the Islamicate World: The Question of Neoplatonic Influence in Sufi Thought." In *Later Platonists and Their Heirs Among Christians, Jews, and Muslims.* Edited by Eva Anagnostou and Ken Parry. 413–544. Leiden, The Netherlands: Brill, 2022.

Mignon, Laurent. "Du mysticisme au nationalisme religieux: les ambiguïtés de Samiha Ayverdi (1905-1993)." *European Journal of Turkish Studies* 25 (2017): e-journal.

Moran, Berna. *Edebiyat Kuramları ve Eleştirileri.* İstanbul: İletişim Yayınları, 1991.

Nasr, Seyyed Hossein. "God is Absolute Reality and All Creation His Tajalli (Theophany)." *The Wiley Blackwell Companion to Religion and Ecology.* Edited by John Hart. 3-11. Oxford: Wiley Blackwell, 2017.

———. *Science and Civilization in Islam.* Cambridge, MA: Harvard University Press, 1968.

Neubauer, Anna. "This is the Age of Women: Legitimizing Female Authority in Contemporary Turkish Sufism." *Journal for the Academic Study of Religion* 29 (2016): 150-166.

Oğuz, Mustafa Cem. "Mustafa Şekip Tunç ve Türkiye'de Bergsonculuk." *Artvin Çoruh Üniversitesi Uluslararası Sosyal Bilimler Dergisi* 1, no. 1 (2015).

Okan, Orçun Can. "Osmanlı'ya Sonlar Yaz((a)ma)mak: İmparatorluk, Devlet ve Ardıllık", *Osmanlı Tarihçiliğinde Yani Çalışmalar: Kaynak, Bağlam, Yöntem*, eds. Fatma Öncel, Sinem Erdoğan İşkorkutan. 245-279. İstanbul: Vakfı Bank Yayınları, 2023.

Öngören, Reşat. "Mevlânâ Celāleddîn-i Rûmî." *TDV İslâm Ansiklopedisi.* 29:441-448. Ankara: TDV Yayınları, 2004.

Özervarlı, Sait. "Positivism in the Late Ottoman Empire: The 'Young Turks' as Mediators and Multipliers." In *The Worlds of Positiv-*

ism: A Global Intellectual History, 1770–1930, edited by Johannes Feichtinger, Franz L. Fillafer, and Jan Surman. Cham: Palgrave Macmillan, 2018.

Pamuk, Orhan. *Secularism and Blasphemy: The Politics of the Turkish Novel*. London: Routledge, 2013.

Parla, Jale. "The Wounded Tongue: Turkey's Language Reform and the Canonicity of the Novel." *Modern Language Association* 1, no. 23 (2008).

Plato. *Fedon: Ruhun Bekası*. Translated by Semiha Cemāl. İstanbul: Orhaniye Matbaası, 1928.

———. *Phaedo*. Translated by David Gallop. Oxford: Oxford University Press, 1993.

———. *Phaedrus*. Translated by Alexander Nehamas and Paul Woodruff. Indianapolis: Hackett Publishing Company, 1995.

———. *Symposium*. Translated by Alexander Nehamas and Paul Woodruff. Indianapolis: Hackett Publishing, 1989.

Platón. *Apologie de Socrate*. Translated by Maurice Croiset. Paris: Librairie Hatier, 1958.

Platon. *Aşk ve Ziyafet*. Translated by Semiha Cemāl. İstanbul: Devlet Basımevi, 1936.

Pulat, Ali and Fatih Bayram. "Nezihe Araz'ın Tiyatrolarındaki Toplumsal Sorunlar." *International Journal of Languages' Education and Teaching* 6, no. 4 (2018): 23-37.

———. "Nezihe Araz Tiyatrolarında Kadın Sorunları." *International Journal of Language Academy* 6, no. 26 (2024): 148-161.

Prahasan, Marimuthu, and Mahir I. L. M. "Human Flourishing by Living in Harmony with Nature and Moral Integrity: Insights from Epictetus the Stoic." *American Journal of Arts and Human Science* 4, no. 1 (2025).

Radpour, Esmail. "Symbolism of Water in Daoism: A Sufi Point of View." *Sophia Perennis* 34, no. 15 (2019): 5–17.

Rifāī, Semiha. "Çoban Kızı." *Mihrap* 28, no. 2 (1925).

———. "Kurban-ı Aşk." *Mihrap* 27, no. 2 (1925).

Said, Edward. *Culture and Imperialism*. New York: Vintage Books, 1993.

Salim Nefes, Türkay. "Ziya Gökalp's Adaptation of Emile Durkheim's Sociology in His Formulation of the Modern Turkish Nation." *International Sociology* 28, no. 3 (2017).

Sargut, Cemalnur. *Ken'ān Rifāī Ile Aşka Yolculuk*. Edited by Sadık Yalsızuçanlar. İstanbul: Nefes Yayınları, 2014.

Sarmis, Dilek. "Conceptualiser Le Mysticisme Dans Une Perspective Académique : La Constitution D'une Histoire Générale Du Mysticisme Chez Mehmet Ali Ayni (1868-1945)." *European Journal of Turkish Studies*, no. 25 (2017): 1–26.

Savaş, Kudret. *Zaman Sürgünü: Semiha Cemal Hayatı ve Eserleri*. Çanakkale: Paradigma Akademi, 2022.

Sawai, Makoto. "From Mysticism to Philosophy: Toshihiko Izutsu and Sufism." *Journal of the Institute for Sufi Studies* 1, no. 2 (2022): 112–21.

Schafer, Murray R. *The Soundscape: Our Sonic Environment and the Tuning of the World*. Vermont: Inner Traditions, 1993.

Schimmel, Annemarike. *Mystical Dymension of Islam*. Chapel Hill: University of North Caroline Press, 2011.

Sedgwick, Mark. *Western Sufism: From the Abbasids to the New Age*. Oxford: Oxford University Press, 2017.

Selvi, Dilaver. "Tasavvufta Marifetin Meyvesi Rahmet Ahlâkı ve Hizmet." *Kafkas Üniversitesi İlahiyat Fakültesi Dergisi* 4, No. Ek.1 (2017): 85-155.

Subaşı, Muzaffer and Derya Nazlıpınar. "Halide Edip Adıvar and Her Perception of the 'New Woman' Identity." *Uluslararası İnsan Çalışmaları Dergisi* 1, no. 2 (2018): 374-382.

Şanal, Mustafa. "Osmanlı İmparatorluğu'nda Kız Öğretmen Okulu'nun (Dârülmuallimât) Kuruluşu, Okutulan Dersler ve Kapatılışı." *Ankara Üniversitesi Osmanlı Tarihi ve Uygulama Merkezi Dergisi (OTAM)*, no. 26 (2011): 222–44.

Şeker, Nesim. "Vision of Modernity in the Early Turkish Republic: An Overview." *Historia Actual Online* 14 (2007): 49-56.

Şen, Cafer. "Tasavvufî Bir Romana Psikanalitik Bir Bakış." *Aşk Peygamberi,* Semiha Cemal, haz. Nurcan Şen. İstanbul: Çolpan Kitap, 2023.

Tahralı, Mustafa. "İlhan Ayverdi." *TDV İslâm Ansiklopedisi.* Ek1:149-150. Ankara: TDV Yayınları, 2020.

Tahralı, Mustafa. "Rifaiyye." *TDV İslam Ansiklopedisi.* 35:99-103. İstanbul: TDV Yayınları, 2008.

Tanpınar, Ahmet Hamdi. *Huzur.* İstanbul: Dergah Yayınları, 2023.

Tatcı, Mustafa. "Yunus Emre." *TDV Islâm Ansiklopedisi.* 43: 600-606. İstanbul: TDV Yayınları, 2013.

Thurot, François. *Epiklet (Epictete).* Translated by Semiha Cemāl. Ankara: Maârif Vekâleti, 1932.

———. *Epiktet (Epictéte).* Translated by Semiha Cemāl. İstanbul: Milli Eğitim Basımevi, 1932.

Topal, Alp Eren. "Against Influence: Ziya Gökalp in Context and Tradition." *Journal of Islamic Studies* 3, no. 28 (2017): 283–310.

Toprak, Zafer. "Nazım Hikmet'in 'Putları Kırıyoruz' Kampanyası ve Yeni Edebiyat." *Toplumsal Tarih* 261 (2015): 35-36.

Tunç, Mustafa Şekip. *Bergson ve Manevi Kudrete Dair Birkaç Konferans.* İstanbul: Muallim Ahmet Halit Kitaphanesi, 1934.

Uçman, Abdullah. "Dergâh." *TDV İslâm Ansiklopedisi.* 9:172-174. İstanbul: TDV Yayınları, 1994.

———. "Hayat." *TDV İslâm Ansiklopedisi.* 17:12-14. İstanbul: TDV Yayınları, 1998.

Uludağ, Süleyman. "Marifet." *TDV İslâm Ansiklopedisi.* 28:54-56. İstanbul: TDV Yayınları, 2003.

———. "Tevhid." *TDV İslâm Ansiklopedisi.* 41:22-24. İstanbul: TDV yayınları, 2012.

———. "Hicab." *TDV İslâm Ansiklopedisi.* 17:430-431. İstanbul: TDV Yayınları, 1998.

Ülken, Hilmi Ziya. "Yusuf Ziya Yörükân (1887-1952)." *İlâhiyat Fakültesi Dergisi* I–II (1954).

Uludağ, Süleyman. "Cemāl." *TDV İslâm Ansiklopedisi.* 7:296. İstanbul: TDV Yayınları, 1993.

Üstün Kaya, Senem. "Women Behind the Pens: A Comparative Analysis of Turkish Female Authors From Reform Period to Modernism." *The Online Journal of Science and Technology* 11, no. 4 (2021): 133–41.

Van Bruinessen, Martin. "Sufism, 'Popular' Islam and the Encounter with Modernity." *Islam and Modernity,* 2009.

Vlastos, Gregory. *The Individual as an Object of Love in Plato.* Princeton: Princeton University Press, 1981.

Wilcox, Andrew. "The Dual Mystical Concepts of Fanā' and Baqā' in Early Sufism." *British Journal of Middle Eastern Studies* 38, no. 1 (2011): 95–118.

Wilson, M. Brett. "The Twilight of Ottoman Sufism: Antiquity, Immorality, and Nation in Yakup Kadri Karaosmanoğlu's Nur Baba." *International Journal of Middle East Studies* 49, no. 2 (2017): 233-253.

———."Putting out the Candle: Sufism and the Orgy Libel in Late Ottoman and Modern Turkey." *Comparative Studies of South Asia, Africa and the Middle East* 41, no. 1 (2021): 72–84.

Yalçınkaya, Arzu Eylül. "Ken'ān Rifā'ī and the Dynamics of Late Ottoman Sufi Poetry: Continuity, Innovation, and Intellectual Engagement." *Journal of the Institute for Sufi Studies* 3, no. 2 (2024): 207–26.

———. *Ken'ān Rifāī: Hayatı, Eserleri ve Tasavvuf Anlayışı.* İstanbul: Nefes Yayınevi, 2021.

———. "Semiha Cemal Hanım'ın Dilinden Ken'ân Rifâî'nin Meşreb-i Şerifleri." Presented at the I. Uluslararası Tasavvuf Araştırmaları Lisansüstü Öğrenci Sempozyumu, 2018.

———. "From Concept to Novel: Tāhirülmevlevī's (1877-1951) Sufi Engagement and Critique of Teşebbüs-i Şahsī (Individual Initiative) in the Late Ottoman Era." *Kadim* 8 (2024): 23-50.

Yakalı, Dikmen and Bora Ataman, "Selfless Subjectivities that (Re) Build the Nation: Remaking the 'Modern Turkish Woman' in the

Early Republican Period in Türkiye." *Journal of Family History* 48, no. 4 (2023): 432-446.

Yeşilyurt, Şamil. "Cumhuriyetin Erken Döneminde Tarihī Roman (1923-1950)." In *Türk Ocakları Derneği Bursa Şubesi'nin Cumhuriyet'in 100. Yılına Armağanı*, Bursa, 2023.

Zürcher, Erik J. *Turkey: A Modern History*. London: I.B. Tauris, 2017.

Dictionary

A

Ağa (pl. *ağalar*): *Master* or *chief*. A historical title for men of authority or status, especially in rural or tribal contexts. In Ottoman times it could denote a landowner, head of a family, or military officer. In modern use it survives in some regions as a respectful form of address for an elder male, akin to "sir."

Ağabey (lit. "big brother"): *Elder brother*. Used both for one's actual older brother and as a polite address for an older male friend. It conveys respect and affection, similar to "bro" or "big brother" in English. In the novel, younger characters address senior male figures as *ağabey* to show respectful familiarity.

Ālamet-i fārika: *Distinctive mark* or *hallmark*. An idiomatic Ottoman expression (lit. "sign of distinction") referring to a unique feature that sets someone or something apart. For example, a person's Ālamet-i fārika might be an unusual birthmark or a signature style.

Allah'a ısmarladık: *"May God protect [you]"*. A formal way to say *goodbye* when one is the person leaving. It literally means "I entrust you to God" and carries the sense of "farewell, God be with you." (The expected reply from those staying is *"Güle güle,"* meaning "go with a smile.")

Amber: *Ambergris*, a waxy substance from whale intestines historically used in perfumery. By extension, **amber** in Ottoman parlance refers to a warm, musky fragrance. Amber is often paired with *gül* (rose) as in "gül ve amber kokusu" to evoke the exotic scent of traditional perfumes.

Asude: *Tranquil* or *at peace*. Describes a state of calmness and serenity. For example, *asude bir akşam* means a peaceful evening. In poetry and prose it often connotes an almost idyllic calm, free from worldly worry.

Aşık: *(1) Lover; (2) Minstrel.* In daily use, *aşık* means a person in love. In a cultural context it also refers to itinerant bards in Anatolian tradition (often called *ozan*), who sing of love and mysticism. In the novel it primarily denotes a passionate lover. An *āşık* is driven by **aşk** (love), sometimes to the point of madness or holy devotion.

Aşina (Persian *āshnā*): *Familiar* or *well-acquainted.* Describes someone or something known intimately. **Aşinalık** means familiarity or intimacy. In Sufi literature, being *aşina* with the spiritual realm implies an innate familiarity or kinship with the divine.

Aşk: *Love.* In everyday Turkish, *aşk* means passionate love (often romantic). In a Sufi philosophical sense, **aşk** signifies a divine, ecstatic love for the Absolute. Sufis distinguish **aşk-ı mecāzī** (metaphorical love, such as human romantic love) from **aşk-ı hakikī** (true love, the love of God). The novel's title *The Prophet of Love (Aşk Peygamberi)* invokes *aşk* in its elevated, spiritual sense, portraying love as a guiding, sacred force.

Ateşin: *Fiery; ardent.* Used to describe something full of fire (*ateş*), whether literally burning or figuratively passionate. An *ateşin güzellik* is a beauty that burns with intensity. In the book, a lover's "ateşin güzel" (fiery beauty) indicates a beloved who is both bright and passionately alive. By extension, *ateşin* can mean lively, spirited, or emotionally intense.

B

Balāter (Persian origin): *Higher; supreme.* An archaic term meaning "much higher" or "loftier." In context it can imply a superior quality or a sound that is above others. For example, a *balāter makam* might mean a higher rank or a more exalted state.

Bayram: *Festival; holiday.* Refers especially to Turkish/Islamic holidays. There are two major religious **Bayrams:** *Ramazan Bayramı* (Eid al-Fitr) and *Kurban Bayramı* (Eid al-Adha). The term is also used for secular celebrations. To "bayram yapmak" ("to make bayram") means to celebrate joyously. In the novel, *donanma gecesi*(Illumination Night) is a kind of bayram celebration with lights and fireworks.

Beşaret: *Good tidings; auspicious sign.* An old word meaning a happy omen or message. If someone's **hālinde bir beşaret** görülüyor, it means "there is seen an auspicious sign in his condition" – indicating hope or good fortune.

Besmele: *The Bismillah*, i.e., the phrase **"Bismillāhirrahmānir-rahīm"** ("In the name of God, the Compassionate, the Merciful"). Muslims utter the *besmele* at the start of any significant task or prayer. In the novel a character declares, "Ey aşk, seni kendime **besmele** ittihaz ettim!" – "O love, I have adopted you as my besmele," equating love with a holy invocation. This underscores how love is elevated to a sacred principle, invoked at the beginning of all endeavors.

Bismillāhi'l-Aşk: *"In the name of Love."* A creative phrase modeled on the besmele. The novel uses **Bismillāhi'l Aşk düsturu** ("the motto 'In the name of Love'") to suggest that love itself has become the deity or guiding force in the speaker's life. It encapsulates the book's theme of love as a religion.

Bey: *Gentleman; sir* (lit. "chieftain"). A Turkish honorific historically given to leaders or nobles, and today used as a polite title after a man's first name (e.g. **Celāl Bey**). It is similar to "Mr." or "sir". In the novel, men are often addressed with **Bey** to show respect. (Plural **beyler** can mean "gentlemen" or, colloquially, "sirs").

Beyhude: *In vain; futile.* Describes an action that is wasted or without result. For example, *beyhude beklemek*means to wait in vain. A character might lament an unrequited effort as **beyhude** – expressing a sense of futility or uselessness.

Bi-pervā (Persian **biparvā**): *Without care; reckless.* Literally "unafraid/uncaring," it describes a heedless or boldly unconcerned attitude. In the text, *bi-pervā türküler* (carefree songs) are sung without concern for who might hear. Someone acting **bi-pervā** behaves boldly, free of worry about consequences or others' opinions.

Bürūdet: *Coldness.* An old-fashioned word (from Arabic *burūdat*) meaning a chilling quality. It can describe literal cold (air, weather) or figurative coldness (an emotional frigidity). The novel uses it for the *bürūdet* that numbs a heart until love's warmth revives it.

C

Canan: *Beloved.* A literary term (from Persian) for one's loved one, especially a woman who is adored. **Can** means "soul," and **canan** implies "soul's beloved." In poetry, the lover (*āşık*) longs for the **canan**, often comparing her to Layla or other idealized beloveds. In the novel, *canan* signifies the adored object of one's love.

Cefa: *Torment; cruelty.* Often paired with *mihnet* (hardship), **cefa** refers to suffering inflicted, especially by a beloved's unkindness or the pain of separation. To "çekmek cefa" is to endure cruel difficulties. Ottoman love poetry frequently speaks of the **cefa** of the beloved – the trials the lover endures for love.

Cihan: *World; universe.* An old term for "world" or "cosmos" (synonymous with *dünya*). **Cihan** can mean the whole world or an age. In phrases like *cihan dolusu aşk* ("love as vast as the world") it emphasizes greatness. The novel says *cihan* had lost color for a character once they found love. Also in idioms like *cihanın anahtarı* ("key to the world").

Cumba: *Bay window; overhanging balcony.* In traditional Ottoman houses, a **cumba** is a wooden bay window that protrudes from the upper floor, often latticed. It allowed those inside (especially women) to see the street while remaining unseen. The text mentions "**kafesleri sökülmüş cumbalar**" – window screens removed from the cumba, symbolizing a house opened to view.

Ç

Çehre: *Face; countenance.* A somewhat elevated word for a person's face or visage. **Çehre** often implies the expression or the radiant appearance of a face. The novel describes a *berrak çehre* (clear, shining face) of a vision. A *gülen çehre* is a smiling face. It can also mean the outward appearance of things.

D

Dārülfünūn: *House of Sciences.* The old Ottoman Turkish term for the university. Istanbul University (founded in the 19th century) was called **Dārü'l-fünūn.** In the novel's foreword, it is mentioned as *Dārülfünūn Emīni* (Dean of the University). It represents the early modern higher education in Türkiye.

Derviş: *Dervish*. A member of a Sufi Islamic ascetic order. Dervishes renounce worldly possessions and practice intense devotion to God – some are known for the **semā** (whirling dance) or other rituals. The term can also mean someone living in poverty or humility for spiritual reasons. In literature, a lover may be metaphorically called a **derviş** for living on the "alm of love" alone. (Plural **dervişler**).

Donanma gecesi: *"Illumination night"*. A festive celebration at night with lights, flags, and fireworks. In Ottoman times, **donanma** referred to decorated nights on special occasions (bayrams, royal birthdays, etc.), when cities would be adorned with oil lamps and fireworks. The text describes a *donanma gecesi* where neighbors gather amid illuminated joy.

Düstur: *Principle; motto; maxim*. Literally "rule" or "regulation," **düstur** in literature often means a guiding principle or slogan. Someone's **düstur** is the motto they live by. In the novel, *"Bismillāhi'l Aşk" düsturu* is mentioned, meaning the guiding maxim "In the name of Love." As an exclamation, *Düstur!* can also mean "Take heed!" or requesting permission to proceed (archaic usage).

E

Entari: *A long robe or gown*. A traditional ankle-length garment worn by both women and men in the Ottoman era (though styles differed). For women it was a flowing dress, often with long sleeves. In the novel's setting (early 20th century), a *pembe entari* (pink gown) might be part of a lady's attire. (Plural **entariler**).

Evza-ı mahsusa: *Specific conditions; particular states*. An Ottoman phrase (pl. *evza* from Arabic *vaz'*, condition). It refers to certain special circumstances or prescribed states one must adhere to. In the text it appears in a scientific or instructional context, implying there are particular conditions to be met for some procedure.

F

Fānī: *Mortal; perishable*. Describes anything transient, subject to death or decay (opposite of *ebedī*, eternal). **Fānī dünya** means "the ephemeral world." A famous line in the book is "Ruh ebedī, madde fānīdir" – "The soul is eternal, matter is mortal". In Sufi thought, recognizing the **fānī** nature of the self is a step toward seeking the eternal truth (see **fenā**).

Fazilet: *Virtue.* Moral excellence, goodness. A person of **fazilet** is virtuous and possesses moral merits. The novel speaks of discovering that there is beauty and **fazilet** in the world. The term often implies a combination of righteousness and honor. (Plural **faziletler**).

Fenā: *"Annihilation" (in Sufi theology).* Short for **Fenā fi'llāh**, the state of annihilating one's ego in the love of God. It means the self fades away until only the Divine remains in one's consciousness. In contrast to **bekā** (subsistence in God after fenā). The term literally means "perishing" – indicating the ephemeral nature of the individual self. In the novel's context, *fenā* is not explicitly named but the theme of the self being lost in love aligns with this concept.

Feyz: *Divine grace; inspirational illumination.* An Arabic-origin word meaning the spiritual energy or enlightenment that "overflows" from God or a spiritual master to the seeker. To **feyz almak** is to receive inspiration or blessing. Students are described as *senden feyz alan çocuklar* ("children who drew spiritual inspiration from you"). It connotes an almost invisible nourishment of the soul.

G

Galiz: *Coarse; vulgar.* Refers to something foul or crude, especially language or behavior. **Galiz söz** means a gross or obscene word. The novel uses *galiz hükümler* ("vile judgments") to indicate harsh, ugly words or curses. It's an old-fashioned term; modern Turkish would use *kaba* or *ağır* in similar contexts.

Gam: *Sorrow; grief.* A Persian loanword frequently used in poetry for melancholic sorrow. Someone *"gamsız"* is carefree (literally "without grief"). In the text, a lover's **gamsız alnı** (untroubled brow) being marked by fate indicates that even the carefree will taste sorrow. *Gam çekmek* means to suffer grief, and *gamze* (from the same root) poetically refers to a coy glance that "inflicts sorrow" on lovers.

Gaşyolmuş: *Enraptured; in a faint.* From **ğaşy** (Arabic, "unconsciousness/ecstasy"), it describes someone who has lost their senses from ecstasy or swoon. In the novel, *gaşyolmuş gibi* is "as if in a trance/faint". It often connotes a spiritual ecstasy – the state of being "blacked out" to the world due to overwhelming emotion or divine love.

Gönül: *Heart; soul.* Not the physical heart (*yürek*), but the seat of emotions and spirituality. **Gönül** is where love and longing reside. One *gönül vermek* ("gives one's heart") to a beloved or cause. In Sufi literature, the **gönül** is the vessel that can reflect divine light once polished of ego. The novel often uses *gönül* to mean the inner heart that yearns and perceives truth beyond intellect.

Gurbet: *Exile; being far from home.* The melancholy of living away from one's homeland or loved ones. **Gurbet elde** means "in a foreign land." It implies loneliness and longing for home (see also *sıla*). The text references *yalnızlık, gurbetin mihnetleri* – the loneliness and unexpected hardships of exile. In Turkish literature, *gurbet acısı* (the pain of exile) is a common theme, evoking homesickness and isolation.

Gurur: *Pride.* It can mean self-respect or, in a negative sense, arrogance. In the novel, someone's **gururuna dokunmak** means "to offend his pride." For instance, when a helping hand wounds Sühā's pride, he recoils – *bu hāl Sühā'nın gururuna dokundu* ("that act touched Sühā's pride"). **Gururlu** describes a proud person (positively dignified or negatively haughty depending on context).

Gurūb: *Sunset.* An archaic form (from Arabic *ghurub*) of modern Turkish *gurup* or *gün batımı*. It denotes the west or the act of the sun setting. The novel's imagery includes "**gurūb cihetinden uçan kuş kafilesi**" – a flock of birds flying from the direction of sunset. Sunset symbolizes endings or the onset of separation (night) in literature. (*Gurup vakti* means at sundown.)

H

Hāşā: *"God forbid!"; far be it!* An interjection used to repudiate something strongly, often to ward off blasphemy or an unwanted suggestion. In the novel, when one character suggests the beloved might be mortal, the lover exclaims **Haşa**, sen mahlûk değilsin – "Perish the thought, you are no mere creature!". It's a way of saying "no, absolutely not" with almost religious emphasis, as if to say the very idea is sacrilegious.

Halecān: *Palpitation; trembling excitement*. A poetic term combining *hāle* (state) and *can* (soul), often used for the thrill or quiver of the heart in intense emotion. It can describe the physical flutter of the heart during passionate excitement or anxiety. In the text, *kalbimi halecān içinde buluyorum* – "I find my heart in a tremor" – denotes feeling an agitated excitement.

Hasret: *Yearning; longing*. Deep emotional longing for someone or something absent. One can feel **hasret** for a lost lover, one's home, or past days. It carries the ache of separation. The novel frequently evokes *bitmeyen bir hasret* ("an unending longing"). *Hasretinden ölüyorum* means "I'm dying of longing for you". The term implies both love and pain – missing someone so much it hurts.

Hatun: *Lady; woman*. An old term for a woman of respectable status, historically akin to "lady" or "mistress of the house." In Ottoman times, **Hatun** was used for noble or royal women (e.g. *Hürrem Hatun*). In the novel, an elderly neighbor is called *Fatıma Hanım* but described as *bu hatun* by the narrator, using hatun in the sense of "woman" or "lady." It can also colloquially mean "wife" (e.g. *evdeki hatun* – the lady at home).

Hayāl: *Image; dream; imagination*. **Hayāl** can mean a vision or apparition as well as the faculty of imagination. In the novel, the protagonist often pursues a **hayal** – an image of the beloved that may be a dream or a spiritual vision. Ottoman poetry calls the beloved's elusive image a *hayal* that haunts the lover's heart. The word captures both the illusory nature of appearances and the creative power of imagination. (Note: *Hayal etmek* means to imagine or daydream.)

Hicrān: *Separation sorrow*. The pain of being separated from one's beloved. **Hicran** is a poetic term for the heartache of love in absence (related to *hicret*, exile). A *hicrān dolu gece* is a night filled with sorrows of separation. In the story a "woman sorrowful from exile" (**hicranlı** bir kadın **gurbetten** gelen) appears, embodying both exile and heartache. The word often implies tears, nostalgia, and lonely suffering.

Hüzün: *Melancholy; wistful sorrow.* A key concept in Turkish culture, **hüzün** refers to a deep, lingering sense of sadness that is not entirely negative – it has an air of spiritual richness or reflection. Istanbul literature often speaks of *İstanbul'un hüznü* (the melancholy of Istanbul). In the novel, characters experience **hüzün** as they confront loneliness or the passage of time. It's a kind of sweet sorrow that fosters introspection. Orhan Pamuk describes *hüzün* as the communal heaviness of heart Istanbulites share – here it is personal, the gloom shadowing a soul in love or loss.

I

Izdırap (modern **ızdırap**): *Anguish; pain.* Intense suffering, usually emotional but sometimes physical. A lover consumed by **ızdırap** is in torment from love or grief. The text says *bütün vücudu ızdırap içinde, ruhu melâl içindeydi* – "his whole body was in pain, his soul in melancholy". The word conveys a protracted agony, often noble or poetic in context (the suffering that deepens the soul).

İ

İhtiras: *Passion; ambition.* Depending on context, it can mean lust, ardent desire, or worldly ambition. **İhtiras** in romance is burning desire; in a negative sense it can imply greed or covetous ambition. The novel refers to *unsurî ihtiraslar* (base elemental passions), suggesting carnal or material lusts. A person *ihtirasla* doing something is doing it with intense, sometimes reckless, passion.

İlahī: *Divine.* Used as an adjective meaning "pertaining to God" or "heavenly." For example, *ilāhī aşk* is divine love. The novel speaks of **ilāhi vücud** – "the divine being" – when a lover describes the beloved in almost godlike terms. *İlahī* can also start exclamations (e.g. *İlahi!* meaning "Oh my, how funny/odd" in a colloquial, different sense). Here it maintains its literal meaning of divine or sacred.

İlham: *Inspiration.* Specifically creative or spiritual inspiration believed to come from an outside source (literally "in-breathing"). A poet or artist receives **ilham** like a breath from the divine muse. In the book, Semiha Cemāl is said to take her **ilham** (inspiration) from her own soul rather than external nature. To *ilham gelmek* is "to get inspired." Often paired with *perī* (fairy) in idiom *ilham perisi* – the muse.

İmtidād: *Extension; lengthening.* Used in the novel to describe something stretching out. For example, *imtidad eden ufuklar* – horizons that extend far. It implies a long, continuous stretch (of time, space, etc.). The root is Arabic *mumtedad* (extended). In modern Turkish, one might use *uzanma* or *yayılma*, but imtidād gives a classical flavor.

İnkiyad: *Obedience; submission.* An archaic term meaning yielding or bending to another's will (from Arabic *inqiyād*). The phrase *mānā-yı inkıyād* is used in the text: *inkıyad manasını okumak* – "to read the meaning of submission", implying understanding true obedience amid wildness. In Sufi context, **inkiyad** is the disciple's submission to the spiritual guide or God's will.

İnşallah: *"God willing."* A common phrase used when speaking of future hopes or plans, expressing the desire that God will grant success. For example, *"İnşallah ikimiz de döneriz"* – "God willing, we will both return." It reflects a cultural habit of humility about the future. In the novel's letters, characters say they will meet again, **inşallah**, acknowledging fate's uncertainty.

İstidād: *Talent; capability.* Refers to an innate ability or aptitude (modern Turkish *istidat* or *yetenek*). The foreword praises Semiha Cemāl's *ateşin istidād* (fiery talent). Someone with **istidād** has the potential for greatness in some art or skill. It can also mean capacity or disposition – e.g., a heart's *istidādı* for love.

İttihāz etmek: *To adopt; to take on.* An Ottoman verb form meaning to assume or treat as. For example, … *seni kendime besmele ittihaz ettim* – "I have taken you as my *besmele* (sacred invocation)".

Here **ittihāz**conveys formally adopting something as one's own. It's a high-register word, replaced in modern language by *edinmek* or *kabul etmek*.

K

Kahvehane: *Coffeehouse*. In Ottoman and Turkish culture, the **kahvehane** (lit. "coffee house") is a social hub where men drink coffee or tea, smoke, and converse or play games. It was a center of community life, story-telling, and even political discussion. The novel references a village youth working at the *kahve* (short for kahvehane). These establishments were important settings for daily socializing and spreading news.

Kemāl: *Perfection; maturity*. Often used in the phrase *kemāle ermek* ("to reach perfection/maturity"). It implies the fullest development of something. In a spiritual context, **kemāl** can mean completeness or the perfect human virtues. The text has *ondan kemāli öğrendik* – "from him we learned perfection", suggesting an ideal example of virtue and excellence. *Kemāliyle* means "completely/fully." The related term *kāmil* means accomplished or perfected (as in **İnsan-ı Kāmil**, the Perfect Human in Sufi thought).

Kısmet: *Fate; one's lot*. A very common Turkish concept meaning the portion or destiny allotted to a person. If something was **kısmet**, it was meant to be. Marriage prospects, wealth, even a piece of bread can be called *kısmet*. The novel's characters occasionally resign their hopes with "kısmet" – accepting that some outcomes lie in God's hands. It can also mean a share (e.g., *ekmek kısmeti* – one's share of bread). Saying *kısmet değilmiş* means "it wasn't fated to happen."

L

Latīf: *Pleasant; delicate*. Describes something gentle, agreeable, or subtly beautiful. **Latif** can refer to a charming person, a fine smell, or an elegant phrase. The novel uses it for the quality of sunset (*batışın doğuşundan daha latifse de...* – "though your setting is gentler than your rise"). As a noun (Latif), it is one of God's names meaning "The Subtle, The Gracious."

Lāyemut: *Immortal; undying.* (Literally "unceasing to die"). Not directly in the text but often found in late Ottoman usage to describe eternal things (e.g. *şöhret-i lā yemut* – undying fame). It combines *lā* (no) and *mevt*(death). If something is **lāyemūt**, it will never perish.

Lāyenkati (also *lāyenkatī*): *Uninterrupted; continuous.* Literally "without cutting/break." In the text, *layenkatı çukurlar* (never-ending potholes) are mentioned, indicating continuous obstacles. It comes from *lā* (no) + *inkıta* (interruption). It's an archaic term; modern Turkish would say *aralıksız*.

Lerze: *Tremor; shiver.* A poetic word for a slight trembling (often from emotion or a gentle motion). The novel poetically notes a **lerze** – a quiver – of a silver-lit object in the breeze. *Lerze-i aşk* would mean a "tremble of love." It's typically used for delicate, subtle vibrations (a trembling light, a quaking heart).

M

Mahviyet: *Humility; self-effacement.* In Sufi ethics, **mahviyet** is the quality of effacing one's ego – being humble to the point of self-annihilation. The foreword describes how Semiha tempered the manifestations of her lyrical genius with **mahviyet** (modesty). It implies a meekness that is spiritual – the opposite of arrogance. A *mahviyetkār* person effaces herself and attributes success to God or others.

Maşuk: *Beloved.* The counterpart to *āşık* (lover). **Ma'şuk** is the one who is loved, often portrayed as the passive object of the lover's passion. In Sufi poetry, the *maşuk* is frequently God or the Divine reality cloaked as a beautiful beloved. While not explicitly used in the novel, the concept underlies the love dynamic: the *āşık* (lover) and *maşuk*(beloved) in an eternal dance of longing.

Meczup: *Enraptured one; mad devotee.* Literally "attracted" (to God). A **meczup** is someone so overwhelmed by divine love that they appear insane or disconnected from normal life. Often applied to wandering holy fools or wild-eyed dervishes believed to be lost in God. In the text, *koyunların meczubane itaatı* ("the sheep's love-struck obedience") uses the adjective **meczubāne** (like one enraptured) to poetically describe complete, rapt compliance. A meczup may babble truths or act strangely – revered in folklore as touched by the Divine.

Menhūs: *Accursed; ill-omened.* Something **menhus** is thought to bring bad luck or to be gloomy and inauspicious. Sühā calls his strict math teacher *menhus* – essentially a "wretched" or "jinxed" person in the students' eyes. It can describe times (a *menhus gün* – unlucky day) or objects as well. The tone is one of superstitious disdain or fear.

Meyhane: *Tavern; wine-house.* A place where alcohol (traditionally wine or rakı) is served – essentially the opposite of a teetotal coffeehouse. In Ottoman times, **meyhanes** were often run by non-Muslims and seen as dens of vice by the pious. The novel briefly notes a *kirli ışık* from a **meyhane** (dirty light emanating from a tavern) in a rundown area. This imagery evokes an atmosphere of melancholy and debauchery. (The word comes from Persian *mey* = wine.)

Mihnet: *Hardship; affliction.* Painful difficulty or suffering, often endured with patience. A classic pairing is **mihnet ve cefa** – trials and tribulations. In one letter, it's said that loneliness in exile brings many unforeseen **mihnets** (hardships). The word suggests hardship that tests one's endurance (as in the saying *"Mihneti kendine zevk edinenler..."* – "those who make hardship a pleasure").

Muallim: *Teacher.* An old-fashioned word (from Arabic) for instructor, used in the early 20th century. The book uses **muallim** for schoolteachers (e.g., *riyaziye muallimi* – math teacher). After language reforms, *öğretmen* became the common term, but *muallim* still implies a mentor with an almost paternal authority in traditional contexts. (Female form: *muallime*).

Muhabbet: *Affectionate love; conversation.* **Muhabbet** can mean deep love (not as fiery as *aşk*, more tender) or a warm, heartfelt chat. To *"muhabbet etmek"* is to engage in friendly, soul-baring conversation. In Sufi terms it can imply love for God or between spiritual companions. The novel speaks of someone *ona muhab-*

betimle ısıtmaya çalıştım ("I tried to warm him with all the heat of my affection"). *Muhabbet kuşu* in Turkish is literally a "love bird" (budgerigar). This word emphasizes a gentle, caring love often expressed through companionship and talk.

Muhacir: *Immigrant; refugee.* Especially refers to Ottoman Muslims who migrated from lost territories back to Anatolia. In the early 1900s, **muhacir** often meant the Muslim refugees from the Balkans or the Caucasus. The novel mentions a *muhacir arabası* (an immigrant's wagon), alluding to people uprooted by war or population exchange. The term carries the poignancy of exile – these communities brought their belongings in ox-drawn carts, seeking a new home in Türkiye.

Muhtez: *Quivering; trembling.* An obscure word derived from *ihtizaz* (tremor). The text uses *muhtez müteheyyiç kalabalık* – "a trembling, excited crowd". **Muhtez** describes a state of vibrating or shaking, often from excitement, fear, or cold. It paints an image of people literally shaking with anticipation or agitation.

Mukaddes: *Sacred; holy.* Something inviolable or highly revered. **Mukaddes** emanet means a sacred trust, **mukaddes görev** a sacred duty. In the novel a dying teacher is called *mukaddes ölü* ("sacred dead") by grieving students, showing deep reverence. The beloved might be put on a **mukaddes** pedestal in a lover's eyes. It denotes that which must be treated with utmost respect. (Opposite: *mundar* – profane, unclean.)

Murad: *Desire; wish; purpose.* Often a *heart's desire.* To *muradına ermek* is to attain one's wish. **Murad** can also mean an intention or goal. In fortune-telling and folk belief, one speaks of *muradının olması* (one's wish coming true). The novel includes a fortune-teller saying, *"Senin bir muradın var ama… bir kalp işi olsa gerek"* – "You have a desire – perhaps a matter of the heart…". The name *Murad* (e.g. Sultan Murad) comes from this word, meaning "the willed one."

Mürşid: *Spiritual guide; mentor.* In Sufism, a **mürşid** is a enlightened master who guides disciples (*mürids*) on the mystical path. The word (Arabic *mürşid*, "one who guides rightly") implies someone who has attained **kemāl** (perfection) and can lead others to God.

A mürşid is also called *şeyh* or *pir*. The novel, steeped in spiritual love, implies that *Aşk Peygamberi* himself acts as a **mürşid-i aşk** – a guide initiating the protagonist into the mysteries of love. In a broader sense, **mürşid** can refer to any mentor or teacher who profoundly influences one's moral or spiritual development.

Müstāğrak: *Immersed; absorbed.* Describes being deeply lost in something (literally "plunged"). For instance, *müstāğrak nazarlar* are gaze absorbed in thought or light. A person **müstāğrak** in prayer doesn't notice the world around them. The text uses *müstagrak ışık bekleyen nazarlarına baktım* – "I looked at her eyes, absorbed, awaiting light", suggesting a transfixed, trance-like state.

Müşevveş: *Confused; disordered.* Often describing the mind or speech. Literally "disturbed/muddled," it indicates a state of chaos or turbulence. The novel mentions **müşevveş lisān-ı elem** – "the confused language of pain". A **müşevveş zihin** is a confused mind. It can also describe a messy situation. The connotation is of something once clear now stirred into disorder (as in a once calm surface now ruffled).

Mütālāa: *Study; reading; contemplation.* In an educational context, **mütalaa** means private study or the act of reading and reflecting. A *mütālāa odası* is a study room or reading hall. The diary in the novel says *mütālāa salonunda toplanmıştık* – "we had gathered in the study hall". It suggests a scene of students quietly reading or doing homework. The word can also mean careful consideration of a text or subject. (Modern Turkish uses *etüt* or *okuma* for study, but *mütalaa* survives in formal usage).

Müteessir: *Moved; affected (with sorrow).* Describes someone emotionally touched, usually in a sad or poignant way. If a character is **müteessir**, they are overcome with emotion (often grief or pity). The novel might describe a person as *yarı müteessir, yarı mes'ud* – "half saddened, half happy". *Teessür* is the noun form for deep sorrow or being affected. It's a gentle word—less intense than *perişan* (devastated)—implying a soft heart that easily feels sympathy or sadness.

Mütehakkim: *Domineering; authoritarian.* Literally "acting like a ruler (hākim)." It describes a person who is overbearingly commanding. The novel uses it for an oppressive tone: *annemin mütehakkim sesi* – "my mother's tyrannical voice". A **mütehakkim nüfuz** is a dominating influence. This adjective often has a negative connotation, suggesting arbitrary or unjust force.

Müteheyyiç: *Agitated; excited.* From **heyecan** (excitement), it denotes a state of stirred-up emotion. A **müteheyyiç kalabalık** is an excited, restless crowd. A heart can be *müteheyyiç* with passion. It implies a high-energy emotional arousal, whether joyous, anxious, or angry. The crowd in the book growing impatient and *müteheyyiç*paints a picture of mounting tension.

N

Nazar: *Gaze; sight; viewpoint.* **Nazar** literally means look or glance, but it has rich connotations. *Nazar değmesi* is the "evil eye" – the belief that a malicious or envious look can cause harm. In the novel, *noktai nazarına nüzūl etmek* means "to descend to someone's point of view", showing empathy. **Nazar** can also mean perspective (e.g., *benim nazarımda* – in my view). *Nazarlık* is an amulet against the evil eye. When used alone ("nazar!"), it might warn that someone is watching or to beware of jealousy.

Nazlı: *Coquettish; shyly demure.* Describes usually a woman who is delicate and playfully reluctant. A **nazlı**beloved makes the lover chase her, giving affection sparingly (performing *naz*, coquetry). In the novel, phrases like *nazlı, dilber hayal* describe the vision of a coy, graceful beauty. *Nazlı* can also simply mean pampered or sensitive (as in *nazlı çiçek* – a flower that needs careful tending). The word paints an image of charming hesitation and tender aloofness that entices others.

Nezāhet: *Purity; innocence.* Connotes moral and physical cleanliness. In the text, a character's love is said to contain such **nezāhet ve ulūhiyet** (purity and divinity) that it inspires reverence. A **nezih** person is pure-hearted or of impeccable conduct. *Nezāhet* is often used for chastity or unspoiled character – e.g., *nezāhet-i aşksızlık* in literature might mean the purity of not having been in love before.

Nefs: *The self; ego.* In Sufi philosophy, **nefs** refers to the lower self or ego which must be disciplined and purified. It's often translated as *"ego"* or *"carnal soul."* Humans are seen as composed of the **rūh** (spirit) which is pure, and the **nefs** which is prone to base desires. The novel has a character afraid of his own nefs: *"kendi nefsimden bile ürküyorum"* ("I even fear my own self"). Sufis speak of **nefs-i emmāre** (the commanding self that incites evil) and progressively higher states of the nefs as one purifies it. In everyday Turkish, *nefsine hakim olmak* means to control one's appetites. The struggle against the **nefs** is the *greater holy war* of the soul.

Nihān: *Hidden; concealed.* An old word for *gizli* (hidden). For example, *gözden nihān olmak* – to become hidden from sight. In the novel, *nihān* is used when the sun/beloved becomes concealed: *"güneş... gözden nihān oldu"*("the sun became hidden from sight"). It implies being out of view or kept secret. A *nihān aşk* is a secret love. The root also gives *istihnān* (occultation).

Nüzūl: *Descent.* Often used to describe the act of coming down or a revelation descending (as in the Qur'an's *nüzul*to Muhammad). In the text, *nüzūl ederek onu mazur görmesini bilir* – "(she) knows how to descend to his point of view and excuse him". Here **nüzul** means to come down to someone's level (figuratively). In old usage, *nüzul* could also mean a slight stroke (medical) or the event of lodging somewhere. But primarily it's "descent" – whether of an idea, grace, or oneself.

O

Ordugāh: *Military camp.* A compound of *ordu* (army) and *gāh* (place), meaning an encampment or barracks area for troops. The novel's war scene references *ordugāhın meydanında* – on the field of the military camp. It evokes the transient living quarters of soldiers at the front. (In modern Turkish, *ordu* = army, and *karargāh* or *ordu kampı* might be used for headquarters or camp, but *ordugāh* is an older term found in historical texts).

P

Perestiş: *Adoration; idolization.* From Persian *parastish* (worship), it means profound love verging on worship. To **perestiş etmek** is to adore or venerate someone/something. In the novel, *ne o per-*

estiş eden muhibleri... kalmıştı – "nor those devotees who adored him remained...". This suggests almost religious reverence by his lovers/followers. *Perestişkār* means adoring. Often used for the kind of love that places the beloved on a pedestal, as an idol (the root *perest* means worshipper, seen in *putperest* – idolator).

Pervāne: *Moth.* A symbol of the lover in Eastern poetry – the moth that flutters around the flame until it burns in it. **Pervane** represents passionate, self-destructive love. In the text a *pervane* flutters around a candle flame, sacrificing itself to the light. This mirrors the lover (*āşık*) drawn to the beloved's fire (or the mystic to the Divine light). A common metaphor is *pervāne gibi yanmak* – to burn like a moth (for love).

Peştemal: *Waistcloth; bath towel.* A long woven cloth wrapped around the waist. In a traditional **hamam** (Turkish bath), one wears a *peştemal.* The novel describes an old villager wearing an *iplikli peştemal* (striped loincloth) with his shirt. It's part of Anatolian dress (especially for workers or when bathing). Today, *peştemal* refers to the thin Turkish bath towels popular as beach wraps.

Peygamber: *Prophet.* Specifically an envoy of God (like Prophet Muhammad, *Hz. Peygamber*). **Peygamber**literally means "bringer of news" (Persian *payām* = message, *-ber* = bearer). The novel's title *The Prophet of Love (Aşk Peygamberi)* is metaphorical – suggesting someone who brings the gospel of love. In Turkish, *peygamber sabrı* means "the patience of a prophet" (extreme patience). Each **Peygamber** in Islam (from Adam to Muhammad) is revered as a model of virtue. By calling a character "love's prophet," the novel elevates that figure to a almost sacred status, as one who reveals divine truth through love.

R

Rahmān: *The Merciful (God).* One of the 99 Names of Allah, emphasizing divine mercy. Often paired with *Rahīm*(the Compassionate) in the besmele. In the text, *"Rahmān'ın rahmetine tevdi olunduğu gün..."* refers to the day she was consigned to **Rahman's mercy** (i.e., the day she died and went to God's mercy). As an adjective, *rahmānī* means merciful or grace-giving. The use of **Rahmān** invokes the all-encompassing mercy of the Almighty.

Rahmet: *Mercy; blessing.* Can mean God's mercy or a merciful blessing like rain. *Rahmet okumak* means to bless the deceased (literally "read mercy for them"). In the novel, when Semiha dies, it's said she *Rahman'ın rahmetine tevdi olundu* – was entrusted to the Mercy of the Merciful. *Rahmetli* is a polite prefix for "the late [person]" (literally "the mercy-ated one"). Also, *yağmur rahmettir* – "rain is a mercy." **Rahmet** embodies compassionate grace, often divine.

Raks: *Dance.* A graceful dance, often with the implication of swirling motion (as in Sufi whirling). **Raks etmek** is an old term for dancing (modern Turkish *dans etmek*). The text describes a *billur şelâleler ortasında raks eden güzel* – "a beauty dancing amid crystal cascades". In Ottoman imagery, **raks** is associated with both secular revelry (dancing at joyous events) and spiritual ecstasy (dervish dances). The word brings an air of elegance and abandon.

Rāyiha: *Fragrance; scent.* A poetic word for a pleasant smell (modern Turkish *rayiha* or *koku*). The novel mentions *onun rāhiyāsını... yer yer ateşledi* – "her fragrance rekindled my love here and there". **Rayiha**often implies a lingering perfume or the nostalgic scent of something beloved (like a flower or a beloved's presence). It appeals to the sense of smell as a trigger of emotion and memory.

Refik: *Companion; spouse.* A somewhat archaic term for a companion on life's journey (from Arabic *rafîq*, friend/comrade). *Refik-i hayat* means life companion (spouse). The novel uses *dadım refik zevkiyle...* – "my nanny, with the pleasure of a companion..." preparing a room, implying she took part as a close helper. **Refik** can also mean partner-in-crime or close colleague. It emphasizes loyalty and sharing the road together. (Feminine: *refika*).

Riyāziye: *Mathematics.* An old term (from Arabic *riyadhiyat*) for math or arithmetic. In the diary, the student dreads *riyāziye dersi* (math class) and calls the teacher *menhus riyāziye hocası* ("accursed math teacher"). The word reflects older educational language (today one says *matematik*). It reminds the reader of a bygone era's terminology. Interestingly, *riyaziye* literally comes from "discipline" (related to *riyazat*, ascetic discipline – implying mathematics disciplines the mind!).

Ruh: *Soul; spirit*. The immaterial essence of a person. **Ruh** is eternal in Islamic thought, in contrast to the perishable body (*ceset*). The text frequently references **ruh**, for example "Ruh ebedī, madde fānīdir" – *the spirit is eternal, matter is mortal*. It also speaks of one's **ruh** as a source of inspiration and depth. In common usage, *ruh* can mean mood or spirit (e.g., *takım ruhu* – team spirit). In Sufism, the **Ruh** is that divine breath in humans that longs to reunite with the Creator. When a character's *ruhu yanıyor* it means his soul is burning (with love, despair, etc.).

S

Saadet: *Happiness; bliss*. A high, often enduring happiness, sometimes with a connotation of blessedness (as in **Darü's-saāde**, the Ottoman palace of felicity). **Saadet** appears when describing someone attaining a long-sought joy: e.g. *saadete ermiş* (attained bliss). *Saadet* can be worldly or heavenly (as in *ebedī saadet*, eternal bliss of paradise). The novel uses it in contexts of emotional fulfillment. (The newspaper *Saadet* in Ottoman times meant *Contentment*).

Secde: *Prostration*. The act of bowing down and placing one's forehead on the ground in worship. Muslims perform **secde** in each unit of ritual prayer (*namaz*). Beyond literal prayer, it symbolizes utmost reverence and surrender. In the novel, an ethereal vision of Sūzān *secde ediyor* (prostrates) before an ilahi vücud (divine figure) – a powerful image of worshipful love. *Secde etmek* can also be metaphorical for bowing deeply to someone. The physical posture of **secde** indicates humility and devotion.

Sehāb: *Cloud*. An archaic term (Arabic *sahāb*) for cloud, modern Turkish *bulut*. The text uses *rakik sehāb geziyor* – "a thin cloud is wandering". It lends a poetic tone (where *bulut* would be plain). Also seen in *sehābeler*(clouds) or *sehābeli* (clouded, having a cloud). *Sehāb* appears in old poetry, e.g. *sehāb-ı mattem* (cloud of sorrow).

Sehhār: *Enchanting; bewitching.* Describes something that fascinates as if by magic (from Arabic *sihir*, magic). The novel says *bu ay yine böyle sehhārdı* – "the moon again was so enchanting". It literally means "charmer" – e.g. *sehhār bakış* (bewitching gaze) or *sehhār gece* (spellbinding night). It implies an almost supernatural allure that captivates the senses.

Serāzād: *Free; unbound.* A Persian-derived word (literally "head free") meaning completely independent, not tied down. The text refers to *serazad çocuk saflığı* – "a childlike innocence that was still freely shining". **Serazad** often describes someone whose spirit is untamed or someone liberated from obligations. It is less common in modern use (replaced by *bağımsız* or *özgür*), but used in literary contexts to emphasize unfettered freedom.

Siyanet: *Protection; safeguarding.* An old word meaning keeping safe (Arabic *siyanah*). The novel uses *gece ile siyanet edilmişti* – "she was shielded by the night". It implies a careful guarding or preservation. One might speak of *siyanet-i İlahiye* (Divine protection). It's not common in modern Turkish (one would use *koruma*), but in context it gives a sense of formal, possibly divine, protection.

Surur: *Joy; delight.* A refined term for happiness (modern Turkish *sevinç* or *neşe*). *Sürur* is often used for the cheerful feeling that comes from good news or fulfillment. The diaries mention *kuş süruruyla uçmak* – "to fly with the joy of a bird", conveying an image of pure, unburdened joy. *Surur duymak* is to feel joy. It is less about loud merriment and more about deep contentment or delight shining from within.

Sūzān: *Burning; fiery.* From Persian (feminine form of *sūz* – burning). It can be a name (as in the character Sūzān) and literally means "burning one." The novel plays on this meaning: Sūzān's presence is associated with fire (her beauty and touch burn like flame). *Suzan suzan* as an exclamation in the text ("Burning, burning!") suggests the intensity of heat or passion. The name thus doubles as an epithet: Sūzān is both a person and "the burning (beloved)."

Sükūn: *Silence; tranquility.* A calm stillness. After commotion, when all is quiet, there is **sükūn**. It can describe a peaceful atmosphere or the state of being at rest. In music, a *sükūn* means a pause. The diaries note *bir müddet sükūn içinde dinledikten sonra...* – "after listening in silence for a while, then...". It implies not just absence of sound, but a serene quietude. (Not to be confused with *sükut* which strictly means silence; *sükūn* is broader, including peace.)

Ş

Şevk: *Enthusiasm; ardor.* A lively excitement or eagerness, often in pursuit of something enjoyable. A person **şevkle** doing something does it with zeal. The diaries mention *fırtınanın şevkiyle koşuyordu* – "she was running with the excitement of the storm". **Şevk** can be positive (youthful zest, creative spark) or even manic. *Şevk içinde* means "in a state of jubilation." An older phrase *şevk-i hayat* means the zest for life.

Şükür: *Thanks; gratitude.* Often specifically **şükür (olsun)** meaning "thank God." To **şükretmek** is to give thanks to God, especially after a hardship has passed or a blessing received. A character might say *çok şükür* ("many thanks [to God]") upon good news. Culturally, it's an expression of relief – *Şükür kavuşturana* ("praise be to the One who let us reunite") when seeing someone after a long time. It implies humility and recognition that fortune or safety is due to divine mercy. In everyday use, *şükür* can be secular "whew, thank goodness." For example, *Hele şükür!* in the diary – "Thank goodness (finally)!" at getting a reprieve from classes.

T

Tahassür: *Regretful longing.* A deep sorrow for something lost or unattained (related to *hasret*, yearning). **Tahassür** is the pang one feels over missed opportunities or irretrievable moments. In the text, *ne tahassürler dökerdi* – "she would shed such tears of wistful regret". It combines sadness and longing – e.g., an old person's **tahassür** for youth. It often implies quietly mourning what might have been.

Tambur (Tanbur): *A long-necked lute.* A traditional stringed musical instrument in Ottoman classical music. The **tambur** has a pear-shaped body and deep, soothing sound. The novel mentions *Zeliha içeride tambur çalıyor* – "Zeliha is playing the tambur inside". The instrument evokes an atmosphere of refined, somewhat melancholic music typical of old Istanbul. It's a symbol of cultured art – a girl who can play **tambur** is musically educated.

Tasahub: *Possessiveness; appropriation.* Literally "taking ownership" (from Arabic *sahip*, owner). It can mean guarding closely or claiming for oneself. In the novel, *Zehrā'nın kalbine tasahub ediyordu* – "(he) was taking possession of Zehra's heart". **Tasahub** implies a protective or jealous ownership. In a negative sense, it's possessiveness; in a positive sense, taking someone under one's wing. It's not commonly used today, but in the text it underscores a strong claim of love or guardianship.

Teabbud: *Worship; servitude to God.* Derived from *abd* (servant). **Teabbud** means acts of devotion or the state of worshiping. The novel uses it in *teabbud ettiğim ilāhi vücud* – "the divine being that I worship". It highlights an almost religious reverence for the beloved, as if she is the object of worship. It is related to *ibadet*(worship), but with a nuance of continuous devotion. *Kulluk* (servanthood) is a similar concept – hence **teabbud**can be translated as "rendering worshipful service."

Tecessüd: *Embodiment; incarnation.* Literally "clothing in flesh" (from Arabic *cism*, body). To take on bodily form. The foreword marvels at a *ruh latifesi nasılsa tecessüd etmiş* – "a delicate spirit somehow incarnated in flesh", referring to Semiha's pure soul in a human body. It's often used in a spiritual sense, e.g., the virtues *tecessüd etmek* (embody) in a saint. In ordinary usage, rarely used except in theological or philosophical contexts (like the **Tecessüd-i İsa** – Incarnation of Jesus).

Tekāsüf: *Condensation; thickening.* It means coming together densely (used for vapor condensing or abstractly for intensification). The novel describes a cloud suddenly solidifying: *birden tekāsüf edi-yor ve meçhul bir güneşin ziyāsı ile eriyip açılıyor* – "suddenly it condenses and then melts away in the light of an unknown sun". Here **tekasüf** conveys the moment a hazy thing becomes concentrated. In general, *düşüncelerimin tekasüfü* would mean "the coalescence of my thoughts." It's a high-register word, replaced by *yoğunlaşma* in modern language for physical condensation.

Tekrim: *Veneration; honoring.* Treating with honor or performing an act of respect. The novel uses it as *tekrimle secde etmek hissi veriyor* – "it gives the feeling of wanting to prostrate in venera-tion". **Tekrim** comes from Arabic *ikram* (honor, respect). It sug-gests not just respect, but actively **showing** reverence or hospital-ity. For instance, *misafire tekdim ve tekram etmek* – to welcome and honor a guest. It's an old-fashioned word implying courte-ous reverence.

Tervīh: *Refreshing; giving relief.* Related to *rahatlatmak*, it means to ease or relieve someone's discomfort, or to freshen the air. In the text: *Yoluna kucak kucak çiçek serip tervih eden yine o olmadı mı?* – "Wasn't it again she who scattered armfuls of flowers in his path to comfort him?". **Tervih** literally can mean increasing the aroma (of incense or flowers) or metaphorically easing some-one's heart. The root *rāhat* (comfort) is present; *tervīh-i nafs* in Ottoman usage meant recreation or relaxation.

Teşrinievvel: *October.* Ottoman Turkish name for the month of October, meaning "First Teşrin" (from Latin *Tishrin* via Syri-ac). **Teşrinievvel** appears in the diary dates (e.g., *2 Teşrinievvel (Ekim)* for 2nd October). After 1925, these old month names (Teşrin-i evvel, Teşrin-i sāni for Nov, etc.) were replaced by modern names, but the novel's diary preserves them, ground-ing the story in its time. *Teşrinisani* was November. So **Teşrin-i evvel** corresponds to October.

Tevahhuş: *Becoming wild or horrified.* It denotes a state of feeling wild fear or alienation (*vahşet* = wildness/horror). The diary says *geceyi tevahhuşla hatırlıyorum* – "I recall the night with a feeling of eerie dread". Or *yalnız geceyi tevahhuş etti* – "she spent the night in fearful desolation". **Tevahhuş** can mean turning feral or, as used here, experiencing a frightful loneliness (like being in a wilderness). Modern Turkish would use *vahşete kapılmak* (to fall into terror) or *yabanīleşme* (becoming wild) depending on nuance.

Tirşe: *Turquoise-blue; aquamarine.* A color term (from French *turquoise* via Persian *tirsheh* meaning sky-blue). The novel describes a *tirşe fanila* – a sky-blue undershirt on a flamboyant girl. It's an old-fashioned way to describe a greenish-blue. Today one might say *turkuaz*. Its usage in the text adds vividness to the scene, painting the figure in bright hues beneath the drab surroundings.

Tuhfe: *Gift; present.* Often implying an exquisite or rare gift. The foreword calls Semiha *"Rabbānī bir tuhfe"* – "a divinely bestowed gift". The word suggests something given as a blessing or with honor (e.g., a book titled *Tuhfe-i Hüsrev* – "Gift for the King"). In everyday use, *tuhaf* (odd) actually comes from the same root, because unique gifts were often curious. But **tuhfe** in our context is entirely positive: a precious offering.

Türkü: *Folk song.* A traditional regional song, usually with simple melody and heartfelt lyrics. **Türküler** are an important part of Turkish folk culture, conveying tales of love, longing, and daily life. In the novel, the *bi-perva ateşin türküler* – "heedlessly fiery folk songs" – of the beloved resound. Typically accompanied by saz (lute), a **türkü** can be joyful or lamenting. The word comes from *Türk* (as in "song of the Turks"). The characters singing **türkü** evoke authenticity and deep emotion tied to the Anatolian soul.

U

Ufuk: *Horizon.* Both literally the line where earth and sky meet, and figuratively one's outlook or scope. The novel uses it in the literal sense: *ömrümün ufkunda nihāyetlendiğini görmek istemiyorum* – "I do not want to see [the day] ending on the horizon of my life". **Ufuk** also appears in phrases like *ufkunu genişletmek* (to broaden one's horizons). In poetic usage, *meçhul ufuklar* (unknown horizons) symbolize the future or destiny.

Ulūhiyet: *Divinity; godhood*. The quality of being God or god-like (*uluhiyyet* in modern Turkish theology). In the novel, the beloved is said to possess "such purity and **uluhiyet**" that the lover feels like worshipping her. This indicates he perceives a divine aspect in her. **Ulūhiyet** is used in discussions of theology to mean the Divine essence or the state of God. To attribute **uluhiyet** to a human is hyperbole, showing how idealized and sacred the beloved has become in the lover's eyes.

Ulvī: *Lofty; sublime*. Describes things that are exalted or heavenly. **Ulvī** duygular are noble feelings. In the foreword, Semiha is called an *ulvī çocuk* (sublime child) whose life seemed too elevated for this world. It's often used for abstract high concepts like *ulvī amaç* (lofty goal) or *ulvī aşk* (sublime love). The word conveys spiritual or moral height. It's the opposite of *süflī* (base, low).

Üryan: *Naked; bare*. A poetic synonym for *çıplak*. In the desert scene, the text says *sahra üzerinde yarı üryan bir kadın* – "a half-naked woman on the plain". **Üryan** can also mean metaphorically stripped of ornament. A dervish might be described as *üryan ve yeksāne* (naked and alone – meaning utterly destitute). It's an evocative term found in older literature, often implying vulnerability and exposure. Today one might encounter it in a phrase like *üryan hakikat* (the naked truth).

V

Vefā: *Loyalty; faithfulness*. A virtue referring to being true to one's promises or relationships (from Arabic *wafa'*, fulfillment). **Vefa** in love is steadfastness through time and trials – the opposite of *vefasızlık*(faithlessness). The diaries counsel that if one perceives disloyalty everywhere, perhaps one's own portion of blame must be considered. Istanbul's old district *Vefa* is named for a lodge of a dervish known for his loyalty. *Ahde vefa* is a common phrase meaning keeping one's covenant. In the novel's emotional world, characters cherish **vefa** as the rare quality that someone will not abandon or betray the love shared.

Y

Yeldirme: *A loose over-garment or cloak*. A traditional outerwear piece, typically a light coat or cape worn by women in rural areas. The text describes a village girl in a faded **yeldirme** and headscarf. It usually had long sleeves and hung down to mid-calf, protecting the wearer from sun or wind. The term is now archaic, but such garments were common attire in early 20th-century Anatolia. Including details like a **yeldirme** helps paint the period setting of the novel.

Z

Zālim: *Cruel; oppressor.* Describes a person who is unjust or abusive in their power. It can be an adjective ("cruel one") or noun ("tyrant"). The novel uses it casually (e.g. *hain Celāl* and *zālim Celāl* to scold a friend in jest or frustration). In love contexts, the beloved is paradoxically called *zālim* for inflicting pain by withholding affection. For instance, *"Zālim yar!"* – "Cruel beloved!" – a commonplace exclamation in folk songs. It conveys both reproach and the lover's helpless admiration. Literally from Arabic meaning "wrongdoer," **zalim** in Ottoman poetry could even refer to fate or time as cruel agents.

Zebūn: *Helpless; defeated.* Often in the phrase *zebun etmek* (to subdue). In the novel, a character says *"Beni... zebun etti felek"* (Fate has rendered me helpless) quoting a classical line. **Zebun** implies being overcome by love or hardship to the point of powerlessness. A lover might be *aşkına zebun* ("subdued by her love"). It carries a sense of rueful resignation – not just defeated, but enthralled or incapacitated.

Zeval: *Disappearance; decay.* Literally "waning" or "coming to an end." *Zeval bulmak* means to perish or cease. In the novel, *ten zevāl olur mu?* – "will the body know decay?" – is asked rhetorically, expressing hope that the beloved's beauty might never fade. **Zeval** is often used for the setting of the sun (hence *zeval vakti* – afternoon prayer time, when the sun starts declining). It's also found in the idiom *zevale ermek* (to come to ruin). The word imbues the text with a fatalistic sense: everything material is fated to decline (*maddī şeyler zevale mahkūmdur* – material things are doomed to perish). In contexts of love, fearing **zeval** means dreading the end of happiness or the loss of the beloved's presence.